Heritage Cuisines

Food is one of the most fundamental elements of culture and a significant marker of regional and ethnic identity. It encompasses many other elements of cultural heritage beyond the physical ingredients required for its production. These include folklore, religion, language, familial bonds, social structures, environmental determinism, celebrations and ceremonies, landscapes, culinary routes, smells and tastes, to name but a few. However, despite all that is known about foodways and cuisine from hospitality, gastronomical, supply chain and agricultural perspectives, there still remains a dearth of consolidated research on the wide diversity of food and its heritage attributes and contexts.

This edited volume aims to fill this void by consolidating into a single volume what is known about cuisines and foodways from a heritage perspective and to examine and challenge the existing paradigms, concepts and practices related to gastronomic practices, intergenerational traditions, sustainable agriculture, indigenous rituals, immigrant stories and many more heritage elements as they pertain to comestible cuisines and practices. The book takes a global and thematic approach in examining heritage cuisines from a wide range of perspectives, including agriculture, hunting and gathering, migration, ethnic identity and place, nationalism, sustainability, colonialism, food diversity, religion, place making, festivals and contemporary movements and trends. All chapters are rich in empirical examples but steady and sound in conceptual depth.

This book offers new insight into and understanding of the heritage implications of cuisines and foodways. The multidisciplinary nature of the content will appeal to a broad academic audience in the fields of tourism, gastronomy, geography, cultural studies, anthropology and sociology.

Dallen J. Timothy is Professor of Community Resources and Development, Director of the Tourism Development and Management Program and Senior Sustainability Scientist at Arizona State University. Professor Timothy is Editor of the *Journal of Heritage Tourism* and serves on the editorial boards of sixteen international journals. His primary research interests include cultural heritage; tourism and sustainable development; globalization processes and supranationalism; political boundaries and border issues; biodiversity and tourism impacts; religion, conflict and security; immigration and global diasporas; and peripheral region dynamics.

Routledge Studies of Gastronomy, Food and Drink

Series Editor: Michael Hall, University of Canterbury, New Zealand

This groundbreaking series focuses on cutting-edge research on key topics and contemporary issues in the area of gastronomy, food and drink to reflect the growing interest in this as academic disciplines as well as food movements as part of economic and social development. The books in the series are interdisciplinary and international in scope, considering not only culture and history but also contemporary issues facing the food industry, such as security of supply chains. By doing so the series will appeal to researchers, academics and practitioners in the fields of gastronomy and food studies, as well as related disciplines such as tourism, hospitality, leisure, hotel management, cultural studies, anthropology, geography and marketing.

Published:

The Business of Champagne: A Delicate Balance
Steven Charters

Alternative Food Networks
David Goodman, Michael Goodman & Melanie DuPuis

Sustainable Culinary Systems
C. Michael Hall and Stefan Gossling

Wine and Identity
Edited by Matt Harvey, Warwick Frost and Leanne White

Social, Cultural and Economic Impacts of Wine in New Zealand
Peter Howland

The Consuming Geographies of Food
Hillary Shaw

Heritage Cuisines: Traditions, Identities and Tourism
Dallen J. Timothy

Forthcoming:

Food Tourism and Regional Development
C. Michael Hall and Stefan Gossling

Heritage Cuisines

Traditions, identities and tourism

Edited by Dallen J. Timothy

LONDON AND NEW YORK

First published 2016
by Routledge

2 Park Square, Milton Park, Abingdon, Oxfordshire OX14 4RN
711 Third Avenue, New York, NY 10017

Routledge is an imprint of the Taylor & Francis Group, an informa business

First issued in paperback 2018

British Library Cataloguing in Publication Data
A catalogue record for this book is available from the British Library

Library of Congress Cataloging-in-Publication Data
Catalog record for this book has been requested

ISBN: 978-1-138-80506-4 (hbk)
ISBN: 978-1-138-59232-2 (pbk)

Typeset in Times New Roman
by Apex CoVantage, LLC

Contents

Figures

Tables

About the contributors

Stephen W. Boyd is Professor of Tourism in the Department of Hospitality and Tourism Management at Ulster University, UK. He is best known for his research on cultural and heritage tourism, national parks, tourism and trails, dark and political tourism. His current research outside of these areas focuses on heritage interpretation, community empowerment in island communities, as well as an interest in food tourism, in particular slow food.

Deborah Che is a Lecturer in the School of Business and Tourism at Southern Cross University where she has been involved in developing and teaching in the online Le Cordon Bleu Master of Gastronomic Tourism. She has researched agritourism, food tourism, and wine tourism in the US and has published on linkages between agritourism and wine tourism destinations, emphasizing food quality/safety, and specialized local foods; the role of winery tasting rooms in education, direct marketing and differentiation; and branding in agritourism and food tourism development and marketing. She is currently examining food and destination branding and the role of farm-based family enterprises in tourism development in Australia.

Sally Everett is the Deputy Dean (Quality and Student Experience) at the Lord Ashcroft International Business School, Anglia Ruskin University, UK, and is a Principal Fellow of the Higher Education Academy. Sally's research interests include innovation in business education, cultural tourism, sustainable development, visitor management and heritage interpretation. She has also published extensively in the field of food and drink tourism.

Warwick Frost is an Associate Professor of Tourism, Hospitality and Events at La Trobe University, Melbourne, Australia. His research interests include heritage, gastronomy, tourism and the media and events. He is Series Editor of the Routledge Advances in Events Research book series and a member of the editorial board of the *Journal of Heritage Tourism*. He is currently working with colleagues on a book titled *Gastronomy, Tourism and the Media*, which will be published by Channel View in 2016.

C. Michael Hall is a Professor in the Department of Management, Marketing & Entrepreneurship, University of Canterbury, New Zealand, and Docent in Geography, University of Oulu, Finland. He also holds positions at Linneaus University, Sweden, and University of Johannesberg, South Africa. Current food research includes honey consumption, artisan breads and cheese, spring lamb, halal and middle eastern cuisine.

Atsuko Hashimoto is an Associate Professor in the Department of Tourism Management at Brock University, Canada. Her research focuses on issues in sustainable tourism development in rural areas, socio-cultural, cross-cultural and human aspects of tourism development. In addition to longitudinal studies on rural development through tourism in Japan, her recent research focuses on dark tourism sites in Japan.

Jennifer Laing is a Senior Lecturer in the Department of Management and Marketing at La Trobe University, Australia. Together with Dr Warwick Frost, Jennifer is a foundation co-editor of the Routledge *Advances in Events Research* series. Her research interests include travel narratives, the role of events in society, heritage tourism and tourism and the media.

Miguel Pena is the Assistant Curator of History at the Barbados Museum & Historical Society (BMHS), since 2007. In addition to developing numerous national exhibitions for the BMHS and programmatic events which highlight Barbados' unique social history, Pena maintains a strong interest in both contemporary tourism issues that have impacted the Caribbean as well as those that are historic in nature. He is a member of the International Council of Museums (ICOM) and The Barbados National Trust.

Gregory Ramshaw is an Associate Professor in the Department of Parks, Recreation and Tourism Management at Clemson University where his research explores the social construction and cultural production of heritage, with a particular focus on sport-based heritage. His recent edited texts include *Sport Heritage* (Routledge, 2015) and (with Sean Gammon and Emma Waterton) *Heritage and the Olympics* (Routledge, 2014). He blogs at The Sport Heritage Review (www.sportheritagereview.com) and tweets at @sportheritage1.

Amos S. Ron is a senior lecturer and head of the Department of Tourism Studies at the Ashkelon Academic College in Israel. A cultural geographer by training, he is a specialist on the geography of monotheistic religions, with an emphasis on contemporary Christian travel, religious culinary tourism, religious themed environments, perceptions of time in pilgrimage, and sacred site management.

Edmund (Ned) Searles is an Associate Professor of anthropology at Bucknell University in Lewisburg, Pennsylvania, USA. He has authored numerous articles and book chapters on the subjects of culture, food, and identity among Inuit peoples in Nunavut, Canada. He teaches courses on environmental anthropology, sense of place, and native peoples of North America. One of his favorite pastimes is also an essential component of his research methodology—eating anything that is served to him, whether raw, cooked, or frozen.

David J. Telfer is an Associate Professor in the Department of Tourism Management at Brock University, Canada. His research focuses on tourism and development, tourism planning, rural tourism and dark tourism. He has been involved in a longitudinal study on rural tourism in Japan.

Dallen J. Timothy is Professor of Community Resources and Development at Arizona State University and Senior Sustainability Scientist in the Julie Anne Wrigley Global Institute of Sustainability. He edits the *Journal of Heritage Tourism* and serves on the editorial boards of 16 international journals. His food-related research interests include food as souvenir, regional cuisines and identity, the politics of food, culinaria and personal heritage, and migration and gastronomy.

1 Introduction

Heritage cuisines, foodways and culinary traditions

Dallen J. Timothy

Introduction

Humans have a habit of eating. For thousands of years, Homo sapiens have foraged for food, including hunting animals, fishing and gathering fruits and wild grains. Throughout human history, hunting methods have changed, gathering techniques have been perfected and with the domestication of plants and animals, farming methods developed. Although most residents of the developed world and many in the developing world have ready access to food products at grocery stores or markets, some people still hunt, fish and forage for the majority of their food. Certain groups in the Arctic and the tropics maintain their hunting and foraging traditions for the sake of expediency and out of necessity (Searles 2001, 2002), especially in remote areas where supermarkets are uncommon.

Others forage as a means of supplementing their household budgets or food supplies, enjoying the recreational element of being out in nature with family and friends, appreciating the naturalness of the wild comestibles they gather, or they forage because it is a tradition – a part of their personal heritage (Hall 2013; Pouta et al. 2006; Vaara et al. 2013). For the same reasons, 'lifestyle' farmers or hobby gardeners choose to cultivate small landholdings, kitchen gardens or minor allotments – because of a deep-seated desire to produce what they eat, to maintain part of their heritage, to preserve heirloom plant and animal varieties and for the obvious health benefits.

Food and foodways, including hunting, gathering, agriculture, aliment preparation and consumption, are an extremely important part of cultural heritage. All components of culture – features of communication, cognition, material objects and behavior – are somehow connected to food. Language describes or represents cuisines, and food elements are commonly used as symbols in societies to represent various meanings. Ideas and human creativity have led, through trial and error, to the development of world-famous gastronomies and epicurean delights. Knowledge and experience inform people about what crops will grow where and how best to cook them, and with knowledge, foodways and recipes are passed down to the next generation. Beliefs, from a religious perspective, determine relationships between humankind and deity, with food being an intermediary influence. Social mores frequently determine who eats first or when certain meals should be consumed, and food plays a crucial role in the ritualization of everyday life and extraordinary events (Di Giovine 2014; Son and Xu 2013). As well, the material culture of food can manifest in many different ways: ingredients, cooking accoutrements and recipe books (Bannerman 1996).

Foodways and cuisines constitute elements of culture and are therefore an important part of human heritage (Anderson 2014; Civitello 2004; Counihan and Esterik 2013; Denker 2003; Katz and Weaver 2003; Kittler et al. 2012; Miele 2006; Miele and Murdoch 2002). This chapter introduces cuisines as cultural heritage. It examines the ways in which cuisines and foodways are preserved or modified by native peoples, colonial powers and waves of migration. It also speculates on the evolution of peasant food to widespread culinary delights, surveys the role of agriculture and *terroir* in regional gastronomic specialties and examines the role of tourism as a consumer of heritage cuisines.

Cultural heritage and its uses

From the cultural industries and conservation perspectives, heritage means what we as humans inherit from the past and use in the present (Graham et al. 2000; Timothy 2011). It may be tangible (e.g. monuments, buildings, coal mines, railway stations, artwork or museum pieces) or it may be intangible (e.g. beliefs, flavors, sounds, activities or social relations). There is a general misperception that heritage refers only to buildings or other physical artifacts. Prevailing confusion, especially within the tourism industry, also seems to suggest that heritage must be very old or ancient, and that it must be lavish or grandiose (e.g. castles, cathedrals, fortresses, palaces, elaborate gardens, mansions and government buildings). However, given the meaning of heritage – inheritances that are used for our benefit today – it is clear that cultural heritage may also be intangible, newer than ancient and in many cases very ordinary (Timothy 2014a, 2014b). There are many uses of the past that render it the consumable product known as 'heritage'.

Education is one of the most pervasive applications of heritage. The past is an important teaching tool and is frequently included in official school curricula. Schoolchildren and university students alike consume the past in their pursuits of knowledge, regardless of their academic majors or courses of study. The past is also utilized as a substance of scientific research. Archaeologists use heritage to reveal truths about people and civilizations that have gone before us. Human geographers use heritage to unpack the meanings inherent in cultural landscapes, urban configurations and other spatial manifestations of human behavior. Biologists and medical scholars utilize formulas, toolkits, paradigms and conjectures that are based on time-tested assumptions and hypotheses.

Government regimes and people in power regularly use heritage for a variety of political purposes (Timothy 2011). The past is used to encourage patriotism and allegiance to a nation, leader or administration. Tangible and intangible heritages are frequently manipulated for propagandizing purposes to build solidarity and unity. Secondly, but similarly, heritage is used to indoctrinate foreign tourists. History can be retold or rewritten to convince visitors of the utopian values of a society or to extol its many virtues. This was a common practice in the former communist countries of Europe and continues to be in several remaining socialist states today. Finally, heritage may also be used to tell a version of history that never existed, or to block embarrassing or disturbing events from history in a form of societal amnesia, or an intentional forgetting of what happened before, which may even include rewriting history books and the educational curriculum.

Heritage is also the focus of artists, architects, art enthusiasts and cooks, and it is prized for its visual, aural, gustatory and olfactory qualities (Boswell 2008; Kong 1999; Stringfellow et al. 2013). Consider the use of Doric, Corinthian or Ionic architecture in New World building designs and the blueprints of modern health spas and resorts that are reminiscent of ancient Roman baths. The co-mingling of wheat flour and cornmeal in tortilla making by Mexican chefs reveals a great deal about the colonial relationships between the Spanish metropole and the indigenes of New Spain, and what it means to be Mexican (Long-Solís and Vargas 2005; Pilcher 1996). Modern jazz and blues are part of an acoustic heritage based upon the musical traditions of African-American slaves (Martin 2012).

Among the most pervasive users of cultural heritage are tourists and other leisure visitors. Cultural heritage–based tourism relies on a supply of places, events, ideas and objects from the past (Timothy 2011). Tourists visit tangible heritage (e.g. museums, churches, cemeteries, factories, temples), partake of intangible heritage (e.g. music, dance, celebrations, folklore), overnight in heritage lodging (e.g. historic hotels, country inns, dude ranches), and dine at heritage food services (e.g. ethnic restaurants, sidewalk cafés, diners, historic restaurants). They may even travel to and from, or within, the destination on heritage transportation, such as historic railways, nostalgic buses, old cars or preserved ships and riverboats.

All of these and many other heritage consumers (e.g. farmers, fishers and religious pilgrims) are directly related to food and gastronomy. Leaders and groups in power are known to use food as a nationalistic instrument for uniting populations, or at least trying to, and they may also use food in direct or indirect ways to determine a country's national dishes through inclusionary or exclusionary practices (Chen 2011; Helstosky 2004; Morris 2013; Watson and Caldwell 2005). Educators and researchers seek to understand historic foods and traditional foodways of people everywhere. Artists not only paint or sculpt images of food, but also in many ways cooking methods and gastronomic customs become art forms in their own right. Tourists' and tourism service providers' use of heritage cuisines hardly needs an explanation. Cultural tourists in particular frequently seek out heritage foods as part of their cultural immersion. Many consume local foods, participate in indigenous alimentary rituals and buy representative food souvenirs (Swanson and Timothy 2012).

Food and cuisine: The cultural heritage of eating

After considering the various uses of heritage and food, it is clear that gastronomic traditions and even the alimentary materials prepared and consumed are among the most pervasive and obvious constituents of cultural heritage (Di Giovine and Brulotte 2014). Perhaps more than any other element of human culture, cuisine and foodways provide indispensable insight into the history of humankind (Timothy 2007). Food's heritage role is most evident in how it reflects the cultural norms and values of people, places and times; elucidates the realities of geography and place; and signals humankind's struggle to survive nature and indeed subdue it. Cuisines tell stories of refinement through contacts with other societies and civilizations, and food's clear imprint on other heritage components (e.g. religion, language, music, folklore, earthly knowledge and family life) is unmistakable.

Indigenous people, colonialism and migration

Prior to their contact with outsiders, aboriginal peoples ate whatever food was available. Their diets were determined by a variety of environmental factors, including weather and climate, abundance or scarcity of water, soil quality and the available range of endemic or indigenous plants and animals. While the tenets of pure environmental determinism have long been debated in the geographical sciences, it is obvious that the environment did govern what native peoples could consume (Frenkel 1992; Kuhnlein and Turner 1991; Nunn 2003; Rotherham 2008).

Ancient travel for trade and exploration in areas such as East Asia and the Mediterranean introduced new food practices and ingredients. The ancient Phoenicians, Greeks and Romans were especially adept at cross-pollinating foods from their travels. Throughout the Roman Empire period, European foods were influenced by flavors and techniques derived from various parts of the imperial hinterland.

Later, during the 'age of discovery', or period of European transoceanic explorations, which extended from the early fifteenth century until the eighteenth century, European foodways, as well as the food of the natives in faraway colonies, were permanently changed through the process Crosby (1972) labeled the 'Columbian Exchange'. This meant the post–Christopher Columbus introduction of plants, animals, cultures, technologies and ideas from the Americas to the European metropoles, as well as the relocation of these same things from Europe to the Americas. Through the Columbian Exchange, crucial food ingredients in contemporary European cuisines (e.g. tomatoes in Italy, potatoes in northern Europe and cocoa/chocolate in Switzerland) were brought from the Americas, although it took a few centuries for some of them to become popular in European cooking. For example, for a few hundred years in Europe, tomatoes were thought to be poisonous and were only used as decorative plants in leisure gardens (Peralta and Spooner 2006). Through the same exchange process, Old World comestibles were introduced to the Americas and other colonial realms and have become staple foods there as well: beef, chicken, pork, a wide range of fruits and spices, wheat, rye, olives, sugarcane and many more.

Some of the purposes of these worldwide explorations were to bring foods (e.g. spices) back to Europe. Along with spices came overseas staples such as potatoes, tomatoes, winter squash (pumpkins), coffee, tea and numerous other foodstuffs upon which much European fare is based today. And of course, as noted earlier, European food products were also introduced to the overseas colonies, melding Continental flavors with local culinary traditions (Staiff and Bushell 2013) (Figure 1.1).

Today, cuisine is still a crucial component of the living culture and heritage identities of indigenous people everywhere. In many colonial societies, especially in the Americas, Australia, New Zealand and parts of Asia and Africa, native peoples struggle to maintain their traditional culinary ways against the incursion of international fast food chains, the infiltration of nonnative ingredients, the adaptation of preparation methods to speed the cooking process, more readily available prepacked supermarket foods and the threats of climate change (Bannerman

Figure 1.1 Sign in Pondicherry, India, illustrates the French colonial influence on Tamil cuisine (Photo: Dallen J. Timothy)

2006; Lynn et al. 2013; Sebastian and Donelly 2013; White 2014). However, with its List of Intangible Cultural Heritage, UNESCO is trying to safeguard the preparation methods, flavors and appearances of time-honored foods around the world. With the exception of a growing number of alimentary customs from Latin America, most of UNESCO's food-related listings are not from colonial countries or settler societies. Nevertheless, the list highlights aboriginal gustatory customs, such as the preparation and appearance of Armenia's traditional bread, *lavash*, and the native ingredients, smells, flavors and preparation methods of indigenous Mexican food, particularly that from the state of Michoacán as a primary example.

Migration trends in modern times have also influenced the development of ethnic cuisines in different ways (Alonso and Krajsic 2013). Food is among the most important memories immigrants carry with them to their adopted lands. For immigrants, cooking traditional foods helps them maintain their cultural identity in a place far away from their familial roots (Avieli 2005; Kaftanoglu and Timothy 2013; Laing and Frost 2013). It is also a means of maintaining their children's connections with their familial homeland and passing down cherished recipes and gustatory traditions. Regardless of how well they try to keep it pure, immigrant food typically is affected in one way or another by acculturation processes or immersion forces surrounding them. Original ingredients might be unavailable, even at specialty shops, so other spices or ingredients substitute as the next best thing. Many diasporic people rely on ethnic restaurants to satisfy their penchant for the authentic tastes of home (Chhabra et al. 2013).

The need to remain connected gastronomically has led many émigrés to put their culinary skills to work feeding themselves and others of the diaspora with home-cooked meals and in public kitchens. Eventually they opened cafés and restaurants, which became popular among non-diasporic peoples as well (Molz 2004), leading to the widespread growth of ethnic restaurants throughout the world. Urban ethnic islands, or ethnic enclaves, and 'ethnoburbs' are known for their array of foreign food (Li 2009). Chinatowns all over the world cater not only to the Chinese diaspora but also to residents of the local majority and to tourists. Chinatowns, Koreatowns, Greektowns and Little Italies are some of the most prominent ethnic enclaves in settler societies, and their offered culinary heritage has become an important part of regional foodscapes.

Many traditional gastronomic methods and their accompanying foodstuffs play a crucial role in the tourism product of places. Out of cultural pride or economic necessity, indigenous people around the world demonstrate their living culture as part of the tourists' heritage experience. Similar to the Fijian *lovo* and the Hawaiian *luau* (O'Connor 2008), the traditional Māori *hāngi* feast, for instance, is carried out on special occasions or when tour groups desire it as part of their native New Zealand experience (Hall et al. 1992). In putting down a *hāngi*, Māoris dig a pit, build a large fire and heat stones with which baskets of food are buried in soil for several hours to cook (Williams 2014). The process itself is an important part of Māori heritage, but even the *hāngi* stones are considered special and may be passed down from generation to generation as tangible artifacts of this culinary tradition.

Vernacular heritage: Cuisine and the peasant past

As already noted, the growing importance of vernacular landscapes and ordinary patrimony reflects a changing heritage narrative. While archaeologists, anthropologists and cultural geographers have long emphasized the importance of ordinary heritage, the cultural industries are at last beginning to realize its potential for diversifying regional heritage portfolios, developing a more democratic sense of place and branding tourist destinations (Clifford 2011; Derrett and St Vincent Welch 2008; Timothy 2014b). This burgeoning trend acknowledges that, while tourism and other heritage-consuming activities have heretofore focused overwhelmingly on large-scale, globally significant and stately built heritage, these big heritages represent the patrimony of only a small fraction of the world's population (Timothy 2014a). What percentage of the world's inhabitants were kings and queens, popes and bishops, generals and commanders, prime ministers or national heroes? It is a very small percentage indeed, yet tourism and other cultural sectors have focused on the built heritage of the privileged. What about the heritage of the rest of humankind? This concern relates directly to heritage cuisines.

Indigenous and peasant foods have long formed the foundations of modern-day gastronomy and haute cuisine. The majority of the world's most beloved dishes originated at some point as poor people food – ordinary subsistence fare

Figure 1.2 Cooked insects in Guangxi Province, China, from peasant food to culinary delicacy (Photo: Dallen J. Timothy)

(Rotherham 2008). In certain areas of Guangxi Province, China, insects are a chief delicacy often served to visiting dignitaries and at special occasions. Bamboo worms, crickets, bees and bee larvae are savored for their crispness when fried, delicious nutty flavor and high protein content (Figure 1.2). Historically, these were the aliment of peasants, who raised chickens, ducks, hogs and cattle for the marketplace. These livestock meats were too valuable to consume themselves, so farmers gathered the cheaper insects for their own families. Today, however, the tides have turned. They still gather these insects but for sale to high-end restaurants and markets, and they now consume the poultry and livestock that were formerly out of reach.

A similar case is tri-tip, a popular cut of beef in North America, Europe and Latin America. Until the mid-twentieth century, tri-tip, or triangle steak, in the United States was generally considered scrap meat and usually minced with other less favored cuts into ground beef or sold at steep discounts to immigrants. In the 1950s, however, it was introduced to the market in California as a whole piece of beef for roasting or grilling, or cut and sold as barbeque steaks. Since then, tri-tip has become one of the preferred cuts of meat in the United States for its flavor and tenderness, and it is one of the costliest cuts of beef on the market (Raichlen 2003).

With the best cuts of meat originally being served to the wealthy and social elites, most of Europe's peasants anciently and in more modern times were relegated to eating the parts of animals the upper classes refused to eat. The peasants were creative in this regard and were able to concoct meals and delicacies from the fat, skin, blood, internal organs and entrails of their slaughtered animals. This is how most European sausages originated. Sausages, including hot dogs, are now consumed all over the world, regardless of their ingredients and humble beginnings. Haggis, the famed Scottish dish (although it is not endemic to Scotland) has similar origins. The haggis was originally prepared by mincing sheep organs, oats, onions and other flavorings and cooking them in the animal's stomach. It was peasant food, which hunters and farmers could carry to eat along the way (Wright 1996). Today, most haggis is cooked in commercial casings, but the ingredients and events associated with the haggis are still an important part of Scottish national identity and culture. Similarly, faggots are a popular, albeit rustic, peasant dish in the United Kingdom, especially in Wales and the English Midlands. The dish is made of pig hearts, fatty meats and liver, minced with bacon, seasonings and bread crumbs. It is usually shaped into balls and served with mashed potatoes, gravy and a vegetable.

According to traditional folklore, *fideuà*, the less famous Catalonian cousin of *paella*, came about in the early twentieth century. The story goes that a group of fishermen, upon realizing they lacked sufficient rice to make paella, decided to substitute *fideu*, a thin noodle, in place of the rice. There are various other versions of the story, but what they all have in common is the improvisation of common folk to make do with what was available. Regardless of the story's details, *fideuà* has become a favorite dish in Catalonia and in cafes and high-end restaurants throughout Spain (Medina 2005).

Thousands of similar examples of poor people food exist all over the world. All of these accounts illustrate how peasant food opens windows to the past. These gastronomic traditions, many of which have permeated the world and become food favorites (e.g. hot dogs and sausages) tell stories of poverty and servitude, preserve memories of vernacular landscapes and valorize the heritage of ordinary citizens.

Agricultural heritage

Since humans began domesticating plants and animals thousands of years ago, farming has been a critical economic activity, providing for the needs of farmers' families but also for everyone else through the market system (Carolan 2012). Through trial and error, agriculturists have learned over the centuries and millennia which products will grow best in their own environments. This, of course, has been a major determining factor in which foods are developed and used, and which items become staples and which agricultural products contribute to regional specialties and national dishes. Rice is most commonly associated with Asian cuisines, pastas with Italian dishes, beans and corn with Mexican and other Latin American gastronomy, and potatoes with traditional European fare.

Through the refining millennia of agricultural history, unique agricultural landscapes have developed. Rice's heavy dependence on water has led to intricate systems of terraced paddies and feeder ditches in many parts of Asia. Terraced landscapes in Asia, the Middle East, South America, Africa and southern Europe derived from the need to utilize sloped terrain as a food source; many of these formations are hundreds, and even thousands, of years old, comprising part of unique cultural landscapes that tell remarkable stories. Inheritance laws, land tenure and land use systems have produced the unique fenced and pastured rural landscapes of Ireland and Great Britain. As well, the landlord-serf relationship under feudalism, historic and modern aquaculture in coastal areas and even the large-scale industrialization of farms in modern times have all produced unique agro-heritage landscapes.

To sell their agrarian goods, people have for centuries gathered occasionally – weekly or biweekly – at rendezvous points in villages, towns or cities to sell or trade the fruits of their labors. These 'periodic markets' and trading posts became the forerunners of today's ubiquitous farmers' markets and grocery stores. In some parts of the world, farmers' markets and fish markets are still the dominant means of acquiring fresh vegetables, fruits, eggs, dairy products and meat (Figure 1.3). In more industrialized countries, supermarkets have taken the place of outdoor vendors to the point that farmers' markets are now more of a leisure pursuit for many consumers, especially those who want to know the origins of their aliment and meet its producers. Nostalgia for an agrarian ideal and the desire to know more about the sources of their food play a role in people shopping at fish bazaars and farmers' markets.

Figure 1.3 Farmers' market in Thimphu, Bhutan. Most urban Bhutanese still buy their produce directly from farmers (Photo: Dallen J. Timothy)

The diversification of rural economies has seen the spread of tourism and other means for farmers to earn money. Farming is a volatile industry, with incomes being at the mercy of world markets, climate change, local weather or insect infestations. As such, many farmers, especially smallholders, are becoming more diverse and not putting all of their economic eggs in one basket, so to speak. Even small-scale subsistence farmers in the Amish and Mennonite communities of North America have begun to understand the importance of selling honey, eggs, fruit, vegetables, quilts and handicrafts to passersby.

An especially popular activity in parts of the United States and Canada, as well as Australia and Europe, is pick-it-yourself farms. This activity fulfills a number of different interests and desires, but chief among these are to harvest fresh fruit for one's own home use, to experience the source of one's food using all the senses, to enjoy a recreational activity outdoors and to satisfy a sense of nostalgia. For many urban residents, getting out into the countryside to u-pick farms, to browse at a farm shop, enjoy a hay wagon ride, ride horseback or undertake other day-trip agricultural activities can satisfy a need to unwind from the pressures of city living and perhaps relive one's own agrarian roots (Timothy and Ron 2013a, 2013b). For Israelis, visiting collective farming communities known as *kibbutzim* or *moshavim* can, through a sense of societal nostalgia, help reinforce a feeling of solidarity for their country and the foundation of the state of Israel in 1948 (Mittelberg 1988; Uriely et al. 2003).

Regional foods, specialty foods and terroir

As previously noted, place-by-place differences in geography determine the types of plants and animals that have thrived in a given area. Geography can certainly determine the taste of food and the range of items produced, reflecting important and place-specific 'geographies of taste' (Montanari 2009). This phenomenon is more broadly known as *terroir*, or the unique characteristics of a locale's climate, soil, sunshine exposure, water and topography that influence growth patterns, seasonality and genetics, and therefore how they influence flavor and other inherent characteristics (Barrey and Teil 2011; Croce and Perri 2010; Montanari 2004; Trubek 2008). For instance, subtle differences between the grasses cows eat in different paddocks can affect the essence of their milk and therefore influence the delicate flavors of cheese and yogurt. Microclimates and soil types, even in neighboring areas, can determine quality and quantity of production. Wine connoisseurs have long understood the role of *terroir* in determining the fragrances and gustation of different grapes and wines.

Subtle differences in flavors that to outsiders seem the same are very different and distinctive to the palates of residents, such as the brine in which a cheese is aged, the type of wood used to make a wine barrel, the length of time something needs to age, or minor differences in spices and flavorings. Even the subtlest differences affect flavors, which can make regions very proud of their unique products. By way of example, Saint-Nectaire cheese from Auvergne, France, gets part of its unique taste by being aged on top of rye straw rather than wheat straw or wood.

There are certain programs and legislative actions in different countries and regions to ensure the genuineness or authenticity of traditional and place-based foods. On a national level, two of the best and most durable examples are the *appellation d'origine contrôlée* (AOC – 'controlled designation of origin') certification in France (Barham 2003; Bertozzi and Panari 1993; Laferté 2006) and the *denominazione di origine controllata* (DOC) in Italy (Croce and Perri 2010; Montanari 2004), which was established after the earlier French model in 1963. The French AOC, which became law in 1919 to protect the place of origin of particular food products, was based on the notion of *terroir* – that the unique flavors and characteristics of certain food and drink products draw from their geographic origins and cannot genuinely be produced elsewhere. To be accepted as true 'Cognac', a brandy must meet all AOC legal requirements. It must be made from certain grapes, produced in the region of Cognac, France, and be distilled in a specific manner. For chicken to be labeled *Poulet de Bresse*, an expensive meat considered by many chefs and aficionados to be the most flavorful chicken in the world, it must be the Bresse breed, raised in a certain geographically bounded area in the vicinity of Bresse, France, and grown using certain feeds and feeding methods. Roquefort, one of the most famous French blue cheeses, must be made from sheep's milk and aged in the Combalou Caves of Roquefort-sur-Soulzon (Table 1.1).

In Mexico, the *Norma Oficial Mexicana* (NOM – Official Mexican Standard) controls the legal requirements for certain heritage foods just as the AOC and

Table 1.1 Examples of famous foods on the European Commission's protected designation list

Product	*Country*	*Status*	*Protection Category*	*Product Class*
Münchener Bier	Germany	Registered	PGI	Beer
Havarti	Denmark	Published	PGI	Cheese
Halloumi	Cyprus	Applied	PDO	Cheese
Feta	Greece	Registered	PDO	Cheese
Pâté de Campagne Breton	France	Registered	PGI	Meat product
Roquefort	France	Registered	PDO	Cheese
Szentesi paprika/ Szentes pepper	Hungary	Registered	PGI	Fruit, vegetables and cereal
Pizza Napoletana	Italy	Registered	TSG	Confectionary, bread, pastry
Kalamata	Greece	Registered	PDO	Oils/fats
Mozzarella	Italy	Registered	TSG	Cheese
Asiago	Italy	Registered	PDO	Cheese
Gouda Holland/ Holland gouda cheese	Netherlands	Registered	PGI	Cheese
Poulet de Bresse/ Bresse chicken	France	Registered	PDO	Fresh meat
Kiełbasa Lisiecka/ sausage	Poland	Registered	PGI	Meat product
Buxton blue	United Kingdom	Registered	PDO	Cheese
Tiroler Bergkäse/ Tirol mountain cheese	Austria	Registered	PDO	Cheese
Českobudějovické pivo/beer	Czech Republic	Registered	PGI	Beer
Prosciutto di Parma/ Parma Ham	Italy	Registered	PDO	Meat product
Canard à foie gras du Sud-Ouest/foie gras	France	Registered	PGI	Meat product
Whitstable oysters	United Kingdom	Registered	PGI	Fresh fish, molluscs, and crustaceans
Lapin poron liha/ Lapland reindeer meat	Finland	Registered	PDO	Fresh meat

DOC do in France and Italy. According to Mexican law, distilled alcoholic drinks from Mexico, can only be labeled 'Tequila' if they come from the region around the city of Tequila and are made from certain blue agave varieties that thrive in the area's volcanic soils. Tequila is recognized globally as a protected designation of origin product. These same sorts of requirements can be found in the production of hundreds of wines, spirits, cheeses, chilies, butters, honeys, meats, lentils, grains and other such heirloom products all over the world (De Roest and Menghi 2000).

On a multinational scale, the European Commission aims to protect heritage food and some non-food agricultural products through a three-pronged program: Protected Designation of Origin (PDO), Protected Geographical Indication (PGI) and Traditional Specialty Guaranteed (TSG). The PDO safeguards comestibles that are produced and prepared exclusively in a specific region with known and verified procedures and where the characteristics of the place determine the quality and properties of the item. The PGI names areas, regions or countries in which food items are closely connected to a specific place, area or country. The item must be traditionally and at least partially produced and processed in the specified region, with the region providing characteristics that could not be produced elsewhere. The TSG quality designation emphasizes the traditional qualities of a food item in terms of its composition and production process, but it does not necessarily link the product to a geographical locale. The determination is based on whether or not the food is traditional, rather than where it is made (Jordana 2000; Ilbery and Kneafsey 2000). These 'brands' provide exclusive rights over the registered product name, so that similar gastronomy from other regions cannot use the same name (Table 1.1).

These three labels pertain to gastronomic items, some beverages and other agricultural products (e.g. hay, herbal oils, and gums and resins); spirits, wines and other aromatic drinks have their own classifications, sometimes described as appellations (Barrey and Teil 2011). As of July 1, 2015, there were 1,472 different foods or drinks on the European Commission's Protected Geographical Status list (Geographical Indications and Traditional Specialties in the European Union) that were applied, published or fully registered with one of the three PDO, PGI or TSG designations. The program aims to provide clear information about a product's origins, to assist rural populations and farmers as they attempt to improve product quality and to promote products that come from rural and marginal areas.

These legislative mechanisms notwithstanding, places regularly utilize their agricultural heritage or gustatory celebrity to build a reputation and create a marketable image for a variety of purposes. Aside from the agriculture or food production industries themselves, many of these efforts to extol their own virtues function to attract tourists and a tourism industry. While the effects of these various official designations on people's tourist experiences have not been well researched, one study concluded that the knowledge of PDO labels did affect tourists' desires to eat or avoid certain products (Mynttinen et al. 2015).

Tourism and culinary heritage

As mentioned earlier, tourism is one of the most substantial consumers of food heritage and heritage food. The culinary heritage associated with indigenous peoples, colonialism and migration, peasant traditions, agricultural practices and *terroir* have salient implications for tourism, as food is no longer seen only as a tourism side-service but also a key attraction. There is a growing academic research literature on the relationships between cuisine and tourism, largely focusing on food as a main attraction (e.g. Bessière 1998; Everett 2008; Febriani 2015; Hall et al. 2003; Hashimoto and Telfer 2006; Hjalager 2004; Hjalager and Richards 2002; Jolliffe 2014; Jolliffe and Aslam 2009; Long 2004; Montanari and Staniscia 2009; Omar et al. 2015; Presenza and Del Chiappa 2013; Tresidder 2015). Special interest tourism is a growing area for the industry and for researchers. Just as tour operators are now beginning to provide travel experiences for railway enthusiasts, sports aficionados and mountain climbers, culinary travel is gaining ground as an increasingly lucrative segment of the broader cultural tourism market (Reynolds et al. 1994; Stanley and Stanley 2015).

Food as archetype and touristic symbol of place

Culinary traditions and agricultural products frequently become iconic symbols of places. This is especially true in regions that are well known for specific products (Alonso 2013; Tellström et al. 2006). Although cheddar cheese is named after the village of Cheddar, England, the village is no longer a major producer of the product, yet its name and alimentary association are an important tourist draw. People visit Tequila, Mexico, because of its name – to see agave farms, observe the production process, taste the product and purchase the spirit. France's Champagne region is visited by fans of champagne, and Hershey, Pennsylvania's, claim to tourism fame is its chocolate factory.

These food-related images also develop famous tourism cuisines on a national scale even to the point of stereotyping. Hungary is best known for goulash and paprika, Italy for pasta dishes, Spain for paella, Mexico for tacos, Japan for sushi, Switzerland for cheese and chocolate, India for curries, Fiji for kava and Grenada for nutmeg. These are only a few examples, but in such locations, gastronomic landscapes become tourism landscapes and are important contributors to national and regional identities (Everett and Aitchison 2008; Metro-Roland 2013; Valadares Teixeira and Ribeiro 2013; Wilk 1999). Most souvenir shops in Prince Edward Island, Canada, and Maine, United States, for instance, feature the ubiquitous lobster (Lewis 1989). Many of Mexico's tourist-oriented handicrafts feature chilies or corn, and the Holy Land's tourist foodscape is essentially a Biblical heritagescape, wherein foods of the Bible dominate souvenirs, signs and advertisements (Ron and Timothy 2013).

This stereotyping of comestibles also leads to the museumification of heritage cuisines. The Idaho Potato Museum, housed in an old railway station in Blackfoot,

Table 1.2 Examples of culinary heritage museums

Name of Museum	*Location*
Currywurst Museum	Berlin, Germany
Kimchi Museum	Seoul, South Korea
Salami Museum	Felino, Italy
Paprika Museum	Kalocsa, Hungary
Amsterdam Cheese Museum	Amsterdam, Netherlands
Southern Food and Beverage Museum	New Orleans, United States
Museum of the Olive Culture	Trevi, Italy
Ramen Museum	Yokohama, Japan
Idaho Potato Museum	Blackfoot, Idaho, United States
European Bread Museum	Ebergötzen, Germany
Chinese Rice Wine Museum	Shanghai, China

Idaho; the Kimchi Museum in Seoul, South Korea; and more than twenty-five olive and olive oil museums in Spain, France, Italy, Tunisia, Turkey, Greece and Israel are prime examples (Table 1.2).

These archetypal place-to-primary product linkages result in substantial commercial advantages for tourism. Regions with famous food-based images offer plethoric lists of cuisine tours and other food activities. Companies, such as Epitourean (2015), offer itineraries of 'Edible Destinations', including Tuscany and Abruzzo, where tour participants visit local vegetable markets, fish markets and fishing huts, vineyards and wineries, olive presses and cheese factories, and participate in antipasti, pizza and pasta cooking courses. Organized multiday wine and cheese tours in France and Switzerland or one-day organized tasting tours or dessert tours on Amelia Island, Florida, are becoming ever more popular with the foodie market segment, which is becoming more aware of their own 'geographies of taste' (Montanari 2009).

Food festivals and tourism

Of particular interest to scholars of heritage cuisine are food festivals and related culinary events. These epicurean events celebrate harvests, famous foods or interesting eating practices. Their heritage value can be seen from two different perspectives. First and most obviously, they showcase heritage foods. The 'cantaloupe capital' of the world, the easternmost onion producer and the original farm where a certain honey was developed are all markers of heritage uniqueness that 'deserve' a celebratory festival. A location's culinary history cements that place's point on the tourist map, especially when a festival is developed to commemorate it.

The second way food events epitomize heritage is when the festival itself becomes a component of local patrimony: an original native event that has become a tourist attraction through an organic process or even a purpose-planned event that has longevity and has brought visibility to its locale. The Gilroy Garlic Festival is an example of the second type and is mentioned frequently in academic writing and industry examples of success. The fête was founded in 1979 in an effort to raise money for various charities. Since that time, it has become an economic mainstay for the town of Gilroy, California, which has dubbed itself the 'Garlic Capital of the World'. The entire heritage identity of Gilroy encompasses garlic. The California community has a long history of growing garlic, which is part of its organically developed heritage, but the festival, now thirty-seven years old, is itself a sure part the area's patrimony. The Gilroy event is only one of thousands of such occasions throughout the world, including the Baltic Herring Festival in Helsinki, Finland; the Crêpe Festival in Gourin, France; the Galway Oyster Festival in Ireland; the Gruyère Cheese Festival in Gruyères, Switzerland; and the Singapore Food Festival, which are all solid representations of local and regional heritage. Of the Singapore Food Festival, its organizers say:

> … this annual food festival brings Singapore's love of food to life through a variety of gastronomic experiences that stimulate the senses and celebrates the richness of our local culinary landscape. Since its inauguration, the festival has consistently whetted the appetites of locals and tourists alike. Closely entwined with our multicultural heritage, Singapore's local cuisines feature a tantalising spectrum of flavours, sights and smells … visitors have gained a deeper appreciation of how Singaporean food has been uniquely shaped by its diverse cultures and growth as a young nation.
>
> (YourSingapore 2015: n.p.)

Food routes and culinary trails

Taste trails, culinary routes, food trails or wine routes all refer to touring circuits that cater to residents who appreciate their comestible heritage, to recreational foodies or to other tourists who are interested in food heritage. These are found primarily in developed countries at different scales. Short taste trails inside a city center may be walkable and connect shops, restaurants, bakeries, vendors, museums or cafes into a linked network of comparable businesses. The Waterloo–Wellington Ale Trail in Canada, which linked breweries, bars and restaurants in Waterloo, Ontario, was a good example (Plummer et al. 2005). Likewise, in the nearby city of Stratford, the Bacon & Ale Trail fuses the area's pork heritage with its beer heritage. Visitors or residents can follow the self-guided trail to taste regional food and drink at ten meat shops, breweries and pubs (Timothy and Boyd 2015). The Dublin Tasting Trail, the Grand Rapids Food Trail and the Singapore Food Trail are a few famous examples of many throughout the world.

There are countless additional food and wine trails at larger scales, including regions or provinces/states and countries. These are obviously meant for car, bicycle or motorbike traffic and typically link together breweries, wineries, restaurants, vineyards, farms, museums, plantations, farmers' markets and other related sites. Successful culinary circuits are themed according to regional specialties. Wine, whiskey, cheese, meat products, pastries, sweets, pasta, fruits and vegetables are examples of extant topical trail themes, while cooking styles or culinary traditions (e.g. Cajun or Tex-Mex) may also link regional chefs, restaurants and processing plants. Taste of the Tropics Savannah Tablelands Food Trail in Australia and the Seafood Trail in Scotland are examples of longer-distance trails with judicious themes for their regions.

These linear attraction systems function as magnets for tourism and investments and provide a critical mass of similar or themed services, resulting in symbiotic relationships between vineyards, wineries and cellars or farms, butcheries and delicatessens. Such routes and trails require strong members and a concerted effort between nodal services that realize selling the whole route as a single feature is more beneficial that each individual business acting on its own. Gastronomic trails and routes are key tools for highlighting a region's specialty items and providing a competitive advantage over other agriculture-based regions that also have famous foods.

Agritourism

Agritourism, or tourism based on agricultural products, landscapes and practices, is widespread and gaining popularity (Che 2006; Che et al. 2005; Sznajder et al. 2009; Torres and Momsen 2011; Veeck et al. 2006; Wilson et al. 2006). Appreciating rural landscapes is a salient part of most tour itineraries, and thus, the age-old terraces, paddocks, fields, barns, fences and other elements of the agricultural landscape not only provide ancillary rural appeal for people traveling for other purposes, but they can in fact form the basis of the primary attraction for many (Timothy 2005).

The growing numbers of people who visit u-pick farms, as noted earlier, attests to the mounting esteem for nostalgic, healthful or recreational values placed upon agricultural regions. Culinary enthusiasts who travel to participate in farm activities best resemble Montanari's (2009) 'tourism of taste', as their goal may not be to visit famous locales but rather to appreciate the vernacular agricultural landscapes that represent heirloom varieties, original flavors and fresh farm-to-table produce. There is something intriguing about harvesting one's own comestibles by hand.

Farmstays and dude ranches are longtime agritourism holiday choices. In these scenarios, people pay to stay on a farm or ranch and help with daily chores – feeding the animals, milking the cows, gathering eggs, slaughtering chickens, herding cattle, branding livestock and gardening. While such entrepreneurial endeavors by farmers takes time, money and patience, many agrarian people are beginning to see the value of diversifying their farm income through tourism.

Conclusion

Most heritage-based research attention and the primary focus of the cultural industries are devoted to the stately tangible heritage of worldwide importance. However, scholars are now recognizing intangible, ordinary and younger elements of the cultural past more frequently. The growing recognition of vernacular heritage, including gastronomy and food, will encourage more research on heritage cuisines – an element of human patrimony that is certainly worthy of further investigation.

From a heritage cuisines perspective, globalization processes (e.g. migration and trade) and neoliberal economics have seen the famous foods of India, Mexico, Italy, China and Thailand, arguably among the most pervasive ethnic foods on a global scale, proliferate even in the remotest parts of the world (Pilcher 2008; Timothy and Teye 2009). At times I have enjoyed excellent Thai food in Greenland, wonderful Mexican food in Asia and delicious Lebanese cuisine in West Africa. Since the late twentieth century, these trends have democratized the availability of global cuisines so that the foods of the world are more accessible to an increasingly diverse and widespread global population. Colonial connections and migration have also increased the (subjective) oft-noted reputation of Great Britain as having the best Indian food outside of India, the Netherlands having the best Indonesian food outside of Indonesia, and Australia and Singapore having the best Chinese food outside of China. In summary, food tells important stories of migration, colonialism, agricultural traditions and hardships, tastes and smells, family traditions, folklore, faith and societal norms (Bower 2007; de la Barre and Brouder 2013; Duncan 2012; Laudan 1996; Santich 2012; Symons 2007; Turner 2005).

This chapter has examined many ways in which food, foodways and culinary traditions meet the definitional requirements of cultural heritage, although I recognize that there are multitudes of other ways of viewing cuisine and gastronomy from heritage perspectives that were not explored in depth here. The chapters that follow in this volume touch on all of the crucial issues described above and many more. They elucidate important and timely concepts, such as sustainability, authenticity, identity, power relations, nationalism, place branding, indigeneity, colonialism, environmental determinism, fair trade and slow food, human welfare, climate change, leisure and tourism. Together the authors provide valuable insights into the salience of food and culinary traditions as consumable elements of cultural heritage.

References

Alonso, A.D. (2013) Tannat: the positioning of a wine grape as symbol and ‘referent’ of a nation’s gastronomic heritage. *Journal of Heritage Tourism*, 8(2/3): 105–119.

Alonso, A.D. and Krajsic, V. (2013) Food heritage down under: olive growers as Mediterranean ‘food ambassadors’. *Journal of Heritage Tourism*, 8(2/3): 158–171.

Anderson, E.N. (2014) *Everyone Eats: Understanding Food and Culture*, 2nd Edn. New York: New York University Press.

Avieli, N. (2005) Roasted pigs and bao dumplings: festive food and imagined transnational identity in Chinese-Vietnamese festivals. *Asia Pacific Viewpoint*, 46(3): 281–293.

Bannerman, C. (1996) *A Friend in the Kitchen: Old Australian Cookery Books*. Kenthurst, NSW: Kangaroo Press.

Bannerman, C. (2006) Indigenous food and cookery books: redefining aboriginal cuisine. *Journal of Australian Studies*, 30(87): 19–36.

Barham, E. (2003) Translating terroir: the global challenge of French AOC labeling. *Journal of Rural Studies*, 19(1): 127–138.

Barrey, S. and Teil, G. (2011) Faire la preuve de l'"authenticité" du patrimoine alimentaire: le cas des vins de terroir. *Anthropology of Food*, 8: n.p. (online). Available at: https://aof.revues.org/6783

Bertozzi, L. and Panari, G. (1993) Cheeses with Appellation d'Origine Contrôlée (AOC): factors that affect quality. *International Dairy Journal*, 3(4): 297–312.

Bessière, J. (1998) Local development and heritage: traditional food and cuisine as tourist attractions in rural areas. *Sociologia Ruralis*, 38(1): 21–34.

Boswell, R. (2008) Scents of identity: fragrance as heritage in Zanzibar. *Journal of Contemporary African Studies*, 26(3): 295–311.

Bower, A. (ed.) (2007) *African American Foodways: Explorations of History and Culture*. Urbana: University of Illinois Press.

Carolan, M. (2012) *The Sociology of Food and Agriculture*. Abingdon: Routledge.

Che, D. (2006) Select Michigan: local food production, food safety, culinary heritage, and branding in Michigan agritourism. *Tourism Review International*, 9(4): 349–363.

Che, D., Veeck, A. and Veeck, G. (2005) Sustaining production and strengthening the agritourism product: linkages among Michigan agritourism destinations. *Agriculture and Human Values*, 22(2): 225–234.

Chen, Y. (2011) Ethnic politics in the framing of national cuisine: state banquets and the proliferation of ethnic cuisine in Taiwan. *Food, Culture and Society*, 14(3): 315–333.

Chhabra, D., Lee, W., Zhao, S. and Scott, K. (2013) Marketing of ethnic food experiences: authentication analysis of Indian cuisine abroad. *Journal of Heritage Tourism*, 8(2/3): 145–157.

Civitello, L. (2004) *Cuisine and Culture: A History of Food and People*. Hoboken, NJ: Wiley.

Clifford, S. (2011) Local distinctiveness: everyday places and how to find them. In J. Schofield and R. Szymanski (eds) *Local Heritage, Global Context: Cultural Perspectives on Sense of Place*, pp. 13–32. Farnham: Ashgate.

Counihan, C. and van Esterik, P. (eds) (2013) *Food and Culture: A Reader*, 3rd Edn. London: Routledge.

Croce, E. and Perri, G. (2010) *Food and Wine Tourism: Integrating Food, Travel and Territory*. Wallingford: CAB International.

Crosby, A.W. (1972) *The Columbian Exchange: Biological and Cultural Consequences of 1492*. Westport, CT: Greenwood Press.

de la Barre, S. and Brouder, P. (2013) Consuming stories: placing food in the Arctic tourism experience. *Journal of Heritage Tourism*, 8(2/3): 213–223.

De Roest, K. and Menghi, A. (2000) Reconsidering 'traditional' food: the case of Parmigiano Reggiano cheese. *Sociologia Ruralis*, 40(4): 439–451.

Denker, J. (2003) *The World on a Plate*. Boulder, CO: Westview Press.

Derrett, R. and St Vincent Welch, J. (2008) 40 sheds and 40 kilometers: agricultural sheds as heritage tourism opportunities. In B. Prideaux, D.J. Timothy and K.S. Chon (eds) *Cultural and Heritage Tourism in Asia and the Pacific*, pp. 73–83. London: Routledge.

Di Giovine, M.A. (2014) The everyday as extraordinary: revitalization, religion, and the elevation of *Cucina Casareccia* to heritage cuisine in Pietrelcina, Italy. In R.L. Brulotte and M.A. Di Giovine (eds) *Edible Identities: Food as Cultural Heritage*, pp. 77–92. Farnham: Ashgate.

Di Giovine, M.A. and Brulotte, R.L. (2014) Introduction: food and foodways as cultural heritage. In R.L. Brulotte and M.A. Di Giovine (eds) *Edible Identities: Food as Cultural Heritage*, pp. 1–27. Farnham: Ashgate.

Duncan, D. (2012) *Nothing More Comforting: Canada's Heritage Food*. Toronto: Dundurn Press.

Epitourean (2015) Edible destinations. Available online at: http://www.epitourean.com/ Accessed June 20, 2015.

Everett, S. (2008) Beyond the visual gaze? The pursuit of an embodied experience through food tourism. *Tourist Studies*, 8(3): 337–358.

Everett, S. and Aitchison, C. (2008) The role of food tourism in sustaining regional identity: a case study of Cornwall, South West England. *Journal of Sustainable Tourism*, 16(2): 150–167.

Febriani, I. (2015) Tasting Indonesia: cosmopolitanism in culinary tourism. *International Journal of Tourism Anthropology*, 4(2): 111–121.

Frenkel, S. (1992) Geography, empire, and environmental determinism. *Geographical Review*, 82(2): 143–153.

Graham, B.J., Ashworth, G.J. and Tunbridge, J.E. (2000) *A Geography of Heritage: Power, Culture and Economy*. London: Arnold.

Hall, C.M. (2013) Why forage when you don't have to? Personal and cultural meaning in recreational foraging: a New Zealand study. *Journal of Heritage Tourism*, 8(2/3): 224–233.

Hall, C.M., Mitchell, I. and Keelan, N. (1992) Maori culture and heritage tourism in New Zealand. *Journal of Cultural Geography*, 12(2): 115–128.

Hall, C.M., Sharples, L., Mitchell, R. Macionis, N. and Cambourne, B. (eds) (2003) *Food Tourism around the World: Development, Management and Markets*. Oxford: Butterworth Heinemann.

Hashimoto, A. and Telfer, D.J. (2006) Selling Canadian culinary tourism: branding the global and the regional product. *Tourism Geographies*, 8(1): 31–55.

Helstosky, C. (2004) *Garlic and Oil: Food and Politics in Italy*. Oxford: Berg.

Hjalager, A.M. (2004). What do tourists eat and why? Towards a sociology of gastronomy and tourism. *Tourism*, 52(2): 195–201.

Hjalager, A.M. and Richards, G. (eds) (2002) *Tourism and Gastronomy*. London: Routledge.

Ilbery, B. and Kneafsey, M. (2000) Registering regional specialty food and drink products in the United Kingdom: the case of PDOs and PGIs. *Area*, 32(3): 317–325.

Jolliffe, L. (ed.) (2014) *Spices and Tourism: Destinations, Attractions and Cuisines*. Bristol: Channel View Publications.

Jolliffe, L. and Aslam, M.S. (2009) Tea heritage tourism: evidence from Sri Lanka. *Journal of Heritage Tourism*, 4(4): 331–344.

Jordana, J. (2000) Traditional foods: challenges facing the European food industry. *Food Research International*, 33(3): 147–152.

Kaftanoglu, B. and Timothy, D.J. (2013) Return travel, assimilation and cultural maintenance: an example of Turkish-Americans in Arizona. *Tourism Analysis*, 18(3): 273–284.

Katz, S.H. and Weaver, W.W. (2003) *Encyclopedia of Food and Culture*. New York: Scribner.

Kittler, P.G., Sucher, K.P. and Nelms, M.N. (2012) *Food and Culture*, 6th Edn. Belmont, CA: Wadsworth.

Kong, L. (1999) The invention of heritage: popular music in Singapore. *Asian Studies Review*, 23(1): 1–25.

Kuhnlein, H.V. and Turner, N.J. (1991) *Traditional Plant Foods of Canadian Indigenous Peoples: Nutrition, Botany and Use*. Amsterdam: Gordon and Breach.

Laferté, G. (2006) *La Bourgogne et ses vins: Image d'origine contrôlée*. Paris: Belin.

Laing, J. and Frost, W. (2013) Food, wine . . . heritage, identity? Two case studies of Italian diaspora festivals in regional Victoria. *Tourism Analysis*, 18(3): 323–334.

Laudan, R. (1996) *The Food of Paradise: Exploring Hawaii's Culinary Heritage*. Honolulu: University of Hawaii Press.

Lewis, G.H. (1989) The Maine lobster as regional icon. *Food and Foodways*, 3(4): 303–316.

Li, W. (2009) *Ethnoburb: The New Ethnic Community in Urban America*. Honolulu: University of Hawaii Press.

Long, L.M. (ed) (2004) *Culinary Tourism*. Lexington: University Press of Kentucky.

Long-Solís, J. and Vargas, L.A. (2005) *Food Culture in Mexico*. Westport, CT: Greenwood Press.

Lynn, K., Daigle, J., Hoffman, J., Lake, F., Michelle, N., Ranco, D., Viles, C., Voggesser, G. and Williams, P. (2013) The impacts of climate change on tribal traditional foods. *Climatic Change*, 120(3): 545–556.

Martin, D. (2012) The musical heritage of slavery: from creolization to "world music". In B.W. White (ed.) *Music and Globalization: Critical Encounters*, pp. 17–39. Bloomington: Indiana University Press.

Medina, X.F. (2005) *Food Culture in Spain*. Westport, CT: Greenwood Press.

Metro-Roland, M.M. (2013) Goulash nationalism: the culinary identity of a nation. *Journal of Heritage Tourism*, 8(2/3): 172–181.

Miele, M. (2006) Consumption culture: the case of food. In P. Cloke, T. Marsden and P.H. Mooney (eds) *Handbook of Rural Studies*, pp. 344–354. London: Sage.

Miele, M. and Murdoch, J. (2002) The practical aesthetics of traditional cuisines: slow food in Tuscany. *Sociologia Ruralis*, 42(4): 312–328.

Mittelberg, D. (1988) *Strangers in Paradise: The Israeli Kibbutz Experience*. New Brunswick, NJ: Transaction.

Molz, J.G. (2004) Tasting an imagined Thailand: authenticity and culinary tourism in Thai restaurants. In L.M. Long (ed.) *Culinary Tourism*, pp. 53–75. Lexington: University Press of Kentucky.

Montanari, A. (2004) Traces of taste. In S. Conti (ed.) *Italian Reflections: The Identity of a Country in the Representation of its Territory*, pp. 165–171. Milan: Touring Club Italiano.

Montanari, A. (2009) Geography of taste and local development in Abruzzo (Italy): project to establish a training and research centre for the promotion of enogastronomic culture and tourism. *Journal of Heritage Tourism*, 4(2): 91–103.

Montanari, A. and Staniscia, B. (2009) Culinary tourism as a tool for regional re-equilibrium. *European Planning Studies*, 17(10): 1463–1483.

Morris, C. (2013) Kai or Kiwi? Māori and 'Kiwi' cookbooks, and the struggle for the field of New Zealand cuisine. *Journal of Sociology*, 49(2/3): 210–223.

Mynttinen, S., Logrén, J., Särkkä-Tirkkonen, M. and Rautiainen, T. (2015) Perceptions of food and its locality among Russian tourists in the South Savo region of Finland. *Tourism Management*, 48: 455–466.

Nunn, P.D. (2003) Revising ideas about environmental determinism: human–environment relations in the Pacific Islands. *Asia Pacific Viewpoint*, 44(1): 63–72.

O'Connor, K. (2008) The Hawaiian luau: food as tradition, transgression, transformation and travel. *Food, Culture & Society*, 11(2): 149–172.

Omar, S.R., Karim, S.A. and Omar, S.N. (2015) Exploring international tourists' attitudes and perceptions: in characterizing Malaysian heritage food (MHF) as a tourism attraction in Malaysia. *International Journal of Social Science and Humanity*, 5(3): 321–329.

Peralta, I.E. and Spooner, D.M. (2006) History, origin and early cultivation of tomato (solanaceae). In M.K. Razdan and A.K. Mattoo (eds) *Genetic Improvement of Solanaceous Crops. Volume 2: Tomato*, pp. 1–24. Boca Raton, FL: CRC Press.

Pilcher, J.M. (1996) Tamales or timbales: cuisine and the formation of Mexican national identity, 1821–1911. *The Americas*, 53(2): 193–216.

Pilcher, J.M. (2008) The globalization of Mexican cuisine. *History Compass*, 6(2): 529–551.

Plummer, R., Telfer, D., Hashimoto, A. and Summers, R. (2005) Beer tourism in Canada along the Waterloo–Wellington Ale Trail. *Tourism Management*, 26(3): 447–458.

Pouta, E., Sievänen, T. and Neuvonen, M. (2006) Recreational wild berry picking in Finland – reflection of a rural lifestyle. *Society and Natural Resources*, 19(4): 285–304.

Presenza, A. and Del Chiappa, G. (2013) Entrepreneurial strategies in leveraging food as a tourist resource: a cross-regional analysis in Italy. *Journal of Heritage Tourism*, 8(2/3): 182–192.

Raichlen, S. (2003) *BBQ USA: 425 Fiery Recipes from All across America*. New York: Workman Publishing.

Reynolds, P., Cooper, C.P. and Lockwood, A. (1994) Culinary heritage in the face of tourism. *Progress in Tourism, Recreation and Hospitality Management*, 6: 189–194.

Ron, A.S. and Timothy, D.J. (2013) The Land of Milk and Honey: Biblical foods, heritage and Holy Land tourism. *Journal of Heritage Tourism*, 8(2/3): 234–247.

Rotherham, I.D. (2008) From haggis to high table: a selective history of festival and feast as mirrors of British landscape and culture. In C.M. Hall and L. Sharples (eds) *Food and Wine Festivals and Events around the World: Development, Management and Markets*, pp. 47–61. Oxford: Butterworth Heinemann.

Santich, B. (2012) *Bold Palates: Australia's Gastronomic Heritage*. Kent Town, SA: Wakefield Press.

Searles, E. (2001) Fashioning selves and tradition: case studies on personhood and experience in Nunavut. *American Review of Canadian Studies*, 31(1/2): 121–136.

Searles, E. (2002) Food and the making of modern Inuit identities. *Food and Foodways*, 10(1/2): 55–78.

Sebastian, T. and Donelly, M. (2013) Policy influences affecting the food practices of indigenous Australians since colonisation. *Australian Aboriginal Studies*, 2: 59–75.

Son, A. and Xu, H. (2013) Religious food as a tourism attraction: the roles of Buddhist temple food in Western tourist experience. *Journal of Heritage Tourism*, 8(2/3): 248–258.

Staiff, R. and Bushell, R. (2013) The rhetoric of Lao/French fusion: beyond the representation of the Western tourist experience of cuisine in the world heritage city of Luang Prabang, Laos. *Journal of Heritage Tourism*, 8(2/3): 133–144.

Stanley, J. and Stanley, L. (2015) *Food Tourism: A Practical Marketing Guide*. Wallingford: CAB International.

Stringfellow, L., MacLaren, A., Maclean, M. and O'Gorman, K. (2013) Conceptualizing taste: food, culture and celebrities. *Tourism Management*, 37: 77–85.

Swanson, K.K. and Timothy, D.J. (2012) Souvenirs: icons of meaning, commercialization, and commoditization. *Tourism Management*, 33(3): 489–499.

Symons, K. (2007) *One Continuous Picnic: A Gastronomic History of Australia*. Carlton: Melbourne University Press.

Sznajder, M., Przezbórska, L. and Scrimgeour, F. (2009) *Agritourism*. Wallingford: CAB International.

Tellström, R., Gustafsson, I.B. and Mossberg, L. (2006) Consuming heritage: the use of local food culture in branding. *Place Branding*, 2(2): 130–143.

Timothy, D.J. (2005) Rural tourism business: a North American overview. In D. Hall, I. Kirkpatrick and M. Mitchell (eds) *Rural Tourism and Sustainable Business*, pp. 41–62. Bristol: Channel View Publications.

Timothy, D.J. (2007) Let them eat Moussaka: cuisine and foodways as cultural heritage. Invited keynote address at the Philoxenia International Symposium on Gastronomy and Wine Tourism, 1–4 November, Thessaloniki, Greece.

Timothy, D.J. (2011) *Cultural Heritage and Tourism: An Introduction*. Bristol: Channel View Publications.

Timothy, D.J. (2014a) Contemporary cultural heritage and tourism: development issues and emerging trends. *Public Archaeology*, 13(3): 30–47.

Timothy, D.J. (2014b) Views of the vernacular: tourism and heritage of the ordinary. In J. Kaminski, A. Benson and D. Arnold (eds) *Contemporary Issues in Cultural Heritage Tourism*, pp. 32–44. London: Routledge.

Timothy, D.J. and Boyd, S.W. (2015) *Tourism and Trails: Cultural, Ecological and Management Issues*. Bristol: Channel View Publications.

Timothy, D.J. and Ron, A.S. (2013a) Heritage cuisines, regional identity and sustainable tourism. In C.M. Hall and S. Gössling (eds) *Sustainable Culinary Systems: Local Foods, Innovation, Tourism and Hospitality*, pp. 275–290. London: Routledge.

Timothy, D.J. and Ron, A.S. (2013b) Understanding heritage cuisines and tourism: identity, image, authenticity, and change. *Journal of Heritage Tourism*, 8(2/3): 99–104.

Timothy, D.J. and Teye, V.B. (2009) *Tourism and the Lodging Sector*. Oxford: Butterworth Heinemann.

Torres, R.M. and Momsen, J.H. (eds) (2011) *Tourism and Agriculture: New Geographies of Consumption, Production and Rural Restructuring*. London: Routledge.

Tresidder, R. (in press) Eating ants: understanding the terroir restaurant as a form of destination tourism. *Journal of Tourism and Cultural Change*.

Trubek, A.B. (2008) *The Taste of Place: A Cultural Journey into Terroir*. Berkeley: University of California Press.

Turner, J. (2005) *Spice: The History of a Temptation*. New York: Alfred A. Knopf.

Uriely, N., Reichel, A. and Ron, A.S. (2003) Volunteering in tourism: additional thinking. *Tourism Recreation Research*, 28(3): 57–62.

Vaara, M., Saastamoinen, O. and Turtiainen, M. (2013) Changes in wild berry picking in Finland between 1997 and 2011. *Scandinavian Journal of Forest Research*, 28(6): 586–595.

Valadares Teixeira, V.A. and Ribeiro, N.F. (2013) The lamprey and the partridge: a multi-sited ethnography of food tourism as an agent of preservation and disfigurement in central Portugal. *Journal of Heritage Tourism*, 8(2/3): 193–212.

Veeck, G., Che, D. and Veeck, A. (2006) America's changing farmscape: a study of agricultural tourism in Michigan. *Professional Geographer*, 58(3): 235–248.

Watson, J.L. and Caldwell, M.L. (eds.) (2005) *The Cultural Politics of Food and Eating*. Malden, MA: Blackwell.

White, L. (2014) Australian native spices: building the 'bush tucker' brand. In L. Jolliffe (ed.) *Spices and Tourism: Destinations, Attraction and Cuisines*, pp. 153–168. Bristol: Channel View Publications.

Wilk, R. (1999) "Real Belizean food": building local identity in the transnational Caribbean. *American Anthropologist*, 101(2): 244–255.

Williams, J. (2014) Food and the Maori. In H. Selin (ed.) *Encyclopaedia of the History of Science, Technology, and Medicine in Non-Western Cultures*, pp. 1–8. Amsterdam: Springer.

Wilson, J., Thilmany, D.D. and Sullins, M.J. (2006) *Agritourism: A Potential Economic Driver in the Rural West*. Boulder: Colorado State University.

Wright, C.D. (1996) *The Haggis: A Little History*. Gretna, LA: Pelican.

YourSingapore (2015) Singapore Food Festival. Available online at: http://www.yoursingapore.com/content/traveller/en/browse/whats-on/festivals-and-events/singapore-food-festival.html Accessed May 30, 2015.

2 The raw, the cooked and the fermented

The culinary heritage of foragers, past and present

Edmund Searles

Introduction

According to Brian Hayden (2003: 222), "Hunting and gathering, or more generally stated as foraging, can be defined as a mode of subsistence in which all food is obtained from wild resources without any reliance on domesticated plants or animals". Hayden continues, stating that foraging "has been the dominant mode of subsistence for 99.5 percent of the 2.5 million years of human existence". Our distant, distant ancestors, so the story goes, started out as foragers and foraged exclusively up until around 10,000 years ago when people began to "domesticate and produce food in some areas, while in other areas hunting and gathering continued up until the nineteenth and twentieth centuries" (Hayden 2003: 222).

When situated in the long arc of human history and the significantly shorter arc of the scientific study of human origins, the foraging mode of subsistence symbolizes an extremely important episode in the evolutionary history of our species. It represents a core foundation of our common heritage as humans. But foraging is more than a set of practices, knowledge, and skills that enabled human species to survive for tens or even hundreds of thousands of years. Foraging is also a set of ideas and images about people, practices, and history with important implications when attempting to understand and theorize the culinary heritage of contemporary foragers. While foraging is frequently undertaken by some in today's modern, Western societies as a salient leisure or lifestyle pursuit (Chipeniuk 1998; Hall 2013; Mears and Hillman 2007), this chapter is concerned with the "heritage cuisines" and living cultural practices of people who continue to forage for their subsistence.

Since there are many different kinds of foragers, there are many different ways in which foragers define heritage. As fully modern subjects seeking justice and equality in various nation-states, foraging peoples have latched on to the idea of heritage as a source of wisdom and pride (shared history, tradition, identity) that is vital in the articulation of a collective past, present, and future. As Clifford (2013: 223) argues, "Heritage projects participate in a range of public spheres, acting within and between Native communities as sites of mobilization and pride, sources of intergenerational inspiration and education, ways to reconnect with the past and to say to others, 'We exist,' 'We have deep roots here,' 'We are different'". By extension, a world of postindustrial non-foragers remains attracted to the image of foragers as being the closest analogs we have of how life was lived during that crucial era of our evolutionary history prior to the widespread domestication of plants and animals. The heritage of contemporary foragers symbolizes what it means to be modern and what it was probably like to be ancient. Drawing on the scholarship of heritage, food and identity among contemporary foragers as well as my own research on food and identity, the purpose of this essay is to reveal the various ways in which heritage and cuisine are woven together in the everyday lives of contemporary foragers.

Modern and ancient

The paradox of being simultaneously modern and ancient is particularly challenging when attempting to generalize about the diet of foraging peoples, past and present, and determining whether or not they have a heritage cuisine. One nagging question that confronts the student of foraging groups of today and the past is whether foragers can be considered as having a cuisine at all. The word "cuisine" does not appear in the *Cambridge Encyclopedia of Hunters and Gatherers* (Lee and Daly 1999), a seminal reference text for experts and non-experts alike. Although its absence does not amount to an explicit endorsement of the claim that hunter-gatherers lack a cuisine, it does suggest rather convincingly that the connection between being a hunter-gatherer-forager and having a cuisine is a somewhat controversial one. One could argue, in fact, that anthropologists studying hunter-gatherers have been reluctant to treat the diet of foraging societies as anything more than a means of obtaining enough food for survival or for evolving nutritional needs. By extension, the culinary dimensions of hunter-gatherer diets have yet to be treated as a valid object of anthropological analysis in their own right, at least until recently as in studies by Starks (2007) and Yamin-Pasternak et al. (2014).

The origins of such an absence can be traced, in part, to scholarly definitions of cuisine, which range on a spectrum from extremely general to extremely specific. At the general end of the spectrum is Solomon Katz, the editor of *Scribner's Encyclopedia of Food and Culture*. He identifies cuisine as any sort of preparation of food that occurs before ingestion, a set of processes that distinguish humans from "related mammals and primates that begin their digestion in the process of chewing their food" (Katz 2003: 479). Katz is convinced that our Paleolithic ancestors had a cuisine and that adapting to a new agriculturally based diet "came from the increased use of cuisine-based technologies that went far beyond the use of tools and fire, already well established in Paleolithic times" (2003: 479). According to this definition, all of humanity has always possessed a cuisine; a cuisine is what distinguishes humans from other animals, culture from nature.

At the other end of the spectrum is Jack Goody (1982: vii), who defines "cuisine" in three distinct ways: 1) as a product of the kitchen; 2) as a culturally differentiated set of high and low cuisines; and 3) as "those highly elaborated forms of cooking found only in a few societies such as China, the Middle East, and post-Renaissance France". Goody's approach reflects in part the etymology of the word "cuisine," which is derived from the French word for kitchen and the Latin word for cooking. Goody's analysis, by extension, relies heavily on the work of Mary Douglas (2013) and Claude Lévi-Strauss, theorists who developed universal systems classification to explain the dietary rules of myriad Western and non-Western groups of people.

Forager heritage and cuisine

Lévi-Strauss's (2013) cross-cultural grammar of food and culture equates raw food with nature and cooked foods with culture. "Rotten" or fermented foods, many of which are consumed by foragers and non-foragers alike, are neither raw nor cooked, but exist in an in-between state of being neither completely raw but not cooked either. This in-between identity also provides a resonant metaphor for the self-identification of many contemporary foraging groups, who understand themselves as having cultures and practices that fuse the modern and the traditional, or to paraphrase a famous scholar of indigenous cultures in the United States, traditions that look several ways (Clifford 2013). Inasmuch as they strive to maintain an image of themselves as possessing a heritage that reflects a powerful connection to nature that is ancient and spiritual, they also seek to be recognized as fully modern subjects of a global community whose aspirations are complex and cosmopolitan; they want their concerns about discrimination and oppression to reach an international audience; they want forms of social and economic justice that enable them to maintain a strong link to the past while creating a lifeline for the future.

As is true of many foraging groups today, the Inuit forage for food but also for identity and heritage. Fienup-Riordan et al. (2000) examined a parallel situation among the Yup'ik of Alaska. As a group that domesticates neither plant nor animal for food, although they continue to raise dogs for hunting and for transport, Inuit provide an ideal case study of how a foraging mode of subsistence is not just about obtaining food, but a way of relating to a world of non-foragers, a world in which being a forager can be a source of pride and envy and/or shame and stigma. Rather than enter the debate about whether or not raw or frozen, unprocessed foods can be considered evidence of a cuisine, I will assume that they do precisely because the very act of producing these foods (through hunting, fishing, trapping, and gathering) and consuming them in whatever form they are consumed (raw, cooked, frozen, fermented) is a powerful and potent way in which foraging peoples produce and express their heritage.

As a student researching the anthropology and history of the foragers of the North American Arctic, I was enchanted by ethnographic portraits of Inuit written by anthropologists who thought they were witnessing the end of an era of human history, the final act of an a foraging way of life that would soon be replaced forever (e.g. Diamond Jenness's [1959] *People of the Twilight*; Franz Boas's [1964] *The Central Eskimo*) by a world of wage-labor employment, bureaucracy, and assimilation. Although later generations of anthropologists discredited such paradigms as not only premature but misguided – anthropologists are much more critical of representations of tradition that equate it with a distant past and a set of unchanging practices and beliefs – early anthropologists such as Jenness and Boas laid the symbolic groundwork for sets of binaries that continue to shape contemporary ideas about Inuit and non-Inuit, foraging and non-foraging, real and not-real food.

As an anthropology graduate student conducting ethnographic fieldwork in the Northwest Territories of Canada in the mid-1990s, I gradually learned how these dichotomies helped Inuit make use of their heritage as a way of relating to their non-Inuit neighbors (Searles 2008) – how basic beliefs and practices became de facto examples of Inuit heritage while heritage was emerging as a key paradigm of contemporary indigenous politics and the politics of contemporary foragers in general. I was conducting research in Iqaluit (pop. 6,000), a town that would later become the capital of Nunavut and which included a sizeable population of Inuit who worked, shopped, and prepared meals like their non-Inuit neighbors who themselves were raised in Toronto, Montreal, or other parts of southern Canada. I also met many Inuit families that continued to spend a great deal of time away from town living in camps or cabins in close proximity to well-known hunting and fishing grounds. My fiancé and I joined the Pisuktie family at Kuyait, one of six "outpost camp" families living along the shores of Frobisher Bay who occupied remote hunting cabins and temporary camps during most of the year. The only way to get to Kuyait from Iqaluit was by boat in summer or snowmobile in winter, a journey of approximately 180 miles that lasted from several hours to several days, depending on the weather and ice conditions (Searles 1998).

To the Pisuktie family, my Inuit hosts, Kuyait was more than a place that had excellent hunting and fishing opportunities throughout the year. It was a place where one could experience *inuktitut*, "the Inuit way", in all of its gory glory and grandeur. It was also a place where a person could access regular and abundant supplies of *niqituinnaq*, real Inuit food (Laugrand and Oosten 2015: 35; Dorais 1997; Wenzel 1991), which was not so readily available in town. It was a place where Inuit heritage was a way of being in the world (an ontology) wholly and seamlessly woven into the fabric of everyday life and not just a resource used by Inuit politicians to celebrate and conserve a particular narrative about collective Inuit identity.

One of my earliest memories from Kuyait is hunting on the sea ice near the floe edge in the outer reaches of Frobisher Bay on a very cold, overcast day in early February. After Pauloosie Piskutie, a son of the camp's leader, shot a bearded seal through a breathing hole about ten miles from his family's cabin, he and his younger brother Ooleetoa hauled the seal onto the sea ice for skinning and butchering. Smiling, Pauloosie handed me a bite-sized chunk of meat he had just sliced from the dead animal's ribs. Still warm and dripping with blood, I was able to swallow the piece after trying unsuccessfully to chew it into smaller portions. Proud that I was able to keep it down, and trying to relay to my Inuit hosts that I was not as squeamish about Inuit foods as other *Qallunaat* ("white people") were, I asked for some more. This was my initiation into the culinary heritage of contemporary Canadian Inuit.

During the course of nine months in 1994 (January through September), I sampled a wide variety of real Inuit foods prepared by my hosts in a variety of different ways, including the muscle, organs, skin, marrow, and other parts of sea mammals (including beluga whale, walrus, bearded seal, ringed seal, and polar bear), land mammals (caribou, Arctic hare), birds (ptarmigan, Canada goose, eider duck), and fish (arctic char). I also ate clams, seaweed, and several species of arctic berries (bearberries, blueberries, and cranberries). I feasted on the fresh brains and blood of a bearded seal fetus carefully removed from the body of its mother.

According to Graburn (2006: 142), Inuit in Nunavut have five different ways of processing foods: "*igunak* (fermented through partial decomposition), *aranaq* (fermented in oil); frozen (*quaq*); with rancid seal oil (*misiraq*); and above all *mikijjipuk, uujungituk* (raw)". I remember eating a dish prepared by Pauloosie's sister. She carefully cleaned and sliced bearded seal intestines into bite-sized squares, which she then marinated in *misiraq*, rancid seal oil. Zona Starks, an independent scholar who researches the cuisines of Alaskan Inupiat and Yupiit, devotes several pages to *quaq*, "one of the Arctic's greatest culinary achievements" (Starks 2007: 47). *Quaq* refers to any food (fish, meat, organ) that is rapidly frozen and then allowed to thaw just enough "to be neither rock hard nor soft" (Starks 2007: 47). It is that in-between state that makes *quaq* food so succulent, "after a quick dunking in seal oil, each bit of the near-freezing razor-thin slices [of walrus meat] shoots explosions through the diner's head" (Starks 2007: 48). In 1990, while participating as a member of a mixed Canadian-US archaeological crew surveying the coast of southern Baffin Island, we met a family of Inuit who shared their supply of fresh caribou with us, including a few morsels of *qisaruaq*, a type of "cheese" created by the stomach of a caribou who was still nursing from its mother before it was killed and butchered.

As someone raised in the middle-class suburbs of Maryland, I did not have much interest in learning the art of hunting, much less eating the partially digested remains of the hunted last meal. So it came as somewhat of a shock when I learned that Inuit and other foraging groups do this regularly. While assisting one of the Pisuktie brothers to butcher a large adult caribou that he killed several miles from his family's hunting cabin, I watched as Pauloosie removed a stomach from the body of the dead animal, being careful not to tear it or spill its contents. I commented on how I read that Inuit regularly feasted on the stomach contents of caribou. Turning to Pauloosie, I asked him if this was a tradition in his family. Rather than answer my question with words, he responded by slicing open the stomach, thereby releasing a powerful odor of a meal of tundra transforming into waste. He then cut a corner of the animal's liver and used it to scoop up bits of the stomach mix, still hot and steaming in the –30-degree cold, before placing it in his mouth and swallowing it with a smile. Just as quickly he cut another piece of liver and handed it to me, exhorting me to follow his lead. Hoping to earn the trust and admiration of my Inuit hosts, I managed to swallow the piece of warm, raw liver smeared with a gooey mix of smelly tundra without complaint. I was unable to ask for more, however.

Many of the animals mentioned above are consumed fresh and uncooked (right after the kill), partially frozen, or thawed on the floor of the cabin's main living and meeting space (Figure 2.1). The dining etiquette of Inuit food at Kuyait (and which extended to other hunting camps on Baffin Island) is simple and straightforward. When someone is hungry, he or she goes to the meat shed next door and grabs an item or series of items to be brought indoors for consumption. Some examples include frozen seal ribs, a frozen caribou leg, a collection of frozen char, or, in summer, a bowl of fresh eider eggs, dried Arctic char (*pipsi*) or dried caribou (*nikku*). A large plastic mat is laid on the floor and covered with cardboard; the food is then placed on top of the cardboard. Whoever is hungry grabs a cutting implement (men use knives; women use a semi-circular knife called an *ulu*) and cuts what she wants from the large slab of meat or organs or other body parts lying on top of the cardboard on the floor. We eat as much or as little as we like or nothing at all. In town, when a hunter brings food to his home, it is customary to send out a message via telephone or the local radio station inviting family and neighbors to join the feast. Many times the family would also boil some of the leftover meat and parts, making a special broth called *qajuq* (which literally means "brown"), which Inuit consume on a regular basis. Sometimes these soups are flavored with salt, pepper, and other spices; the Pisuktie family preferred to add the seasoning packet from the Lipton Cup of Soup mix to flavor theirs.

Figure 2.1 Eating *quaq* (partially thawed Arctic char) outpost camp–style (Photo: Edmund Searles)

Our Inuit hosts encouraged and expected us to eat as much as we liked whenever we liked, a rule that initially I had difficulty following. Except on especially appointed occasions, to eat without restraint is evidence of gluttony and avarice among the people who taught me how to eat and value food. To my Inuit host family, it was just the opposite. To eat abundantly and without restraint is to honor and respect the animals that have been caught and killed by the hunter. As an extension of respect for the animal being consumed, Inuit have strong injunctions against wasting food, hence the variety of parts consumed by Inuit others might not or do not consider to be edible. To waste food, or to refuse to share it freely with others, is not only a source of public shame but is also bad luck. Hunters who refuse to share their catch or who refuse to allow themselves to get bloody while butchering risk angering the soul of the animal itself, which will curse the hunter by ensuring that no animals ever come to that hunter again.

In addition to foods that were hunted, harvested, fished, and trapped locally, there are also foods that are made with non-local ingredients and that are also considered to be examples of real Inuit food. An item we ate regularly at the hunting cabin and in town is bannock, a type of bread that Inuit refer to as *palauraq* ("bread flour"). This food also belongs to the culinary heritage of Arctic peoples in general (including the various groups of Indians whose territories span the subarctic region of northern Canada and Alaska) who have been preparing it since becoming involved in the commercial fur trade beginning several centuries ago. My Inuit hosts always had a regular supply of this bread available for themselves and for guests. While living at Kuyait, we usually began our days with a morning meal of bannock, sliced and smothered with butter and jam, and tea.

Inuit make bannock with wheat flour; baking powder; milk powder; and shortening, margarine, or butter, all of which are available for purchase at grocery stores in Iqaluit. When money and/or shortening is scarce or nonexistent, Inuit can also make bannock with the backfat of a caribou (*tunnuk*) or seal blubber. Although each family typically has its own special way of making bannock, every batch contains more or less the same basic ingredients and is cooked in more or less the same way – on top of the stove in an iron skillet. Inuit have been making bannock since its ingredients first became available to them a century or more ago when the fur trade and whaling industries began to have a steady presence in the region.

When his sister was not able to be present at Kuyait, Pauloosie was in charge of making the daily supply of bannock (Figure 2.2). Later, he taught my wife and me how to make it when he moved to a neighboring outpost camp to take a job supervising young offenders serving their sentences. Although his sister complained that our bannock always made her sick to her stomach, her cousin gave me one of the most memorable compliments I received while conducting research with her extended family on Baffin Island. She said that my bannock tasted so good that I must be half-Inuk ("half Inuit"), a reference to the notion that making delicious bannock is something that Inuit do (are born to do) but that Qallunaat – white people like myself – do not. By contrast, Qallunaat eat loaves of bread made with yeast and baked in an oven.

Figure 2.2 Pauloosie's homemade *palauraq* (bannock) (Photo: Edmund Searles)

This is also when I began to piece together a complicated identity politics that inform how and what Inuit think about food, diet, identity, and heritage. Like so many other objects that Inuit consume on a regular basis, food provides a vast repertoire of symbols and narratives that they use to express not just how to be Inuit but what it means to be Inuit as well (Graburn 2006; Searles 2002). Although eating a slice of bannock is sometimes no more than just filling an empty stomach or satiating a particular craving, it also takes on cultural and ethnic meanings of much larger proportions. When consumed at a reception or meal to honor Inuit elders and leaders, or to celebrate the anniversary of an important historical event or institution (e.g. a museum or cultural center, an Inuit organization, the creation of Nunavut), or an event in which northern culture itself is an object of celebration (the annual Toonik Tyme spring celebration in Iqaluit, Nunavut, features a bannock making competition) it becomes a highly recognizable and recognized symbol of Inuit culinary heritage.

The Ottawa-based organization that represents and promotes the interests of all Canadian Inuit, Inuit Tapirisaat Kanatami (ITK), hosted its fifth annual "A Taste of the Arctic" on March 10, 2015. A few of the dishes served that night included, "carved caribou hip with Saskatoon berry sauce; seal jambalaya . . . with seared chunks of seal and seal sausage on paprika rice; mini muskox burgers with sesame-soya mayo; and crepes with chokecherry chutney, Labrador tea chantilly cream, and salted caramel sauce" (Gregoire 2015: n.p.). Interestingly, the president of ITK stressed that "[t]his is Canadian cuisine at its finest – and I truly believe that these dishes could find a home on any fine dining menu in the country or around the world" (Gregoire 2015: n.p.). Later, the head of ITK added, "Seal meat is delicious and nourishing. . . . Inuit culture is not exotic. It is Canadian culture – all of ours, everyone in this room" (Audla quoted in Gregoire 2015: n.p.).

Attempts to de-exoticize and even de-ethnicize Inuit food (the claim that seal meat reflects Canadian culture, not just Inuit heritage) reflect an ongoing trend to control and even dismantle the boundary separating Inuit and non-Inuit and to create a heritage cuisine that combines the best of foraging and non-foraging flavors and ingredients. For just as much as the savoriness and succulence of certain Arctic foods (*palauraq*, caribou, Arctic char) are a source of collective pride – heritage to be celebrated and shared with the rest of the world – so are they (or can be) a source of shame and social stigma that make Inuit diets strange and exotic.

In the mid-1990s, I learned that a sister-in-law of Pauloosie refused to allow Pauloosie's brother to eat and cook seal meat in their home in Iqaluit. The wife, who moved to Iqaluit from Nova Scotia, found the sight and smell of seal repulsive. Her views typified the views of other non-Inuit in town who found it difficult to visit the homes of those Inuit who lived on a traditional diet of country food (i.e. food hunted, fished, and harvested locally) and whose homes and clothes smelled of boiled seal, walrus, polar bear, and whale. Following Sahlins's (1976: 175) argument that "edibility is inversely related to humanity", so the food preferences and dining styles of Inuit made them seem more raw and less civilized than their non-Inuit neighbors. One Inuit woman I worked with told me that her family kept a set of plates and cutlery on hand so they could eat in the way of white people whenever they had non-Inuit guests. The rest of the time they ate like we ate at Kuyait, sitting on the floor with no plates, forks, or spoons – just knives and fingers and often a great deal of blood and other parts spread out for the eating.

Although many Inuit adapted to sharing their world with non-Inuit by conforming to the stranger's dining traditions while hiding their own, it was apparent that eating the Inuit way, no matter how repulsive and exotic it seemed to non-Inuit, had also become a source of status and cultural capital. Those who can relish the stomach contents of a caribou, or eat *igunaq* ("rotten, stinky walrus meat") could also claim to be the bearers of an emerging Inuit heritage cuisine that is proudly different and distinct from the cuisine of non-Inuit. Many Inuit still honor and value the connection between eating and being Inuit: "Although I have learned more about the white man's ways . . . I am still [Inuit] because I grew up on Inuit food" (Idlout quoted in Laugrand and Oosten 2015: 34). Graburn (2006: 142) documents that during his fieldwork in 2000 he "observed conscious efforts to continue eating and, importantly, to get children to eat *niqituinak* – that is, an Inuit diet or particular Inuit foods".

And yet in other parts of the Arctic, as well as Nunavut, it is unclear to what extent traditional dishes such as boiled seal meat, raw seal brains, and fermented walrus meat will continue to be relished as examples of real food. Graburn (2006: 142) also reports that many adults he met in 2000 could not eat raw meat because they "missed the opportunity when young". A recent study of diet and sense of smell among foraging communities in western Alaska and eastern Siberia discovered that the younger generation of youth "are proud, in accordance with traditional values, to honor and care for the elders so long as the time they spend with grandparents does not come too close within the dinner hour of the latter" (Yamin-Pasternak et al. 2014: 633). It is the smell of a walrus feast in the adjacent room that a young Yupik granddaughter cannot tolerate. Her tastes and desires, so the argument goes, are being inspired by a global food industry that is causing cuisines to converge at a rapid pace on a global scale. On a recent trip to Iqaluit in March 2014, for example, I learned that country foods (foods hunted, fished, trapped, and harvested locally) are becoming more difficult to obtain for a number of reasons – changing ice conditions, rising costs of fuel and equipment, declining populations of game. At the same time, however, residents of Nunavut have access to an ever-increasing array of processed foods and restaurants. The local grocery store has several sections devoted to international cuisine, including a selection of Mexican and South Asian ingredients and meals. I can eat pizza at a Pizza Hut or buy donuts from Tim Horton's, both international restaurant chains that opened franchises in Nunavut. The extension of international markets and products to the most remote regions of the globe has resulted in an increased reliance on store-bought food among contemporary foraging groups like the Inuit, throwing into question the future of heritage cuisine.

Conclusion

The heritage cuisine of contemporary foragers is at a crossroads. The relative cultural value of local foods and dishes derived from locally produced ingredients has grown more important than ever, particularly as a response to the increased availability of non-local foods and diet trends that saturate local markets. Indeed, some still contend that Inuit are Inuit precisely because they eat foods enjoyed by their parents and grandparents – what I refer to as Inuit heritage cuisine – some of which also happen to be foods that many non-Inuit find disgusting if not inedible. As a set of practices and an ever-expanding body of knowledge, heritage has come to play an important role in the identity politics of contemporary foraging peoples. When combined, heritage cuisine is more than a collection of foods that many Inuit and other groups enjoy eating and sharing. It is an important source of symbolic capital Inuit use to battle those forces (regional, national, and global) that threaten to undermine the continuity and viability of traditional Inuit culture and beliefs. This is likely to be the same situation with many different indigenous groups throughout the world.

Looking more broadly, I argue that the heritage cuisine of foraging peoples in general will always have this dual identity. It will include a set of distinctive foods, flavors, and methods of preparation that are traditional, local, distinctive, and even radically different from the cuisine of their non-foraging neighbors. Many foragers consider their foods to be the very same foods prepared and consumed by their ancestors many thousands of years ago. But foraging cuisine is also a set of symbols that encapsulate and condense a wide range of meanings and narratives about who foraging peoples are and how they relate to non-foragers. For the most part, these dual identities are not in conflict with each other; foragers can have their cake and eat it too. But as recent studies show, changing dietary preferences on the part of younger generations of foragers, themselves raised on more mixed diets of local and non-local cuisines, may lose their appetite for the heritage cuisine of their elders. If that is the case, then the heritage cuisine of foragers may become more of a collection of meals and methods of processing country food whose function is more political than nutritional.

References

Boas, F. [1888] (1964) *The Central Eskimo*. Lincoln: University of Nebraska Press.

Chipeniuk, R. (1998) Childhood foraging as regional culture: some implications for conservation policy. *Environmental Conservation*, 25: 198–207.

Clifford, J. (2013) *Returns: Becoming Indigenous in the Twenty-First Century*. Cambridge: Harvard University Press.

Dorais, L. (1997) *Quaqtaq: Modernity and Identity in an Inuit Community*. Toronto: University of Toronto Press.

Douglas, M. (2013) The Abominations of Leviticus. In C. Counihan and P. van Esterik (eds) *Food and Culture: A Reader*, 3rd Edn, pp. 48–58. London: Routledge.

Fienup-Riordan, A., Tyson, W., John, P., Meade, M. and Active, J. (2000) *Hunting Tradition in a Changing World*. New Brunswick, NJ: Rutgers University Press.

Goody, J. (1982) *Cooking, Cuisine, and Class: A Study in Comparative Sociology*. Cambridge: Cambridge University Press.

Graburn, N. (2006) Culture as narrative. In P. Stern and L. Stevenson (eds) *Critical Inuit Studies: An Anthology of Contemporary Arctic Ethnography*, pp. 139–154. Lincoln: University of Nebraska Press.

Gregoire, L. (2015) Arctic food lovers pack the house for Inuit org event. *Nunatsiaq News*, March 20, 2015. Available online at http://www.nunatsiaqonline.ca/stories/article/65674arctic_food_lovers_pack_the_house_for_inuit_org_event/ Accessed May 20, 2015.

Hall, C.M. (2013) Why forage when you don't have to? Personal and cultural meaning in recreational foraging: a New Zealand study. *Journal of Heritage Tourism*, 8(2/3): 224–233.

Hayden, B. (2003) Hunting and gathering. In S.H. Katz (ed.) *Encyclopedia of Food and Culture. Volume 2*, pp. 222–226. New York: Charles Scribner's Sons.

Jenness, D. [1928] (1959) *The People of the Twilight*. Chicago: University of Chicago Press.

Katz, S. (2003) Evolution of cuisine. In S.H. Katz (ed.) *Encyclopedia of Food and Culture. Volume 1*, pp. 479–482. New York: Charles Scribner's Sons.

Laugrand, F. and Oosten, J. (2015) *Hunters, Predators, and Prey: Inuit Perceptions of Animals*. New York: Berghahn.

Lee, R.B. and Daly, R. (eds) (1999) *The Cambridge Encyclopedia of Hunters and Gatherers*. Cambridge: Cambridge University Press.

Lévi-Strauss, C. (2013) The culinary triangle. In C. Counihan and P. van Esterik (eds) *Food and Culture: A Reader*, 3rd Edn, pp. 40–47. New York: Routledge.

Mears, R. and Hillman, G. (2007) *Wild Food*. London: BBC.

Sahlins, M. (1976) *Culture and Practical Meaning*. Chicago: University of Chicago Press.

Searles, E.Q. (1998) *From Town to Outpost Camp: Symbolism and Social Action in the Canadian Eastern Arctic. A study of Inuit ethnicity and symbolic action in Nunavut*. PhD Dissertation, University of Washington, Seattle.

Searles, E. (2002) Food and the making of modern Inuit identities. *Food and Foodways*, 10(1): 55–78.

Searles, E. (2008) Inuit identity in the Canadian Arctic. *Ethnology*, 47(4): 239–255.

Starks, Z.S. (2007) Arctic foodways and contemporary cuisine. *Gastronomica: The Journal of Food and Culture*, 7(1): 41–49.

Wenzel, G. (1991) *Animal Rights, Human Rights: Ecology, Economy, and Ideology in the Canadian Arctic*. Toronto: University of Toronto Press.

Yamin-Pasternak, S., Kliskey, A., Alessa, L., Pasternak, I. and Schweitzer, P. (2014) The rotten Renaissance in the Bering Strait: loving, loathing, and washing the smell of foods with a (re)acquired taste. *Current Anthropology*, 55(5): 619–646.

3 Cuisine, migration, colonialism and diasporic identities

Warwick Frost and Jennifer Laing

Introduction

Conventionally, we see cuisines and food cultures as rooted in place. The distinctive environment, history and characteristics of a particular place combine to provide authenticity and provenance. Two examples illustrate this. The first occurs around the Mediterranean, an environment where olives thrive and have accordingly become the staple of a variety of cuisines. Moving northwards, the climate becomes too cold for olives and historically they have had little place in cooking in northern Europe. The second example is of rice. In Southeast Asia and southern China, paddy rice is the staple of the agricultural economy and cuisine. To the north, away from the tropics, the environment is unsuitable for rice and its role as a food diminishes.

There is, however, an exception to this link between place and food. Diasporas – born of migration and separation – develop their own cuisines in new environments. Complex and fluid, they are influenced by the tensions between old and new countries and their cultures. In migrating far from home, these cuisines both function as ongoing markers of cultural identity and evolve with new hybridised forms and characteristics. To use the examples from the opening paragraph, diaspora communities take olives and rice with them to their new homes, valuing them as integral components of their heritage and introducing their new neighbours to these unfamiliar foods. Our aim in this chapter is to examine the processes behind the making of diaspora and colonial cuisines and explore their contribution to heritage and culture.

Global expansion and migration

Migration is produced by the interaction of push and pull factors. Conditions at home push some to think about leaving. Tales of better opportunities elsewhere provide the pull. For safety and support, migration and settlement tend to be in groups, based on established kinship or local ties. Once established in a new place, successful migrants send news and subsidies to family and friends in their former homes, encouraging others to follow – a process known as 'chain migration'. Whilst not all migrants follow this path, these factors lead to the tendency for migrants to cluster, particularly if they are an ethnic minority in their new location (Simon 1989).

Migration has always been part of the human experience (see Coles and Timothy 2004 for a summary of different diasporas). What we are mainly concerned with in this chapter are the consequences of the accelerated migration resulting from European global expansion in modern times. While this expansion was initiated by Europeans, its consequences for migration extended to many non-European societies.

Following the Fall of Constantinople in 1452, the Mediterranean economies were negatively affected by the disruption of established trade routes. As the economic balance of power shifted, the Atlantic countries took the lead, embarking on the search for new trading routes and colonies. The subsequent patterns of colonisation and migration were shaped by biology (Crosby 1986). In Asia, the Europeans established colonies, though there was little permanent settlement. Instead, government was often through established local elites and military forces comprised of local soldiers with European officers. In the New Worlds of the Americas and Australasia, isolation had made the indigenous peoples highly vulnerable to the diseases the Europeans carried. In temperate areas such as the United States, Canada, Australia and Argentina, the decimation of the indigenous people was followed by massive settlement of Europeans. Reaching a peak in the nineteenth century, the establishment of these settler societies drew migrants from across Europe and integrated their commercial farming into a global commodities market (Belich 2009). In addition, economic opportunities in these settler societies drew labour forces from Asia (particularly China) and the Pacific. In tropical areas of the New Worlds, the mortality rates for both indigenes and European newcomers were high, resulting in the need to recruit non-European labour. Sugarcane is a good example of the links between the commodification of food crops, colonisation and migration. Originating in Asia, it was brought to Europe by Arab traders, but the European climate was unsuitable for its cultivation. The establishment of European colonies in the tropics allowed the farming of this valuable crop. In the West Indies, the collapse of the indigenous population led to the importation of slaves from West Africa. The high demand for labour in the West Indies and southern United States would spawn a forced diaspora of slaves. After the abolition of slavery, indentured labour for the West Indian plantations was recruited from China and India.

The above is a simplified sketch of what were often highly complicated and fluid processes. Coles and Timothy (2004) provide an overview of these nuances, though we would like to add some further brief qualifications. Some diaspora communities are now quite old, others relatively new. In some cases, diaspora communities remained quite separate from others in their new countries. Contrastingly, in other instances there was significant intermarriage, resulting in hybridised *Creole* or *Mestizo* societies. Migration could involve more than one journey. The Cajuns, for example, originally were French settlers to Canada. After the British took over, they shifted again to Louisiana. Similarly, Indian migrants to Uganda were expelled by Idi Amin and resettled in the British Midlands. Economic opportunity seemed consistently to be the main driver, though escaping from war or persecution has increasingly become a major factor, especially in the last hundred years. Another recent development has been the flow of non-Europeans into Europe. In some cases, this was connected to colonialism, as in the influx of West Indians and South Asians to Britain. However, in others there is no colonial connection, such as the movement of Turkish people into Germany, the Chinese into Italy, and Scandinavians into North America (Shortridge 2004). Similarly, the Turkish diaspora in the United States is a product of recent times, rather than colonialism or nineteenth-century history (Kaftanoglu and Timothy 2013).

In considering these patterns of migration, it is critical to understand that social structures and relationships evolved significantly. It is often held that diaspora communities tended towards being insular, quarantining these cultures from change as if they were in a museum. Popular culture has actively reinforced this view, as in the portrayal of Amish culture in the film *Witness* (1985). Whilst such entropy has occurred at times, generally diaspora communities are far more dynamic, fuelled by economic opportunism and influenced by other cultures and new environments. While elements of diaspora cultures, including cuisines, may be framed by nostalgia and heritage, they are also subject to ongoing evolution and adaptation (Simon 1989). Furthermore, the degree to which others adopt aspects of diaspora culture is dependent on the attitudes of these other, often dominant, societies (Mokyr 1990).

The role of food and cuisine

The retention of foods, food culture and rituals was important to these diaspora communities. Food was a means of social bonding, retaining identity and dealing with homesickness (Timothy and Ron 2013a). The first generation of some migrant populations was dominated by single men. Cut off from established relationships and networks, they quickly sought to develop new connections. Even if they saw themselves as sojourners, simply earning money quickly and with an aim of returning home, they tended to seek out the company of others from their homeland. At the end of the working day they would congregate together, seeking company, news and familiarity. Food was important to this coming together. Some migrants saw the entrepreneurial opportunities in providing food using recipes from home for their compatriots. For postwar Italian migrants in Australia, for example, nostalgia was fed by small cafes serving espresso coffee and pasta (Frost et al. 2010; Pricolo and Swan 2013).

A wide range of cultural markers might quickly disappear. Language, seemingly the essence of any culture, often fell away within a generation or so, especially if there was intermarriage with other groups. In contrast, food was important and resilient enough in many cases to be retained (Frost et al. 2009). Very quickly, cuisine retention became the major marker of a diaspora culture. Indeed, as migrants assimilated, it might be one of their few remaining distinctions.

The example of Chinese gold miners in Australia illustrates how cuisine was tightly held onto. In 2005, one of the authors (Frost) was involved in an archaeological scoping study to determine whether 1850s house sites near Castlemaine were Chinese or not. Within minutes, the archaeologists were certain that these were Chinese, even though the houses and mining shafts were indistinguishable from those of European miners. The key evidence was the pottery shards that littered the site. The majority of these were from jars of soy and fish sauce. In terms of the material remains, the Chinese had quickly duplicated European designs and methods in everything except for food condiments.

As diasporas produced and consumed their own foods, others looked on with interest. Intrigued by seeing and smelling these exotic dishes, some of their new neighbours wanted to taste them as well. While some were repulsed, there were plenty who were adventurous enough to try these cuisines. Rituals, strange implements, and unknown ingredients all added to the experience – as did the low price. Accordingly a range of diaspora cuisines, including Chinese, Italian, Indian and Hispanic, crossed over. Restaurants and cafes that had originally catered to fellow migrants began to attract a broader clientele. Interestingly, Gabaccia (1998) places this crossover amongst poorer classes in crowded cities such as New York, whereas Pilcher (2006) emphasises the role of Bohemians and intellectuals. Today, these adventurers might be characterised as the creative classes or foodies. Not all diasporas, however, followed the same path. For example, following the failed rebellions and land clearances of the eighteenth century, Scotland generated strong flows of migrants around the world. Though many customs were retained, such as Highland Games and Hogmanay, their food did not generate a restaurant culture.

Food production followed similar patterns. The larger migrant groups, including the English, Scottish and Irish, tended towards mainstream grazing and broad-acre cropping. Those from smaller ethnic groups tended to be opportunists. At first they functioned as cheap labour in intensive agriculture. Their employers found that they tended to work better in self-organised groups, leading to sharecropping and other collaborative arrangements. Focusing on intensive agriculture and horticulture avoided competition from mainstream farmers and workers. Sales to consumers were through compatriot shops and hawkers. The Chinese, in particular, were noted for filling these niches, but other small diaspora groups were attracted to micro-production (Chan 1986; Frost 2002; Gabaccia 1998).

Some migrants brought specialist knowledge of food production as part of their cultural baggage. Smallholders from Europe and Asia knew about intensive horticulture. Perhaps the most well-known example was of Europeans with knowledge of viticulture. In nineteenth-century California, the Hungarian Agostin Haraszthy promoted the importance of using named varieties. His friend, the German Charles Krug, pioneered the Napa Valley. He recruited a winemaker from Germany in Jacob Beringer, who after six years established his own winery. Another German, Jacob Schram, popularised the idea that quality wines came from hillsides rather than fertile valley bottoms (Frost and Laing 2014).

Mythology and authenticity

Our conceptions of diaspora cuisine are strongly shaped by mythology. It is simple – and comforting – to imagine and romanticise a picture of simple folk maintaining traditions and rituals for generations after they have left the old country. However, diaspora cuisines and customs are often examples of what Hobsbawm (1983: 1) called 'invented traditions', where "traditions which appear or claim to be old are very often quite recent in origin and sometimes invented".

The concept of invented traditions raises issues of authenticity. Due to space constraints, we will do no more than acknowledge the extensive literature on this issue and direct readers towards recent scholarship on authenticity and heritage cuisines (Avieli 2005; Chhabra et al. 2013; Timothy and Ron 2013a, 2013b). A further important consideration is why diaspora communities are so prone to mythologising their food cultures. Hobsbawm (1983) argued that invented traditions were a reaction to modernity and change, which seems particularly appropriate to the case of diasporas. Nostalgia and the importance of preserving shared memory also play a part (Timothy and Ron 2013b). A third factor may be media framing. This concept explains how media producers frame their stories around certain themes or tropes, arguably familiar to audiences and making them easier to comprehend. The notion of restaurants and chefs preserving their traditional heritage, often with recipes passed on from parents and grandparents, is a common example of such media framing (Frost et al. forthcoming).

In the second half of this chapter, we consider these issues of preservation, evolution, adaptation and authenticity through an examination of four well-known diaspora cuisines: Italian, Chinese, Indian and Mexican.

The Italians

Paradoxically, the food most associated with Italian cuisine is from the New World. Though ubiquitous as a base for pizza, pasta and salata, it was practically unknown in Italian cooking until the nineteenth century (Dickie 2008). Initially, tomatoes – along with a range of New World foods – were adopted into Spanish cuisine. They then spread into Italy through Spain's possessions there. When the great Italian emigrations began late in the nineteenth century, tomato-based dishes were relatively new. However, in the diaspora societies they were quickly reimagined as traditional fare.

Italian migration to the United States was fundamentally economic. As the newcomers prospered, they found they enjoyed a much higher standard of living. This allowed the everyday consumption of what had traditionally been festival foods (Gabaccia 1998). Sauces and desserts were richer and meat consumption rose well above that of their relatives who had remained behind. In turn, remittances and migrants returning home changed Italian cuisine with these new richer styles (Pilcher 2006). A similar pattern of food maintenance occurred for Greek and Turkish diasporas (Kaftanoglu and Timothy 2013). Italians and Greeks initially grew Mediterranean crops for their own consumption, but over time, they became 'food ambassadors', encouraging others to try their produce (Alonso and Krajsic 2013).

It was not so much what the Italians ate that attracted others but rather how they ate. Drawing on the traditions of the festa, their foodways were based around family and friends. Meals were long and convivial, with shared plates and wine as the chief drink. The latter was particularly attractive to Anglo societies beset by such high spirit consumption that they experimented with prohibition. Epitomised by *La Dolce Vita* (the Sweet Life), Italian culture was an attractive exotic blend of food, music, drinking and companionship. Furthermore, whereas French cuisine held elite status, Italian restaurants were viewed as cheap and egalitarian. Around the globe, Little Italy urban neighbourhoods became the place to head for a good time, and many of these distinctive neighbourhoods became the foundation for modern tourism and entertainment precincts (Frost et al. 2010; Gabaccia 1998; Pricolo and Swan 2013). Interestingly, in recent times Little Italies have been seen as potentially in need of heritage protection, as new waves of migrants from other cultures have moved in (Conforti 1996).

The Italian festa was also reimagined as a tourism festival accessible to all. In Australia, the Italian winemakers of the King Valley created an annual event called La Dolce Vita, characterised by food, wine and music at the wineries. We interviewed the members of the organising committee, who emphasised that it was the Italian food culture that attracted an audience that was predominantly non-Italian. As one organiser commented:

> [Women are] making salamis and cooking up all this pasta and food to die for … there's all that love and it's just like she's cooking for her own family … [customers] really like that we literally go out the back to pick our herbs as we need them or the tomatoes have just come off the vine this morning.… They all say about how wonderful the atmosphere is and how authentic it is.
>
> (these interviews are considered in greater detail in Laing and Frost 2013)

With such a festival, Italian culture is reimagined and enjoyed as old fashioned and traditional. Attendees from urban areas appreciate the rural setting and produce, even if they do not have home vegetable gardens and purchase most of their needs from supermarkets. The emphasis on women undertaking the bulk of the preparation and cooking highlights a past quite different to today and indeed has been highlighted in criticisms of Slow Food (Frost and Laing 2013). Nonetheless, it is an evocative image of how many people would like to live.

The Indians

Indian cuisine has spread around the globe but is particularly identified with Great Britain, in part because of its imperial history but also due to the waves of immigration from the sub-continent since independence in 1947. The period of the Raj saw a number of dishes partaken by the British while living in India become part of their traditional diet back home: the so-called Anglo-Indian cuisine (Procida 2003). The Victorian enthusiasm for Indian food was shared by the Empress herself, Queen Victoria. She was first served a curry by one of her personal attendants, Abdul Karim, who later taught the Queen how to read and write in Urdu. Victoria loved it and curry was cooked every day for lunch during the last ten years of her reign. While this appeared to have influenced her grandson, George V, who always ate a curry with his meals, Victoria's son, Edward VII, was not similarly enamoured and ordered all the Indian servants, including Karim, to return to India after Victoria's death (Basu 2010). His actions reflected the broader societal view of those who were not ex-colonials that Indian cuisine was suspect and had "negative connotations" (Buettner 2008: 874).

Some of these dishes, however, were not traditionally Indian but were invented for their colonial rulers, a form of 'food colonialism' linked to the "imaginary India whose allure was necessary to provoke an imperial interest in incorporating this Jewel into the British Crown" (Narayan 1995: 66). Thus, curry powder was created, a mixture of the kinds of spices that would have been used in various Indian dishes, and named after a dish (curry) which itself is an invention and might stem from the Tamil word *kari* (Narayan 1995). Mulligatawny soup was created by a chef at the Madras Club during the nineteenth century and contains curry powder. Kedgeree, a spicy rice dish with smoked fish, hard-boiled eggs and peas and another symbol of the Raj, was a staple dish at a Victorian aristocratic breakfast. It was said to be based on *khichri*, an Indian dish of rice and beans or rice and lentils from the fourteenth century, but its pedigree is unclear (Pilcher 2006).

South Asian immigrants in the 1950s and 1960s turned to cooking as a way to make a living, although few Britons patronised their restaurants then, other than those nostalgic for life back on the sub-continent. In the late 1960s and 1970s, younger people, particularly students, sought out cheap alternatives for a meal, and the number of curry houses across the nation grew tenfold between 1960 and 1980 (Buettner 2008). The Indian restaurant is now a staple of the high street, although it still retains an unfortunate image as the place to go when the pubs are closed, often to soak up an alcohol-fuelled binge (Buettner 2008). In response, a new type of Indian restaurant developed in the 1980s, which eschewed the tawdry decor and clichéd names of the curry houses (such as Taj Mahal or Tandoori Palace), and branded itself as upmarket and sophisticated. These were aimed at the knowledgeable (and wealthier) traveller who has stayed in one of the palace hotels in Rajasthan or experienced the ethnic cuisines found in Goa or Kerala, and the menus focused on regional specialties and home-style dishes, rather than the pastiche that is Chicken Tikka Masala (Buettner 2008). Despite this movement away from the cheap and cheerful curry house, a number of British cities are seeking to trade on their links with 'curry culture' and rebrand themselves as 'curry capitals'. Bradford promotes a 'curry trail', Manchester has a 'Curry Mile' and Birmingham refers to its 'Balti Quarter' or 'Balti Triangle' (Buettner 2008).

Interestingly, the menus that many British diners were exposed to and thought of as 'Indian' were in fact something quite different. As the chef Rick Stein points out in his television series *Rick Stein's Far Eastern Odyssey* (2009) and *Rick Stein's India* (2013), many of the Indian restaurants in Great Britain were in fact owned and run by immigrants from the Bangladesh port city of Sylhet. Most were Muslims, which Buettner (2008: 891) argues is rarely brought forward by commentators "worrying about British Muslims' loyalty to the nation and capacity for integration". Ethnic food is often used as an example of the benefits of a multicultural society, and its 'nonthreatening' face (Buettner 2008), yet the acceptance of South Asian food by mainstream Britain has not been accompanied by the widespread embrace of the people who make and serve it. A similar phenomenon can be witnessed in the case of Mexican food in the United States (Haverluk 2003). Fish (1997: 378) argues that it is 'boutique multiculturalism', "which is characterized by its superficial or cosmetic relationship to the objects of its affection". And like Indian food, Mexican food has also been criticised for being a pale imitation of the original (Ferrero 2002), as "the very standardization that proved decisive to a food's gaining wider acceptance beyond the migrant group was held against it by individuals who counted themselves better judges of quality and authenticity" (Buettner 2008: 881). Thus Madhur Jaffrey (1978) in *An Invitation to Indian Cooking* extoled the virtues of learning to cook Indian food at home, rather than patronise 'second-class establishments'. Rick Stein, on the other hand, urged his viewers during his *Far Eastern Odyssey* (2009) to ask for more traditional Bangladeshi dishes at their local restaurant such as a *fish dampokht* – "they'll all know it". The question of the nature of authenticity with respect to diaspora cuisine, however, is not straightforward (Chhabra et al. 2013), and some ethnic communities may be happy to present a hybrid product to their customers if it contributes to their economic prosperity (Narayan 1995).

The Chinese

Food is a critical element of 'cultural capital' for Chinese diaspora communities (Avieli 2005; Khun Eng 2006) and a strong marker of identity retention (Timothy and Ron 2013b). Paradoxically, the great wave of Chinese migration in the nineteenth century occurred during a period in which China was trying to remain distant from global influences. Primarily economic migrants, hundreds of thousands were drawn to the Gold Rushes of Australia, California, New Zealand and Canada. Others were attracted by trading opportunities or were recruited as indentured labour for agriculture in European colonies in the tropics.

When gold yields declined, many of the Chinese turned to agriculture, including market gardening (also known as truck farming) and high-value intensive crops. Their competitive advantage was prior experience with irrigation and small-scale cropping. Occupying a niche that many Anglos did not wish to engage in allowed them to avoid the discrimination they found in other jobs. Recent research has recognised that the Chinese were highly market focussed and entrepreneurial, working in well-organised groups and often in partnerships with Anglos who provided land and capital (Chan 1986; Frost 2002).

Nonetheless, recent reinterpretations have tended towards mythologising the Chinese diaspora. For example, at the Columbia State Historic Park in California, an interpretive panel shows two families at work in their gardens (Figure 3.1). One is Chinese, the other Anglo. Over a white picket fence, an Anglo woman and a Chinese man exchange produce. In the background their spouses and children watch on. The Chinese family has a vegetable garden, and the Anglos do not, but they do have fruit trees and chickens. Accordingly, the exchange suggests they are seeking mutual benefits from their different comparative advantages. It is an idyllic picture, firmly rooted in twenty-first-century ideals of multiculturalism. Was gold rush California like this? Most likely not. Nearby interpretation tells the visitor that the Chinese were marginalised, settled into a distinct camp on the outskirts of the European township.

Some Chinese established themselves as restaurateurs and cooks. The Australian goldfields artist S.T. Gill recorded an example in *John Alloo's Chinese Restaurant, Main Road, Ballarat* (1855). When Sovereign Hill Outdoor Museum was established in 1970, Gill's detailed drawing was used to create a replica of Alloo's business. The goldfields ports of San Francisco and Melbourne were the scenes for extensive Chinatowns which, like the various Little Italies (Conforti 1996), developed as restaurant precincts.

Early Chinese restaurants mainly served European food. Over time, a number of hybridised dishes evolved to satisfy curious diners. Chop Suey, for example,

Figure 3.1 Interpretive panel portraying Chinese-Anglo relationships at Columbia State Historic Park, California (Photo: W. Frost)

originated in California (Pilcher 2006). As with many diaspora cuisines, patrons were drawn from other cultures, partly due to novelty and partly due to the appreciation of value in cheap and hearty meals. One curious example of the enthusiasm for Chinese food occurred among the Jewish diaspora in New York, where they "have incorporated Chinese restaurant food into their new Jewish-American culture. Indeed, New York Jews love Chinese restaurant food so much that they have made it a second cuisine" (Tuchman and Levine 1993: 383). Adding to the intrigue, this seems to be despite Kosher sumptuary laws against pork and shellfish.

Ongoing shifts in Chinese cuisine are demonstrated in the example of Kylie Kwong, owner of the Sydney restaurant *Billy Kwong* and a fifth-generation Chinese-Australian. Her great-grandfather, Kwong Sue Duk, came to Australia in the 1850s during the gold rushes (Wahlqvist 2002). While neither of her parents speak Cantonese (nor does Kylie), their heritage expresses itself through food. Kylie learned the fundamentals of Cantonese cuisine from her mother, Pauline. Growing up in the same suburban Sydney street as one of the authors of this chapter (Laing), Kylie exposed the local children in the early 1970s to Chinese culture through the food that her family prepared. The Kwongs were the only Asian family in that neighbourhood and at the local primary school. Kylie recalls: "The Kwong kids were very popular at school because we always had birthday parties where mum would put on the most incredible spread of delicious Chinese dishes like soy sauce chicken wings, fried rice, Hokkien noodles and sweet and sour fish. All the kids used to come running" (Holden 2014: n.p.).

Kylie constantly stresses the importance of family with respect to her cooking when talking to the media and in her cookbooks and television programs: "I have always said that Italian people and Chinese people are very similar in that we consider food and family are sort of the centre of everything" (Dumbo Feather 2014: n.p.). She also makes it clear that her family, with its multicultural background, embraces multiple cultures through the food they eat. For example, she explains how Christmas offers an opportunity for the Kwong family to showcase both the diaspora cuisine and local delicacies:

> The feast directly reflects my incredible Australian–Chinese family in all its diversity. Alongside Mum's comforting red-braise of pork belly, potato and Chinese mushrooms, and the delicious pork wontons my Uncle Jimmy and his daughter, Bianca, fill and boil to order, sit bowls of Aunty June's refreshing, very Aussie coleslaw and a platter of her pineapple-studded glazed leg ham.
>
> (Kwong 2013: n.p.)

In the same vein, Kylie uses Chinese ingredients fused with Australian native bush foods such as finger limes, wallaby, yabbies and saltbush in her restaurant and cookbooks, to create 'high status' and award-winning cuisine from what was formerly "peasant and working-class food" (Khun Eng 2006: 231). Thus, Kylie is not cooking precisely the dishes she learnt from her mother. She observes: "The

[Australian] flavours are unique. It really has made me re-assess the whole notion of what Australian-Chinese food is. I've found that many of these ingredients are naturally in harmony with the Chinese flavour profile" (Burgess 2012: n.p.). Despite this, there are certain ingredients that Kylie would never contemplate using in a Chinese dish, as they are antithetical to its spirit or are strongly identified with another culture. We saw this when she appeared on the cooking reality show *Masterchef Australia* in 2014. During a challenge based around Chinese cooking, one of the contestants used prosciutto in fried rice, which Kylie frowned upon, commenting that it did not match, as "it's Italian". Kwong is an intriguing example of a diaspora 'food ambassador', combining both a traditional view and a new hybridised perspective. The latter allows her to look for new products and ingredients in the diaspora environment and then to adapt them to a traditional cuisine. Such innovation is evident in other diaspora communities, and this is a subject that would benefit significantly from further research.

The Mexicans

The Mexican restaurant is as ubiquitous across North America as the Indian restaurant is across Great Britain, and ingredients and culinary products relevant to the diaspora cuisines are commonly available for purchase in both countries. Tomato salsa, guacamole dip and taco shells are standard items on shelves around the globe, as are their Indian equivalents of basmati rice and spices such as curry leaves, cumin and turmeric. Another parallel between the two diaspora cuisines is the derision with which they were originally met. Chiles were feared in nineteenth-century North America, as it was thought that they "rotted the stomach and infected the skin and breath" (Haverluk 2003: 172). The initial reaction to curry among the British populace was no less damning (Buettner 2008). The difference in the American context is that people outside the diaspora have appropriated a Mexican theme to promote what is essentially fast food. The most famous is Taco Bell. The first Taco Bell restaurant was opened in 1962 by Glen Bell, a non-Mexican "serving fake Mexican food (in hard taco shells) in [a] fake Mission building in Downey, California" (Glick Kudler 2015: n.p.). There is no Indian equivalent in Great Britain. Perhaps memories of the Raj made this a bridge too far to cross.

Many Mexican restaurants across the world are seen as 'staged' for non-Mexican diners. The menus are highly standardised (Ferrero 2002), revolving around permutations of tacos, tortillas, nachos, enchiladas and frijoles. The décor is often composed of props, such as sombreros and Mexican flags, as well as imagery that evokes "Spanish missions, the Mexican revolution, or the rural ancestry of Mexican culture" (Ferrero 2002: 200). Themes are adopted throughout the year that link back to Mexican holidays and traditions. The May 5 (*Cinco de Mayo*) anniversary of the defeat of the French (1861–1865) in Puebla is celebrated in these restaurants but is "identified with Corona beer and margaritas" (Walker 2013: 660). Mexicans living outside of Puebla, however, disdain this commodification (and lack of respect) of what is a purely local holiday. Some restaurants feature motifs associated with the Mexican Day of the Dead, including skulls painted with flowers and skeletons, as a cultural twist to the Halloween decorations sported by many Anglo restaurants, given the two holidays are celebrated at the same time of the year (Figure 3.2). In Tijuana, this focus on the Day of the Dead is more pointed than it is in the United States, representing "a rejection of the commercialization of Halloween" (Walker 2013: 660). In a similar way, Tijuana restaurants celebrate Three Kings Day on January 6, which marks the visit of the Three Wise Men to the infant Jesus and prepare 'cod and turkey for Easter', rather than dyeing Easter eggs and teaching children about the Easter Bunny (Walker 2013). These festivals, including the food that is served at them, make political as well as cultural statements, on both sides of the border.

Mexican food is another example of a diaspora cuisine that has attempted to move away from its down-market roots in recent years. According to Rinderle (2005: 303), even the use of the term *Mexican* "carries class connotations", which leads some people towards a preference for the terms *Spanish* or *Hispanic* when referring to themselves or their culture. More authentic restaurants can be found clustered in certain districts, such as East and downtown Los Angeles, or the Mexican border town of Tijuana (Ferrero 2002; Walker 2013). Some of these restaurants feature *alta cocina mexicana*, a food movement which aims to fuse "Old World techniques with New World ingredients" and shuns stereotypical dishes "in favour of dishes associated with Central Mexico [which is] both a conscious act of nation-building and a performance of maintaining and creating authenticity"

Figure 3.2 Day of the Dead imagery in a Mexican restaurant in the university town of Davis, California (Photo: J. Laing)

(Walker 2013: 650). Yet without a certain degree of commodification, it is unlikely that Mexican food would have the foothold that it has and thus provide members of the diaspora with a livelihood and degree of economic status. This is another commonality with the story of the diffusion of Indian cuisine throughout Great Britain. The romantic view of what was essentially peasant food has also been criticised (Walker 2013), similar to the eulogising of Slow Food, which overlooks issues of economic inequality and hardship (Donati 2005; Frost and Laing 2013).

While Ferrero (2002: 208–209) argues that Mexican food provides the diaspora with an opportunity to "demonstrate entrepreneurial skills" and gives it "cultural empowerment", this is an overly rosy view of how widespread its acceptance has been more generally throughout American society. As Haverluk (2003) observes, while Mexican food has become a staple part of the American diet, Mexican holidays are observed and Mexican-themed festivals burgeon, such as the chile festival, this does not mean that the Mexican diaspora has been accepted as an integral part of mainstream American society. This dilemma for members of this diaspora, like others we have discussed in this chapter, is how to leverage on the interest in their traditional cuisine without losing the integrity of their culture in the process, and in a way that avoids marginalisation.

Conclusion

In our recent book examining traditional rituals in the modern world, we argued that traditions and customs continue to persist through four processes. These are: preservation, adaptation, appropriation and invention (Frost and Laing 2015: 3). Applying that framework to cuisines and foodways, we argue that diaspora cuisines are primarily distinguished by adaptation.

Such a contention perhaps conflicts with what is held in the popular imagination. Diaspora cuisines are often presented – particularly in the media – as the preservation of traditional heritage, albeit transferred to another place. Such a view sees recipes, customs and ingredients as historic artefacts in a sort of culinary living museum. The persistence of this culture is linked popularly to notions of ethnic groups maintaining their identity intact and unchanged in the face of forces of globalisation and assimilation (Codesal 2010; Sim and Leith 2013; Thursby 2004).

In this chapter, we have presented an alternative view. This recognises that the processes and outcomes related to diaspora cuisines are far more dynamic and complex than popularly held. Rather than museum pieces, these are evidence of the constantly evolving nature of migrant communities. Drawing on examples from Chinese, Indian, Mexican and Italian diaspora cuisines, we have demonstrated that while persisting as identifiable ethnic cultures, they have changed greatly over time.

The migrant experience is inextricably linked to changing cultures. In leaving their homelands, migrants come into contact with new environments and cultures. In terms of cuisine, they encounter new ingredients and foodways. At the same time, nostalgia and homesickness influence them to cling to certain comforting elements.

Over generations, certain foods and rituals become mythologised. Festival foods, for example, become the norm, and past experiences of drudgery and poor nutrition get forgotten. Interactions with other groups lead to further adaptations. Primarily motivated by economic opportunities, some migrants modify their cuisine, changing recipes and experimenting with new ingredients to better suit the tastes of broader communities. The result is that most diaspora cuisines quickly become hybridised, consumed and enjoyed by many who are not part of the diaspora community.

References

Alonso, A.D. and Krajsic, V. (2013) Food heritage down under: olive growers as Mediterranean food ambassadors. *Journal of Heritage Tourism*, 8(2/3): 158–171.

Avieli, N. (2005) Roasted pigs and bao dumplings: festive food and imagined transnational identity in Chinese-Vietnamese festivals. *Asia Pacific Viewpoint*, 46(3): 281–293.

Basu, S. (2010) *Victoria & Abdul: The True Story of the Queen's Closest Confidant*. New Delhi: Rupa & Co.

Belich, J. (2009) *Replenishing the Earth: The Settler Revolution and the Rise of the Anglo World*. Oxford: Oxford University Press.

Buettner, E. (2008) "Going for an Indian": South Asian restaurants and the limits of multiculturalism in Britain. *The Journal of Modern History*, 80: 865–901.

Burgess, K. (2012) Kylie Kwong on bush tucker. *Gourmet Traveller*, September. Available online at http://www.gourmettraveller.com.au/restaurants/restaurant-news-features/2012/8/kylie-kwong-on-bush-tucker/ Accessed January 15, 2015.

Chan, S. (1986) *The Bittersweet Soil: The Chinese in California Agriculture, 1860–1910*. Berkeley: University of California Press.

Chhabra, D., Lee, W., Zhao, S. and Scott, K. (2013) Marketing of ethnic food experiences: authentication analysis of Indian cuisine abroad. *Journal of Heritage Tourism*, 8(2/3): 145–157.

Codesal, D.M. (2010) Eating abroad, remembering (at) home: three foodscapes of Ecuadorian migration in New York, London and Santander. *Anthropology of Food*, 7: n.p. (online). Available at: https://aof.revues.org/6642?lang=fr

Coles, T. and Timothy, D.J. (2004) My field is the world: conceptualizing diasporas, travel and tourism. In T. Coles and D.J. Timothy (eds) *Tourism, Diasporas and Space*, pp. 1–29. London: Routledge.

Conforti, J.M. (1996) Ghettos as tourism attractions. *Annals of Tourism Research*, 23(4): 830–842.

Crosby, A.W. (1986) *Ecological Imperialism: The Biological Expansion of Europe 900–1900*. Cambridge: Cambridge University Press.

Dickie, J. (2008) *Delizia! The Epic History of the Italians and Their Food*. New York: The Free Press.

Donati, K. (2005) The pleasure of diversity in slow food's ethics of taste. *Food Culture and Society*, 8(2): 227–242.

Dumbo Feather (2014) Kylie Kwong is a chef. *Dumbo Feather*. Available online at http://www.dumbofeather.com/conversation/kylie-kwong-is-a-chef/#sthash.5UWrV2XW.dpuf Accessed January 15, 2015.

Ferrero, S. (2002) *Comida sin par*. Consumption of Mexican food in Los Angeles: "Foodscapes" in a transnational consumer society'. In W. Belasco and P. Scranton (eds) *Food Nations: Selling Taste in Consumer Societies*, pp. 194–219. New York: Routledge.

Fish, S. (1997) Boutique multiculturalism, or why Liberals are incapable of thinking about hate speech. *Critical Inquiry*, 23(2), 378–395.

Frost, W. (2002) Migrants and technological transfer: Chinese farming in Australia, 1850–1920. *Australian Economic History Review*, 42(2): 113–131.

Frost, W. and Laing, J. (2013) Communicating persuasive messages through slow food festivals. *Journal of Vacation Marketing*, 19(1): 67–74.

Frost, W. and Laing, J. (2014) Old World winemakers in the New Worlds of California and Victoria. In M. Harvey, L. White and W. Frost (eds) *Wine and Identity: Branding, Heritage, Terroir*, pp. 17–28. London: Routledge.

Frost, W. and Laing, J. (2015) From pre-modern rituals to modern events. In J. Laing and W. Frost (eds) *Rituals and Traditional Events in the Modern World*, pp. 1–19. London: Routledge.

Frost, W., Laing, J., Strickland, P., Lade, C., Best, G. and Williams, K. (forthcoming) *Gastronomy, Tourism and the Media*. Bristol: Channel View Publications.

Frost, W., Laing, J., Wheeler, F. and Reeves, K. (2010) Coffee culture, heritage and destination image: Melbourne and the Italian model. In L. Jolliffe (ed.) *Coffee Culture, Destinations and Tourism*, pp. 99–110. Clevedon: Channel View Publications.

Frost, W., Reeves, K., Laing, J. and Wheeler, F. (2009) Villages, vineyards and Chinese dragons: constructing the heritage of ethnic diasporas. *Tourism, Culture & Communication*, 9(2): 107–114.

Gabaccia, D.R. (1998) *We Are What We Eat: Ethic Food and the Making of Americans*. Cambridge MA: Harvard University Press.

Glick Kudler, A. (2015) The oddball original locations of Los Angeles's most famous fast food chains. *LA Curbed*, January 28. Available online at http://la.curbed.com/archives/2015/01/the_oddball_original_locations_of_los_angeless_most_famous_fast_food_chains.php Accessed February 1, 2015.

Haverluk, T.W. (2003) Mex-America: From margin to mainstream. In G.J. Hausladen (ed.) *Western Places, American Myths: How We Think about the West*, pp. 166–183. Reno: University of Nevada Press.

Hobsbawm, E. (1983) Introduction: inventing traditions. In E. Hobsbawm and T. Ranger (eds) *The Invention of Tradition*, pp. 1–14. Cambridge: Cambridge University Press.

Holden, M. (2014) Kylie Kwong's wallaby with black bean and chilli. *Good Food*, October 10, 2014. Available online at http://www.goodfood.com.au/good-food/cook/kylie-kwongs-wallaby-with-black-bean-and-chilli-20141003–10pmj0.html Accessed January 15, 2015.

Jaffrey, M. (1978) *An Invitation to Indian Cooking*. Harmondsworth: Penguin.

Kaftanoglu, B. and Timothy, D.J. (2013) Return travel, assimilation, and cultural maintenance: An example of Turkish-Americans in Arizona. *Tourism Analysis*, 18(3): 273–284.

Khun Eng, K-P. (2006) Transnational self in the Chinese diaspora: a conceptual framework. *Asian Studies Review*, 30: 223–239.

Kwong, K. (2013) Australian Christmas feasts: the Kwong clan's Christmas. *The Guardian*, December 20, 2013. Available online at http://www.theguardian.com/lifeandstyle/australia-food-blog/2013/dec/20/australian-christmas-feasts-the-kwong-clans-christmas Accessed January 15, 2015.

Laing, J. and Frost, W. (2013) Food, wine . . . heritage, identity? Two case studies of Italian diaspora festivals in regional Victoria. *Tourism Analysis*, 18(3): 323–334.

Mokyr, J. (1990) *The Lever of Riches: Technological Creativity and Economic Progress*. New York: Oxford University Press.

Narayan, U. (1995) Eating cultures: incorporation, identity and Indian food. *Social Identities: Journal for the Study of Race, Nation and Culture*, 1(1): 63–86.

Pilcher, S.M. (2006) *Food in World History*. New York: Routledge.

Pricolo, A. and Swan, S. (2013) *Lygon St – Si Parla Italiano* (Documentary). Melbourne: Two Taps Productions.

Procida, M.A. (2003) Feeding the imperial appetite: imperial knowledge and Anglo-Indian discourse. *Journal of Women's History*, 15(2): 123–149.

Rinderle, S. (2005) The Mexican diaspora: a critical examination of signifiers. *Journal of Communication Inquiry*, 29(4): 294–316.

Shortridge, B.G. (2004) Ethnic heritage food in Lindsborg, Kansas, and New Glarus, Wisconsin. In L.M. Long (ed.) *Culinary Tourism*, pp. 268–296. Lexington: University Press of Kentucky.

Sim, D. and Leith, M. (2013) Diaspora tourists and the Scottish homecoming 2009. *Journal of Heritage Tourism*, 8(4): 259–274.

Simon, J. (1989) *The Economic Consequences of Migration*. Oxford: Basil Blackwell.

Timothy, D.J. and Ron, A.S. (2013a) Heritage cuisines, regional identity and sustainable tourism. In C.M. Hall and S. Gössling (eds) *Sustainable Culinary Systems: Local Foods, Innovation, Tourism and Hospitality*, pp. 275–290. London: Routledge.

Timothy, D.J. and Ron, A.S. (2013b) Understanding heritage cuisines and tourism: identity, image, authenticity, and change. *Journal of Heritage Tourism*, 8(2/3): 99–104.

Thursby, J.S. (2004) Culinary tourism among Basques and Basque Americans: maintenance and inventions. In L.M. Long (ed.) *Culinary Tourism*, pp. 186–205. Lexington: University Press of Kentucky.

Tuchman, G. and Levine, H.G. (1993) New York Jews and Chinese food: the social construction of an ethnic pattern. *Journal of Contemporary Ethnography*, 22(3): 382–407.

Wahlqvist, M. (2002) Asian migration to Australia: food and health consequences. *Asia Pacific Journal of Clinical Nutrition*, 11: S562–S568.

Walker, M.A. (2013) Border food and food on the border: meaning and practice in Mexican haute cuisine. *Social & Cultural Geography*, 14(6): 649–667.

4 Food, heritage and nationalism

Gregory Ramshaw

Introduction

Few aspects of heritage instill as much pride – and, perhaps, dissonance and debate – as nationalism, particularly how national identities are practiced and by whom. Similarly, cuisine is one of the chief symbols of nationalism, and can equally be a source of pride, a vehicle for social and economic development, and a basis for deep divisions. Indeed, food and its preparation are part of virtually every aspect of the personal and collective heritages. If we accept Lowenthal's (1998) assertion that heredity is the most basic and innate form of heritage, then even inherited food allergies such as Celiac disease may be considered a form of (unwelcome) heritage. However, food – and, perhaps more specifically, cuisine – plays a prominent and integral role in the creation, maintenance, and promotion of regional and national identities (Bessière 2013; Pilcher 1996).

The sourcing of local ingredients, regional food preparation techniques, and dishes associated with specific people and places are paramount in the creation and maintenance of national mythologies, as well as a potent tool in place promotion and marketing for tourism. However, in the age of globalization, especially as food cultures become more mobile and accessible, particular challenges and tensions have also become apparent. This chapter therefore explores the relationship among food, cuisine, and heritage, with particular emphasis on how cuisine interacts with regional and national identities. It also examines food and cuisine as a source of heritage dissonance.

Relationship among heritage, cuisine, and nationalism

Heritage, best described by Timothy (2011) as the present use of the past, is used for a variety of purposes that can run from political legitimization of regimes and rulers to the economic development of regions and communities through tourism. It is no surprise, therefore, that a strong and enduring relationship exists between heritage and cuisine. Indeed, one could even say that to know a people, one needs to know something about the food they eat. Ingredients, preparation, and consumption can reflect a great deal about a region or nation. Even something as banal as coffee from a franchise café chain can become a symbol of national pride and identity, as is the case with the Tim Horton's brand in Canada (Foster, Suddaby, Minkus and Wiebe 2011). However, beyond simply consumption, cuisine plays a central role in the creation of heritage identities and, often, as a source of differentiation.

The sourcing of ingredients is pivotal in the creation of cuisine-based heritages. In particular, the establishment of 'traditional' foods requires a supply chain that includes both human geography, including local sourcing, long-standing regional relationships (often built over generations), history, politics and folklore, and physical geography, including abilities of the local landscape and environment to produce particular foodstuffs. While the procurement of local produce was once a necessity and, as Grasseni (2011) suggests, has only recently been explicitly given a patrimony and been heritagized, it nevertheless suggests an historical basis for the foundation of cuisine-based heritage – the ingredients themselves. Further, as Pilcher (2014) suggests, ingredients were also a result of particular political, geographical, and historical circumstances. Of course, the idea of some sort of objective authenticity for the 'original' ingredients of particular foods is contested, not only by the aforementioned political, geographical, and historical circumstances but also through the dynamism of taste and consumption. In other words, the 'originators' of particular dishes almost certainly improvised based on the availability (or lack thereof) of particular ingredients. Similarly, historical circumstances, such as the availability of foodstuffs based on trade routes and colonialism, also played role. Foods commonly viewed as being linked to a particular national identity often originated in other locations, or can be shared between different and often disparate cultures. Tea, for example, is linked to many different cultures, though its preparation and the social meanings and contexts behind its consumption will vary widely (Jolliffe 2003, 2007).

Preparations of particular cuisines are another way in which heritage meanings are created. Food preparation is, of course, based on the availability of particular ingredients; however, the ways in which cuisine is prepared are part of many different scales of heritage. Many families have 'secret recipes' that are passed down from generation to generation, just like any other heirloom, and many forms of food preparation remain largely part of family pride and may generally only be experienced and consumed within small community contexts (the ubiquitous community bake sales perhaps being the best example). The idea of a 'home-cooked meal' and the 'secret family recipe' is often reflective of broader values, including the importance of home in heritage (Ramshaw and Gammon 2010) and the idea that home, as Burns and Novick (1994: n.p.) contend, "brings us back to where we're safe, and where we care, where we're cared about, and where we're loved". In some ways, the home-cooked meal prepared by someone who loves us enough to cook something special, just for us, becomes an authentic antidote to mass production and industrialization. Of course, the values of a home-cooked meal and the secret family recipe too have been broadly commodified and industrialized. Perhaps most famously, the secret family recipe of Colonel Harland Sanders's fried chicken, and the image of both southern American food and culture that his restaurant promotes, reflects a kind of glocalization of heritage and food preparation whereby the intimate and familial becomes a globally consumed product.

Preparation of regional cuisines can be, as Bessière (1998: 23) argues, an emblem of local heritage and identity, "a kind of a banner beneath which the inhabitants of a given area recognize themselves". Food preparation becomes reflective of particular community or regional values, social connections, and as a means of establishing a particular (and often different) identity. While much regional food preparation is, again, subject to the availability (particular historical availability) of particular ingredients, the notion of a community sharing ingredients and knowledge, or that a regional people are in some ways legitimized in creating particular cuisines reflects particular heritage values. Goris (2014), for example, examines the role of moonshine in South Carolina, finding that the way the beverage is distilled and by whom plays a significant role in regional-based heritage identities. Similarly, national cuisines are subject to particular legitimizing practices as well that protect and enshrine heritage values. In other words, the heritage value of cuisine is not just in what is prepared but how it is prepared, by whom, and in which context.

The experience of consuming cuisine – how cuisine is consumed and the context in which it is consumed – also reflects particular cultural heritage values and is often part of the ways in which heritage identities are created and consumed. The kinds of utensils (if any), the order of the meal, the forms and types of conversation or entertainment, and the room and décor in which the cuisine is consumed may all reflect aspects of heritage and, in particular, regional or national heritages. Particular meanings associated with meals may be, as Hobsbawm (1983) termed it, a form of invented tradition that is frequently linked to forms of national identity and heritage. The traditional Thanksgiving day feast in the United States, which almost invariably includes turkey, root vegetables, and pumpkin pie, is meant to harken symbolically back to the beginnings of the nation and, in particular, the sharing of the feast between the early Pilgrims and local aboriginals. The turkey, in particular, plays an important national role, as each Thanksgiving the president of the United States 'pardons' a turkey from slaughter. However, as Adamczyk (2002) notes, the 'traditions' of American Thanksgiving have been exceptionally malleable and have been constructed and discarded based on a variety of social, political, and economic circumstances.

The context in which meals take place is also important. As Veblen (1899) described, setting, particularly for meals, denotes forms of conspicuous leisure and class. Invariably, the context for meals both in décor as well as pace will denote national values around various (and, often, conflicting) ideas of civility and refinement. Indeed, the entire Slow Food Movement is, in part, a reaction to both the perceived global industrial production and consumption of food (largely as a result of convenient and cheap fast-food options) as well as the social, environmental, and health benefits of locally grown and consumed products (Petrini 2003). Though not explicitly citing national values, the underlying discourse of the Slow Food Movement pits an Old-World, European approach to food production and consumption in opposition to a contemporary, American view of food being rapidly produced and consumed.

The conservation of food and cuisine, an element of the Slow Food Movement, is also part of the contemporary cultural heritage landscape. The idea of threat is paramount to heritage conservation as well as nationalism (Lowenthal 1998), and food-based heritages are no different. Again, returning to the Slow Food Movement, the idea of conserving particular agricultural and food preparation practices is integral to its philosophy, in part because of the threat that global food monoculture poses. However, the conservation of cuisines is linked to other forms of nationalism as well. The recent First World War commemorations included the reissuing of ration-based cookbooks as well as the experimentation with professional chefs attempting to cook the recipes. Although ostensibly the cookbooks are souvenirs and the cooking a form of experimental archaeology, the widespread dissemination of cooking and cuisine in wartime points to larger links between food, heritage, and nationalism. Indeed, understanding how our forbearers did 'more with less' also suggests a form of national sacrifice, particularly in contrast with our contemporary consumer culture. Wartime cuisine not only helps to conserve a particular past, but it also provides a form of national remembrance.

All of the local sourcing and legacy of ingredients, the traditions and meanings associated with preparation and consumption of cuisine, and the conservation of particular food-based heritages often invariably lead to the use of food and cuisine in heritage and cultural tourism. As Hall and Sharples (2003) suggest, food and cuisine are expressions of regional cultures and environment, so there are naturally ties to heritage identities and marketing for heritage tourism (Figure 4.1). Indeed, food and cuisine can be a strong maker and marker of place, and can be a source of differentiation and uniqueness in a globally competitive tourism environment (Hall and Sharples 2003). Conversely, culinary heritage tourism, particularly that which involves extreme foods (such as insects), may also be viewed less as a means of experiencing other cultures and nationalities and more as a way of expressing personal identities and acquiring capital (Molz 2007). At a national level, distinctive cuisine can be one of the main ways destinations attract tourists and are often some of the most memorable parts of journeys for tourists. The fact that many of the top countries for international tourism arrivals, such as France, Italy, and Spain, also have well-known and significant culinary heritages certainly is not a coincidence.

While having an 'authentic' regional or national dish is almost invariably part of a broader leisure tourism experience, the fact that many destinations have specifically focused on food and culinary heritages as a means of developing new and innovate products demonstrates the potency of cuisine in heritage tourism development (Alonso 2013; Febriani 2015; Metro-Roland 2013; Timothy and Ron 2013). In particular, many heritage trails have been developed along regional food-based narratives. The development of food-based trails is also viewed as a more sustainable strategy for cultural tourism, as well as for enhancing rural tourism development (Timothy and Boyd 2015). According to Boyne, Hall, and Williams (2003), food-based heritage trails can offer positive economic and social

Figure 4.1 *Fideuà*, one of the distinctive dishes of the Catalonia region of Spain (Photo: Dallen J. Timothy)

benefits for regions, including strengthening an area's tourism products, enhancing visitors' experiences, and helping to maintain and enhance the viability of the local food production and processing sectors. Furthermore, Telfer (2001) argues that the development of food-based trails, such as the winery routes in the Niagara region, can help in creating successful partnerships and alliances between tourism operators and food and beverage providers. In particular, Telfer notes that regional wineries that recognized the potential of tourism and have taken an aggressive approach to tourism including marketing benefitted through additional on-site wine and related merchandise sales. Food-based trails are particularly popular in regions where attractions are spatially diverse, such as in the United States (Timothy and Boyd 2015). Linear and nodal trails such as the Moonshine Trail in Tennessee and the BBQ Trail in South Carolina both provide an expression of regional cultural identities through specific culinary heritages as well as aid in rural tourism development. In terms of national and regional heritage identities, Everett and Aitchison (2008) found that, in Cornwall, England, the development of food-based heritage narratives helped in the retention and development of regional identities and traditions, aided in the awareness of environmental and sustainability issues for providers and guests alike, positively contributed to higher levels of tourist spending, and helped to facilitate the extension of the tourist season. Ideally, culinary trails would have the same impact.

Constructions of place and place identity are another important relationship between tourism and culinary heritage. In addition to creating 'real' and 'authentic' experiences through culinary experiences, food is one of the mechanisms by which distinctive heritage-based place identities are created. In the global race between places for tourism, investment, and attention, heritage is one of the ways in which increasingly homogenous communities differentiate themselves from their competitors (Morley and Robins 1995), and it stands to reason that regional or national cuisines, being a particularly sensuous and memorable heritage experience, play a vital role in place construction and competition (Figure 4.2). As such, it is not just the cuisine itself but also the context in which the cuisine is consumed that plays a vital role in heritage-based place construction. The restaurant or setting of the meal, who serves it and how it is served, the fellow diners (particularly if they are not tourists), and the décor will all play a role in place construction. Furthermore, these contexts will also be either consciously positioned as reflecting regional or national identities, or tourists will interpret them as reflecting 'typical' and authentic reflections of regional or national cultures (Urry 2002). Destination branding also plays a vital role in place construction, though heritage cuisines can also be somewhat Janus-headed in terms of how they are promoted. Gyimóthy and Mykletun (2009), for example, explored the use of traditional Nordic dishes, such as a cooked sheep's head, as a form of

Figure 4.2 A day's tuna harvest in the Maldives. Tuna is the primary ingredient for many Maldivian national dishes, and the fish is a significant source of national pride in this island nation (Photo: Dallen J. Timothy)

both heritage cuisine and extreme, 'scary' foods. In this case, the old, traditional, heritage-based 'scary' food is also a contemporary reinvention for adventurous travelers.

Issues

In late 2014, the BBC reported on an online backlash directed at British celebrity chef Jamie Oliver based on the fact that he had created an 'interpretation' of Jollof rice, a traditional West-African dish ("Africans reject" 2014). The controversy, in which Oliver took the basic tenants of the Jollof rice recipe while creating something new and contemporary, highlights some of the issues that exist in heritage cuisines, specifically which nations or peoples 'own' particular cuisines, who is able to cook and adapt these cuisines, and how the global consumption of traditional cuisines (and, seemingly, heritage cuisine-based media) may create simulacrums from traditional foods. As such, issues of heritagization and dissonance, production and distribution, and commodification all play significant roles in how heritage cuisines are created and consumed, particularly through the lens of regional or national identities.

Heritagization, as described by Poria (2010), is the manner and process by which the past is represented and interpreted in the present. All heritage, in some respects, goes through the heritagization process, as a past has to be consciously plucked and used in the present for a variety of reasons and circumstances. However, one of the consequences of the heritagization process is that particular pasts can become ossified and inflexible to innovation, which is particularly challenging when culture (viewed as the present) and heritage (viewed as the past) are often created and consumed at the same time (Roberts 2014). Bessière (2013), for example, discusses the heritagization of food-based rituals and preparation and suggests there is a tension between incorporating traditional 'heritage' products and practices with modern styles and techniques. Although heritagization could also be used as a means of resurrecting and protecting particular traditions and places, galvanizing support for present issues and anticipated future needs, and creating pride and economic development out of the remnants of the past (Howard 2003), all of which could be used in the creation and conservation of heritage-based cuisines, the tension between petrification and innovation remains a challenge.

Fusion cuisines are now commonplace, and the blend of past and present in cuisine preparation is now, perhaps, an expectation of many consumers. However, the tension between keeping a cuisine 'traditional', no matter how complex the lineage or untraditional a 'traditional' cuisine may be (Pilcher 2014), and the desire, both from the creators' and consumers' points of view, of creating a 'new' dish from a heritage template is an issue. Of course, this issue is compounded when considering the significant role food plays in the creation of regional and national identities. Ossifying a particular dish, to be made in a particular location by local people, using tradition ingredients, has significant economic, social, and political consequences.

Graham, Ashworth and Tunbridge (2000) suggest that dissonance is, perhaps, the one unifying characteristic of heritage. The notion that every heritage could potentially spark discord amongst rival claimants suggests that food-based heritage could be one of the major battlegrounds of heritage ownership. The aforementioned Jamie Oliver case is but one widely broadcast example of food-based heritage dissonance, but certainly the links between food and national heritages are certain to spark discord in much less public venues. Hall's (1999) critique of contemporary constructions of national heritage suggests that intangible heritages become symbols of the national story and national traditions. Of course, who belongs to the nation, and who is authorized to use its heritage, can be a source of immense discord. When considering intangible heritages such as food and cuisine and their importance to heritage identities, the contemporary mobilities of people and cultures may mean that food becomes a place where, to borrow Smith's (2006) phrase, authorized heritage discourses are entrenched as a means of creating ownership of cuisine-based traditions. In other words, who has the 'right' to particular heritage cuisines, how cuisines are prepared, who prepares the cuisine, and how and where the cuisine is served could be a source of debate and disagreement.

The production and distribution of heritage cuisines is another area of concern, particularly when considering the pressures contemporary globalization place on food-based heritages. Grasseni (2011: n.p.) notes that "food is being rediscovered and reinvented: both as a means of local development and as a bearer of collective territorial identities". Although the rediscovery of heritage-based cuisine is, in part, to (re)establish and (re)enforce regional and national identities while also warding off rival claimants, ultimately there is a tension between the traditional means of preparation and distribution and the demands of the global market. An example of this 'glocal' tension exists in one particular ongoing study (of which the author is a member) that is looking at the establishment of a seafood trail on the South Carolina coast.

Ostensibly, the study is looking at a vehicle for rural tourism development outside of the main coastal tourist nodes (e.g. Myrtle Beach, Charleston, and Hilton Head Island) while also supporting the local seafood industry, which has been hard-hit in recent generations. However, one of the central findings of the study to date has been that the demands of the coastal tourism industry far outstrips the supply of local seafood and that imported seafood must be used by the tourism industry to meet demand. Similarly, there is a large external market (i.e. non–South Carolina) that has an interest in South Carolina seafood. As such, traditional South Carolina coastal cuisine has to be both supplemented by external providers as well as promoted and sold well beyond the local market. Grasseni (2011) argues that local food production is subject to broader, globalized standardization protocols, such as bilateral or multilateral trade agreements. Applied to the example above, South Carolina seafood is subject to the rules of global trade in terms of its broad distribution, while often the produce from which 'traditional' South Carolina seafood dishes are created originates from China because of advantageous bilateral trade agreements with the United States. Ultimately, the tension between global and local heritage foods is multilayered, complex, and frequently invisible to consumers.

The commodification of heritage cuisines, particularly for the global tourism market, is another area where tensions exist in food-based heritages, particularly as they relate to nationalism and national identities. Of course, many foods reflect Baudrillard's (1994) ideas of signs and symbols as essentialist modes of particular places, values, or ideas. The sugar maple tree – and its sap from which maple syrup is created – is widely connected to representations of Canada. Any tourist shop in virtually any region in Canada will sell Canadian maple syrup, despite the fact that sugar maple trees only grow in a few regions of Canada and that maple syrup production is largely confined to a small part of the country. Maple syrup is a symbol of Canada, however, and as such, is broadly commodified as an authentic Canadian food product despite its relatively small geographical footprint. Though commodification and authenticity, in this case, appear in opposition to one another, Waterton and Watson (2015: 8) warn that commodification and authenticity are, more often than not, connected based in large part because "commodities are not the basis of exchange in the heritage economy". To illustrate, they use the example of a visitor to Venice sipping a coffee in the Piazza San Marco, whereby it

> is more than the infusion of the coffee bean; it is more than a complex product of the tourism industry; it is an experience writ large around you, keenly felt. And, if you have any doubts that it is more than a commodity, you will find evidence in the bill.
>
> (Waterton and Watson 2015: 8)

As such, the commodification of food-based heritage becomes very much about the perceptions and experience of the consumer and whether cuisine becomes a way to represent an authentic heritage practice. However, perhaps the issue becomes whether the cuisine becomes a symbol by which a people express their identity, and of which outsiders may partake, or that a version the cuisine is self-consciously produced for one audience (tourists/outsiders) as a commodity, whereby the 'authentic' production and consumption happens in some version of MacCannell's (1973) tourism backstage.

Conclusion

The relationship between heritage and nationalism is complex. As Winter (2015) explains, heritage is a key player in the tension among local, national, and transnational identities, whereby we are in an era of post-nationalism, cosmopolitanism, and flexible citizenship, while also cementing the nation-state as the key symbol of identity. Food and cuisine appear to be one of the central facets of this tension, as cuisine is one of the ways in which we engage with the 'global bazaar' at home while also desiring something unique, authentic, and representative of a particular cultural heritage while abroad. Certainly, food has been one of the ways that regional and national heritages have been practiced, entrenched, and commodified, and it has become a key promoter of place differentiation, particularly in tourism. However, the ossification of particular heritage cuisines has also caused tension and dissonance, particularly as food has become a focal point of distinction between regions and nations. Furthermore, the commodification of heritage cuisines also contributes to the inflexibility of national identities, echoing Hewison's (1987) critique of heritage as a reactive rather than progressive process. In some respects, food and cuisine are some of the best ways to practice, promote, and experience regional and national heritages, while also being a potential barrier to contemporary, dynamic identities.

References

Adamczyk, A. (2002) On Thanksgiving and collective memory: constructing the American tradition. *Journal of Historical Sociology*, 15: 343–365.

Africans reject Jamie's Jollof rice recipe. (2014, October 30). Available online at http://www.bbc.com/news/blogs-trending-29831183 Accessed April 3, 2015.

Alonso, A.D. (2013) Tannat: the positioning of a wine grape as a symbol and 'referent' of a nation's gastronomic heritage. *Journal of Heritage Tourism*, 8(2/3): 105–119.

Baudrillard, J. (1994) *Simulacra and Simulation*. Ann Arbor: University of Michigan Press.

Bessière, J. (1998) Local development and heritage: traditional food and cuisine as tourist attractions in rural areas. *Sociologia Ruralis*, 38: 21–34.

Bessière, J. (2013) 'Heritagisation', a challenge for tourism promotion and regional development: an example of food heritage. *Journal of Heritage Tourism*, 8(4): 275–291.

Boyne, S., Hall, D. and Williams, F. (2003) Policy, support and promotion for food-related tourism initiatives. *Journal of Travel & Tourism Marketing*, 14(3): 131–154.

Burns, K. (director/producer) and Novick, L. (producer) (1994) *Baseball: A Film by Ken Burns, The Ninth Inning: Home 1970–1994* [motion picture]. United States: PBS Home Video.

Everett, S. and Aitchison, C. (2008) The role of food tourism in sustaining regional identity: a case study of Cornwall, South West England. *Journal of Sustainable Tourism*,16(2): 150–167.

Febriani, I. (2015) Tasting Indonesia: cosmopolitanism in culinary tourism. *International Journal of Tourism Anthropology*, 4(2): 111–121.

Foster, W.M., Suddaby, R., Minkus, A. and Wiebe, E. (2011) History as social memory assets: the example of Tim Horton's. *Management & Organizational History*, 6(1): 101–120.

Goris, L. (2014) *Moonshine in South Carolina (USA): A Case of Food-based Heritage Tourism Development and Identity.* Unpublished Masters Thesis, University of Leuven, Belgium.

Graham, B., Ashworth, G.J. and Tunbridge, J.E. (2000) *A Geography of Heritage: Power, Culture & Economy*. London: Arnold.

Grasseni, C. (2011) Re-inventing food: Alpine cheese in the age of global heritage. *Anthropology of Food*, 8: n.p. (online). Available at at http://aof.revues.org/6819.

Gyimóthy, S. and Mykletun, J. (2009) Scary food: commodifying culinary heritage as meal adventures in tourism. *Journal of Vacation Marketing*, 15(3): 259–273.

Hall, C.M. and Sharples, L. (2003) The consumption of experiences or the experience of consumption? An introduction to the tourism of taste. In C.M. Hall, L. Sharples, R. Mitchell, N. Macionis and B. Cambourne (eds) *Food Tourism around the World: Development, Management and Markets*, pp. 1–24. Oxford: Butterworth Heinemann.

Hall, S. (1999) Whose heritage? Un-settling 'the heritage', re-imagining the post-nation. *Third Text*, 13(49): 3–13.

Hewison, R. (1987) *The Heritage Industry: Britain in a Climate of Decline*. London: Continuum.

Hobsbawm, E. (1983) Introduction: inventing traditions. In E. Hobsbawm and T. Ranger (eds) *The Invention of Tradition*, pp. 1–14. Cambridge: Cambridge University Press.

Howard, P. (2003) *Heritage: Management, Interpretation, Identity*. London: Continuum.

Jolliffe, L. (2003) The lure of tea: history, traditions, attractions. In C.M. Hall, L. Sharples, R. Mitchell, N. Macionis and B. Cambourne (eds) *Food Tourism around the World: Development, Management and Markets*, pp. 121–136. Oxford: Butterworth Heinemann.

Jolliffe, L. (2007) *Tea and Tourism: Tourists, Traditions and Transformations*. Bristol: Channel View Publications.

Lowenthal, D. (1998) *The Heritage Crusade and the Spoils of History*. Cambridge: Cambridge University Press.

MacCannell, D. (1973) Staged authenticity: arrangements of social space in tourist settings. *The American Journal of Sociology*, 79(3): 589–603.

Metro-Roland, M.M. (2013) Goulash nationalism: the culinary identity of a nation. *Journal of Heritage Tourism*, 8(2/3): 172–181.

Molz, J.G. (2007) Eating difference: the cosmopolitan mobilities of culinary tourism. *Space and Culture*, 10: 77–93.

Morley, D. and Robins, K. (1995) *Spaces of Identity: Global Media, Electronic Landscapes and Cultural Boundaries*. London: Routledge.

Petrini, C. (2003) *Slow Food: The Case for Taste*. New York: Columbia University Press.

Pilcher, J.M. (1996) Tamales or timbales: cuisine and the formation of Mexican national identity, 1821–1911. *The Americas*, 53(2): 193–216.

Pilcher, J.M. (2014) "Old Stock" tamales and migrant tacos: taste, authenticity, and the naturalization of Mexican food. *Social Research*, 81(2): 441–462.

Poria, Y. (2010) The story behind the picture: preferences for the visual display at heritage sites. In E. Waterton and S. Watson (eds) *Culture, Heritage and Representation: Perspectives on Visuality and the Past*, pp. 217–228. Farnham: Ashgate.

Ramshaw, G. and Gammon, S. (2010) On home ground? Twickenham Stadium tours and the construction of sport heritage. *Journal of Heritage Tourism*, 5(2): 87–102.

Roberts, L. (2014) Talkin bout my generation: popular music and the culture of heritage. *International Journal of Heritage Studies*, 20(3): 262–280.

Telfer, D.J. (2001) Strategic alliances along the Niagara Wine Route. *Tourism Management*, 22: 21–30.

Timothy, D.J. (2011) *Cultural Heritage and Tourism: An Introduction*. Bristol: Channel View Publications.

Timothy, D.J. and Boyd, S.W. (2015) *Tourism and Trails: Cultural, Ecological and Management Issues*. Bristol: Channel View Publications.

Timothy, D.J. and Ron, A.S. (2013) Understanding heritage cuisines and tourism: identity, image, authenticity, and change. *Journal of Heritage Tourism*, 8 (2/3): 99–104.

Smith, L. (2006) *Uses of Heritage*. London: Routledge.
Urry, J. (2002) *The Tourist Gaze*, 2nd Edn. London: Sage.
Veblen, T. (1899) *The Theory of the Leisure Class: An Economic Study of Institutions*. New York: Penguin Books.
Waterton, E. and Watson S. (2015). Heritage as a focus of research: past, present and new directions. In E. Waterton and S. Watson (eds) *The Palgrave Handbook of Contemporary Heritage Research*, pp. 1–20. London: Palgrave Macmillan.
Winter, T. (2015) Heritage and nationalism: an unbreachable couple? In E. Waterton and S. Watson (eds) *The Palgrave Handbook of Contemporary Heritage Research*, pp. 331–345. London: Palgrave Macmillan.

5 Personal heritage, intergenerational food and nostalgia

Dallen J. Timothy

Introduction

Heritage is all around us, manifesting in many forms and at many scales. Every individual has a heritage or set of heritages. They may be genetic, such as blond hair, brown eyes, dark skin, small stature or hereditary diseases; learned behavior, such as language, beliefs, interests and tastes; or physical objects, such as a summer cottage, a family Bible, a car, a coin collection, a grandmother's ring or a recipe book. The Latin word *patrimonium* (patrimony/heritage) refers to that which is inherited from a father or ancestor (Vecco 2010). Scholars often concentrate on social or collective heritage, but in a very real sense, everyone literally inherits his or her own patrimony.

Heritage can be seen from a scalar perspective (Timothy 1997) with the momentous and most famous elements of the built environment being marked as universal heritage. UNESCO's World Heritage List is a clear manifestation of the importance placed upon patrimony that is deemed globally important. Such places are awe inspiring and deeply meaningful. Further down the scale is national heritage, which typically emphasizes memorials to national heroes, buildings associated with famous public events or monuments that commemorate important happenings in the development of a nation-state. Visiting such sites may evoke strong nationalistic emotions within an individual and solidarity within a social group. Local heritage is equally important on a parochial level and it is usually interpreted for, and appreciated by, a resident audience, which takes pride in its community and its history. At the lowest scale, one's own inheritance is most plentiful because each person inherits his or her own legacy and leaves a portion of it to the next generation (Timothy 1997, 2011), be it genetic traits, learned actions or tangible objects, all of which influence our daily lives.

This personal heritage commonly manifests as an interest in personal origins, such as a desire to discover one's roots, a deeper sense of intimate nostalgia for bygone days or memories of yesteryear or a desire to visit ancestral homelands. All of these situations can be mitigated, enhanced or embodied through heritage cuisines. Food is central to personal heritage and the nostalgia surrounding it. This chapter examines the crossover between food and personal heritage, in particular as this relationship expresses itself in terms of nostalgia, intergenerational recipes and genealogy-based travel.

Food traditions, recipes and personal nostalgia

Food practices and gastronomic personal heritage play an important role in people's created identities. Nostalgia has received the most attention in the scholarly literature as regards how food and personal heritage relate to one another, and it is nostalgia that often determines someone's favorite food (Baker et al. 2005). Some people experience nostalgia as a sense of melancholy or homesickness, a bittersweet yearning for home or a different time (Davis 1979). Others may experience nostalgia as a blissful 'aching' for childhood memories. Either way it is typically part truth and part fiction as it causes people to see through 'rose-colored glasses' and "gloss over difference, paradox and conflict by constructing a harmonious past" (Lupton 1996: 50).

There are three primary ways in which food nostalgia manifests. The first of these occurs when immigrants use traditional food to preserve their ethnic identity and the embodied memory of their pre-emigration life, or when subsequent generations of diasporic peoples use recipes to revive waning memories of their immigrant forebears.

For immigrants, culinary traditions convey memories of primordial home and nostalgia for the flavors of the homeland (Holtzman 2006; Iszler and Mayer 2005; Kaftanoglu and Timothy 2013; Mannur 2010; Philibert-Ortega 2012; Renko and Bucar 2014). Home cooking ethnic foods from the homeland is a crucial way of preserving one's ethnic identity. As well, dining in 'authentic' ethnic restaurants can help diasporic people preserve their sense of identity or relive gustatory memories of the motherland (Chhabra et al. 2013). One older Hungarian immigrant to Canada noted, "Although I have become very Canadian in my eating palate, my fond memories of the aromas of great Hungarian cooking always bring me back"(Czégény 2009: 7). Food plays a key role in immigrants' desires to keep their ethnic identities alive in an immersion of otherness that can, if not guarded against, supplant the traditions of home. In Holtzman's (2006) thinking, however, for the most part, diasporic associations with food are more a manifestation of mourning their dislocation than of constructing an identity in the adopted country. Immigrant relationships with gastronomy probably more accurately reflect a combination of the two – the adaptation to a hybridized identity in the adopted land and an anxious attempt to grasp onto something of the homeland.

The second manifestation of personal food-based nostalgia is food as a trigger of childhood or early-life memories, not necessarily in relation to immigrant predecessors, but of personal experiences in time and place. This can and does commingle with the first type when childhood memories represent a parent, grandparent or great-grandparent from the ancestral homeland. One second-generation Italian American wrote:

> My great-grandmother came to America on a ship from Italy around 1900 to begin a new life in America. A century later, the smell of spaghetti sauce bubbling up from an iron kettle on my grandmother's stove tells the tale of Italian immigrants, stretching from the olive groves and vineyards of southern Italy.

> There's a story in the sauce, of courage and culture and the perseverance to plant new roots in a new land. Food comforts, soothes, and nurtures. Long perfected recipes – soups and stews made with the loving hands of a mother, grandmother, or great-grandmother – reach across continents, oceans, and generations.
>
> (Coblentz and Williams 2013: 46–47)

Most people's earliest and fondest memories involve family, faith, festivities and food. Homemade food and family gatherings elicit amiable childhood memories (Renko and Bucar 2014; Sandvidge et al. 2008), and favorite recipes are frequently linked to blissful occasions during childhood (Baker et al. 2005). The work of Cuevas Contreras and Zizaldra Hernández (2015) illustrates how Mexican-Americans in El Paso, Texas, reflect on their holidays and the importance of 'Easter food', family and faith in the pleasantest of memories in a complicated borderland. Past Thanksgiving feasts are among the most prized memories for Americans. Recollections of enjoying turkey dinners with extended families reflect a simpler, more virtuous and wholesome past (Pleck 1999). Holidays are also important times for bringing family together to share meals, tell stories (many of which pertain to food) and share and collate recipes for future generations to appreciate (Tietze and Tunick 1998).

The smell or taste of certain dishes can educe the memory of a particular person (Baker et al. 2005: 402). Mothers and grandmothers are the commonest family members associated with one's comestible past (Anthopoulou 2010). In the contemporary era of McDonaldized fast food and the increasingly impersonal nature of eating out, grandma's cooking, whether tasty in reality or not, becomes, through time and perhaps masked by nostalgia, the most delicious food ever eaten! At the very least, family foods are emblematic of dishes "steeped in tradition and prepared with love" (Mannur 2010: 32).

Relatedly, people frequently wax nostalgic when they fall ill or experience depression. The impulse to consume 'comfort foods' derives from their memories of childhood succor: soup, peanut butter sandwiches, sweets or macaroni and cheese (Lupton 1996).

The third category of food-based nostalgia is a broader societal wistfulness for simpler times and old-fashioned ways in a beleaguered world of materiality, harried lifestyles, disruption and placelessness. For many people, home cooking and traditional foods help to affix 'place' and secure our "positionings within it" (Duruz 2001: 22). There is a tendency for that 'place' to be synonymous with rurality, which is in the North American and European mind an idealized space of wholesomeness, where food is better and memory banks are unlocked and liberated. This 'agrarian nostalgia' is nearly always connected with food – homegrown, traditional, intergenerational and somehow very personal to the one consuming it, especially when city dwellers remember their own personal experiences of farming, hunting, fishing and foraging for wild berries and mushrooms (Autio et al. 2013).

This societal nostalgia for a comestible past may also relate to objects rather than just places and activities. The meat pie is one of New Zealand's most cherished snacks and takeaway foods. Until very recently, they were the bread and butter of roadside vendor wagons known as 'pie carts'. The vintage pie cart wields considerable nostalgic power in the New Zealand public memory. While not all of today's pie wagons sell pies, their lingering name and public image depict an important New Zealand culinary tradition that "live[s] on in the memories and narratives of patrons" (Bell and Neill 2014: 49).

Middle-aged and older people often reflect on how things 'used to be' (Duruz 1999). I recently asked my eighty-something father-in-law, Donald Law, about his youthful memories of food. I learned that food tasted much better in the 'olden days': "We used butter and bacon fat. It was healthy enough then because we worked hard, physically, and oh did it make everything taste good. Food was better back then".

Passing it down

Teasing these diasporic, personal and societal food-induced memories is a foundational principle of food advertising (Renko and Bucar 2014), wherein " 'mother's home cooking' and 'old-fashioned' tastes are frequently employed as selling points" (Lupton 1996: 50). Caldwell (2006: 104) describes how a Russian dairy firm sells its products with "stylized representations of grandmothers and summer cottages". To sell cookbooks, publishers print images of kitchens, utensils and foodways of bygone eras that return cooks to a 'better' past (Duruz 1999). These approaches appear to work, because they continue to be widely used in the field of advertising. As long as people connect local food from their past as 'authentic', idyllic and wholesome, where the 'past' in a general sense is "glorified as the period in time when 'real' food existed" (Autio et al. 2013: 568), such images will continue to sell.

Culinary heritage also involves the ways in which families pass gastronomic knowledge from generation to generation (Bessière 1998, 2013; Clark and Zimmerman 2000; Humphrey 1989; Oum 2005; Sharif et al. 2013; Taylor 1999; Trichopoulou et al. 2007) and particularly how in the transmission of food knowledge, personal adaptations are made with each successive generation (Metro-Roland 2013; Sharif et al. 2014).

The passing of recipes and recipe books has long epitomized the traditional place of women's work in the home and family (Anthopoulou 2010; Sharif et al. 2014). Almost without fail, this has been a gendered experience, but this is changing today as more men spend more time in the kitchen. Women have traditionally preserved family recipes, which in Supski's (2005) estimation, imbued them with a certain level of cultural authority in the home as they controlled not only the family's health and nutrition but also acted as the guardian of the family's alimentary heritage.

Cookbooks are typically published and sold at bookshops, shopping malls or through online booksellers. Recipe books, on the other hand, represent an intimate heritage not only in the ingredients and instructions they contain but also in the annotated comments, adaptations and insertions within. For pioneer generations, recipe books were often a cook's most valuable possession (Figure 5.1). These gustatory notebooks functioned as household history books and were carefully protected by purveyors of familial patrimony (Philibert-Ortega 2012). These collections acted "both as a repository of practical, useful knowledge and as a family archive ... that were by nature ever-expanding books of knowledge which changed according to the needs of the current owners" (Leong 2013: 89, 93). This is reflected in the following account of Berzok (2011: xvi–xvii): "Some women leave diaries. My mother left recipes.... My mother's [recipe] collection was a combination of diary, family Bible and social notes.... Reading my mother's recipe collection, I learned not only about her life and times but also about ... who I am and where I've been". Like family Bibles and photo albums, original family recipe books were a centerpiece of one's inheritance. They were ordinarily handed

Figure 5.1 The author's copy of his grandmother's prized recipe book, an important part of her epicurean legacy (Photo: Dallen J. Timothy)

down through matrilineal lines or given to daughters and granddaughters as wedding gifts (Leong 2013) in hopes that "they will be appreciated and recalled as special times with the giver" (Baker et al. 2005: 402).

In the experience of one woman receiving recipes from her mother and co-compiling them into a tangible recipe book, "my dear loving mother … guided me through an incredible pile of recipes, notes, torn pieces of paper, and scribbles of ingredients and cooking instructions that took me back to my childhood. We went down memory lane; we laughed and we cried" (Czégény 2009: 5). Recipes help construct families and impart intergenerational continuity in a discontinuous world (Baker et al. 2005; Hocking et al. 2002) and can be crucibles of family history (Holtzman 2006).

But historically, many women had no written recipes. Cooking skills and ingredients, and their intergenerational transmission depended on knowing (Collings Eves 2005). For African-American slaves, most of whom could not read or write, knowing the recipes by heart was vital, and food-based oral traditions emerged out of circumstantial necessity. Cooking and passing along their perfected techniques were ways of showing motherly love in a dark situation when there were few other options and no alternatives for bequeathing (Collings Eves 2005). Born from poverty, racism and slavery, these known recipes now comprise the foundations of the beloved Cajun and Creole cuisines of the American Deep South (Halloran 2012).

With the widespread use of typewriters, mimeograph machines, photocopiers and scanners in the late twentieth and early twenty-first centuries, family favorite recipes could be typed, printed and copied for wider distribution, so that each grandchild could receive instructions for making their own family favorites. With the current use of online media, such as Facebook and Twitter, family food heritage can now be shared with a person's online contacts. With web-based tools such as Pinterest and YouTube, recipes can now be shared and demonstrated universally, opening what was once very personal heritage to the entire globe to become the food heritage of the world.

Genealogy tourism and the search for a personal past

Gastronomy and embodied memory also reach into the personal heritage-laden realm of tourism. Genealogy (recording dates, places and names) and family history (researching stories, events and personal narratives of ancestors and putting faces to names) are important leisure and professional pastimes today. Some people are passionate about undertaking family history, while others do it more passively. Either way, the desire to understand where we come from is an innate part of being human (Lowenthal 2015).

For serious genealogists who have achieved many of their research goals, traveling to a filial homeland or region is the natural next step in the experience of connecting with those who went before (Higginbotham 2012; Meethan 2004; Timothy 2008). These journeys of discovery are steeped with an inimitable mix of autobiographical and collective memory (Baker et al. 2005), for while diasporic progeny may never have visited their ancestral lands before, they often feel a primordial sense of belonging and/or the melancholy sting of sadness (Basu 2007), learning of the hardships and sacrifices experienced by their progenitors. Some roots tourists describe these as spiritual experiences that connect them both corporeally to their native soil and transcendentally to their predecessors (Timothy 2008; Timothy and Teye 2004).

These ancestral encounters typically involve spending time in clan settlements or villages, calling upon old family homesteads, visiting cemeteries and churches, undertaking archival research, meeting distant relatives who remain in the motherland, touring the countryside, taking short-term language lessons and feasting on local gastronomy (Timothy 1997, 2008; Timothy and Schmidt 2011). There are typically five types of food-related pursuits undertaken by genealogy tourists: eating/tasting, finding recipes, taking cookery classes, agricultural immersion and buying food souvenirs.

Tasting local food, particularly based on recipes from the time of their antecedents and often served in restaurants that specialize in 'traditional' fare (Figure 5.2), is a highlight of many roots vacations. Eating foods typical of the home *terroir* contributes to heredity pilgrims' impressions of belonging. Imaginations can run wild if there is even a chance that the foodstuffs they eat germinated in, and sprung forth from, their own primeval soil.

Figure 5.2 'Traditional' Irish food establishments appeal to roots travelers from the Irish diaspora (Photo: Dallen J. Timothy)

Seeking out period recipes in local libraries, restaurants, bookstores and archives, or from local residents, is another important activity for personal heritage tourists. Cooking classes on location taught by a local culinary specialist have deep meaning, for they teach about the recipes passed down from generation to generation in the area, but they also embrace the flavors of the place and utilize available products. Cautiously, Krosbacher (2010) rightfully points out that geopolitical boundaries change over time. Thus, an ancestor who emigrated from Prussia, a country that no longer exists and is now included in parts of Belgium, the Czech Republic, Denmark, Germany, Lithuania, Poland, Russia and Switzerland, means that the homeland has changed. This has a bearing on 'authentic' or 'traditional' food. Regardless, what roots travelers learn in these cookery lessons is an intangible souvenir that can last a lifetime and embody their personal patrimony.

While not very common, some tourists choose to immerse themselves in the agricultural heritage of their ancestors by volunteering to participate in the farming labor their ancestors were employed in (Timothy and Schmidt 2011). Finally, food souvenirs are one of the most common categories of tourist souvenir (Swanson and Timothy 2012). These edible mementos (e.g. smoked meats, desserts, bread, cheeses, beverages or dried fruits) become especially meaningful when they can be brought back to be shared with those who stayed home.

Many countries with large diasporic populations abroad, such as Hungary, Croatia, Italy, Ireland, Scotland, Ukraine, Poland and Wales, have developed intricate networks of roots-travel service providers. There are plethoric genealogical tour agencies in these and other countries that will help arrange roots travel for the posterity of their émigré compatriots, offering group tours, clan reunions or individual guiding services. Many national and regional government tourism offices also recognize the potential of this lucrative, albeit small in the greater scheme of tourism, market and have produced websites, brochures and promotional campaigns to lure diasporics 'home' to spend their holidays (Sim and Leith 2013; Timothy 2008). Food is a crucial part of these promotional campaigns, playing on visitors' desires to eat local cuisine and visit farmsteads and farmers' markets. Local agents promise to help visitors identify and consume typical regional cuisine where it is produced.

Conclusion

Personal memories frequently revolve around family, festivities and food. Some of our fondest memories are entrenched in holiday food, dining out with the family or consuming everyday meals prepared by a parent or grandparent. Diasporic groups routinely employ their ethnic cuisine as a means of satisfying a longing for their primordial homeland by reliving their pre-emigration lives, fulfilling religious obligations, maintaining a close link to the motherland, forwarding culinary knowledge to the next generation, documenting their migratory experiences or simply enjoying a delicious meal. For modern societies, collective nostalgia becomes an imperative way of maintaining an element of stability in a volatile world where the only constant is change. As society ages, people frequently wax nostalgic for the simpler, slower and more wholesome ways of the past, including food and foodways. In these ways, food, cuisine and foodways are redolent with meaning and become a salient part of our personal or societal patrimony. Food companies and kitchenware merchants have realized considerable success in tapping into these elements of nostalgia to sell products that 'take people back' to their culinary roots.

Preserving personal food heritage occurs in different ways. Recipe books, which traditionally have been pseudo family records enhanced by each successive generation, have long been treasured keepsakes within families and important tools for preserving alimentary heritage and documenting domestic lineages. Until the late twentieth century, the question of who would inherit the family recipe book was the fodder of family quarrels and intergenerational rebellions. Today, however, modern technology allows filial food heritage to be copied, tweeted, video recorded and posted online for the entire world to see, making global what once was very personal.

Personal nostalgia, which may include one's own autobiographical recollections or broader familial remembrances of times, places and people, often manifests in a rather extreme form known as roots tourism, genealogy tourism or personal heritage travel. Undertaking the intimate pilgrimage of doing genealogy and family history a step further, millions of people leave home each year to seek out the homes, farms and villages of their forebears where they connect to their deceased ancestors and touch the same ground their predecessors knew. A natural extension of these emotive experiences is a desire to consume the comestible products of an ancestral land. Eating their own heritage food in the place of its origin is a salient part of the adventure and can be deeply meaningful. This 'sacred substance' is capable of connecting people with their selves at their deepest roots.

Humans will always have an emotional connection to food, whether good or bad. We are wired that way. While affluence brings opportunities to dine out often, eat different ethnic foods or buy processed meals from a supermarket, most food consumed throughout the world is still prepared at home based on locally available ingredients, time-tested family recipes and cherished social settings. Although the methods for preserving and disseminating family recipes have changed, their importance in people's nostalgic repertoires will remain for generations to come.

References

Anthopoulou, T. (2010) Rural women in local agrofood production: between entrepreneurial initiatives and family strategies. A case study in Greece. *Journal of Rural Studies*, 26(4): 394–403.

Autio, M., Collins, R., Wahlen, S. and Anttila, M. (2013) Consuming nostalgia? The appreciation of authenticity in local food production. *International Journal of Consumer Studies*, 37(5): 564–568.

Baker, S.M., Karrer, H.C. and Veeck, A. (2005) My favorite recipes: recreating emotions and memories through cooking. *Advances in Consumer Research*, *32*: 402–403.

Basu, P. (2007) *Highland Homecomings: Genealogy and Heritage Tourism in the Scottish Diaspora*. London: Routledge.

Bell, C. and Neill, L. (2014) A vernacular food tradition and national identity in New Zealand. *International Journal of Multidisciplinary Research*, 17(1): 49–64.

Berzok, L.M. (2011) *Storied Dishes: What Our Family Recipes Tell Us about Who We Are and Where We've Been*. Santa Barbara, CA: Praeger.

Bessière, J. (1998) Local development and heritage: traditional food and cuisine as tourist attractions in rural areas. *Sociologia Ruralis*, 38(1): 21–34.

Bessière, J. (2013) 'Heritagisation', a challenge for tourism promotion and regional development: an example of food heritage. *Journal of Heritage Tourism*, 8(4): 275–291.

Caldwell, M.L. (2006) Tasting the worlds of yesterday and today: culinary tourism and nostalgia foods in post-Soviet Russia. In R. Wilk (ed) *Fast Food/Slow Food: The Cultural Economy of the Global Food System*, pp. 97–112. Lanham, MD: AltaMira Press.

Chhabra, D., Lee, W., Zhao, S. and Scott, K. (2013) Marketing of ethnic food experiences: authentication analysis of Indian cuisine abroad. *Journal of Heritage Tourism*, 8(2/3): 145–157.

Clark, G. and Zimmerman, E. (2000) Greater understanding of the local community. *Art Education*, 53(2): 33–39.

Coblentz, E. and Williams, K. (2013) *The Amish Cook: Recollections and Recipes from an Old Order Amish Family*. New York: Random House.

Collings Eves, R. (2005) A recipe for remembrance: memory and identity in African-American women's cookbooks. *Rhetoric Review*, 24(3): 280–297.

Cuevas Contreras, T.J. and Zizaldra Hernández, I. (2015) A holiday celebration in a binational context: Easter experiences at the US-Mexico border. *Journal of Heritage Tourism*, 10(3): 296–301.

Czégény, C.M. (2009) *Helen's Hungarian Heritage Recipes*. London: Dream Machine.

Davis, F. (1979) *Yearning for Yesterday: A Sociology of Nostalgia*. New York: Free Press.

Duruz, J. (1999) Food as nostalgia: eating the fifties and sixties. *Australian Historical Studies*, 29: 231–250.

Duruz, J. (2001) Home cooking, nostalgia, and the purchase of tradition. *Traditional Dwellings and Settlements Review*, 12(2): 21–32.

Halloran, V.N. (2012) Recipes as memory work: slave food. *Culture, Theory and Critique*, 53(2): 147–161.

Higginbotham, G. (2012) Seeking roots and tracing lineages: constructing a framework of reference for roots and genealogical tourism. *Journal of Heritage Tourism*, 7(3): 189–203.

Hocking, C., Clair, V.W.S. and Bunrayong, W. (2002) The meaning of cooking and recipe work for older Thai and New Zealand women. *Journal of Occupational Science*, 9(3): 117–127.

Holtzman, J.D. (2006) Food and memory. *Annual Review of Anthropology*, 35: 361–378.

Humphrey, L.T. (1989) Traditional foods? Traditional values? *Western Folklore*, 48(2): 162–169.

Iszler, D. and Mayer, M. (2005) *Connecting Generations: Fond Recollections of German-Russian Heritage, Traditional Family Recipes and Reminiscent Stories from Five Generations of "Cooking with Mom"*. Bismarck, ND: North Dakota State University.

Kaftanoglu, B. and Timothy, D.J. (2013) Return travel, assimilation and cultural maintenance: an example of Turkish-Americans in Arizona. *Tourism Analysis*, 18(3): 273–284.

Krosbacher, M.C. (2010) *Authenticity and the Use of Multimedia at Cultural Tourist Attractions*. Doctoral Thesis, Dublin Institute of Technology, Dublin, Ireland.

Leong, E. (2013) Collecting knowledge for the family: recipes, gender and practical knowledge in the Early Modern English household. *Centaurus*, 55(2): 81–103.

Lowenthal, D. (2015) *The Past Is a Foreign Country, Revisited*. Cambridge: Cambridge University Press.

Lupton, D. (1996) *Food, the Body and the Self*. London: Sage.

Mannur, A. (2010) *Culinary Fictions: Food in South Asian Diasporic Culture*. Philadelphia: Temple University Press.

Meethan, K. (2004) "To stand in the shoes of my ancestors": tourism and genealogy. In T. Coles and D.J. Timothy (eds) *Tourism, Diasporas and Space*, pp. 139–150. London: Routledge.

Metro-Roland, M.M. (2013) Goulash nationalism: the culinary identity of a nation. *Journal of Heritage Tourism*, 8(2/3): 172–181.

Oum, Y.R. (2005) Authenticity and representation: cuisines and identities in the Korean-American diaspora. *Postcolonial Studies*, 8(1): 109–125.

Philibert-Ortega, G. (2012) *From the Family Kitchen: Discover Your Food Heritage and Preserve Favorite Recipes*. Blue Ash, OH: Family Tree Books.

Pleck, E. (1999) The making of the domestic occasion: The history of Thanksgiving in the United States. *Journal of Social History*, 32(4): 773–789.

Renko, S. and Bucar, K. (2014) Sensing nostalgia through traditional food: an insight from Croatia. *British Food Journal*, 116(11): 1672–1691.

Sandvidge, S., Seckar, D.S., Wouters, J.S. and Florence, J.S. (2008) *Apple Betty and Sloppy Joe: Stirring up the Past with Family Recipes and Stories*. Madison: Wisconsin Historical Society Press.

Sharif, M.S.M., Zahari, M.S.M., Nor, N.M. and Muhammad, R. (2013) How could the transfer of food knowledge be passed down? *Procedia-Social and Behavioral Sciences*, 105: 429–437.

Sharif, M.S.M., Zahari, M.S.M., Nor, N.M. and Salleh, H.M. (2014) The adaptations of Malay food knowledge among Malay generations in Kuala Lumpur, Malaysia. In N. Sumarjan, M.S.M. Zahari, S.M. Radzi, Z. Mohi, M.H.M. Hanafiah, M.F.S. Bakhtiar and A. Zainal (eds) *Hospitality and Tourism: Synergizing Creativity and Innovations in Research*, pp. 395–405. Boca Raton, FL: CRC Press.

Sim, D. and Leith, M. (2013) Diaspora tourists and the Scottish Homecoming 2009. *Journal of Heritage Tourism*, 8(4): 259–274.

Supski, S. (2005) 'We still mourn that book': cookbooks, recipes and foodmaking knowledge in 1950s Australia. *Journal of Australian Studies*, 28: 85–94.

Swanson, K.K. and Timothy, D.J. (2012) Souvenirs: icons of meaning, commercialization, and commoditization. *Tourism Management*, 33(3): 489–499.

Taylor, M.A. (1999) *Through the Eyes of Your Ancestors: A Step-by-Step Guide to Uncovering Your Family's History*. New York: Houghton Mifflin.

Tietze, R.B. and Tunick, S.L. (1998) Oral History. *Activities, Adaptation & Aging*, 23(1): 39–59.

Timothy, D.J. (1997) Tourism and the personal heritage experience. *Annals of Tourism Research*, 34(3): 751–754.

Timothy, D.J. (2008) Genealogical mobility: tourism and the search for a personal past. In D.J. Timothy and J. Kay Guelke (eds) *Geography and Genealogy: Locating Personal Pasts*, pp. 115–135. Aldershot: Ashgate.

Timothy, D.J. (2011) *Cultural Heritage and Tourism: An Introduction*. Bristol: Channel View Publications.

Timothy, D.J. and Schmidt, K. (2011) Personal heritage and return visits to American colonies in Mexico. *Tourism Review International*, 14(4): 179–188.

Timothy, D.J. and Teye, V.B. (2004) American children of the African diaspora: journeys to the motherland. In T. Coles and D.J. Timothy (eds) *Tourism, Diasporas and Space*, pp. 111–123. London: Routledge.

Trichopoulou, A., Soukara, S. and Vasilopoulou, E. (2007) Traditional foods: a science and society perspective. *Trends in Food Science & Technology*, 18(8): 420–427.

Vecco, M. (2010) A definition of cultural heritage: from the tangible to the intangible. *Journal of Cultural Heritage*, 11(3): 321–324.

6 Agricultural heritage, agritourism and rural livelihoods

Deborah Che

Introduction

Agriculture and the agricultural countryside have long been connected with national and cultural heritage, in contrast to multicultural, global cities. In part this stems from an anti-urban, romantic longing for nature, positioned as pure and restorative, particularly in Western urban industrial societies (Nilsson 2002). The rural agricultural countryside, although shaped by major economic and social changes and global forces, has long been tied to the culture and identity of nations. Williams (1973), in his classic, *The Country and the City*, detailed how agrarian capitalism, industrial development and imperialism shaped the English countryside where first a small, landed aristocracy enclosed and concentrated land ownership. Then the rural estates were acquired and/or expanded upon utilizing profits earned through trade in domestic cities, which were otherwise associated with social disorder, plague and crime, and later with agricultural commodities and raw materials extracted from the British colonies.

Even as England became increasingly urbanized, agriculture declined, and the land-owning aristocracy lost much of its political power as the nation industrialized, the social imagery of rural gentility predominated. According to Lowenthal (1991), the English national collective identity and heritage is tied to Britain's old landed elite and their created, maintained pastoral English landscapes of villages, fields, meadows, pasture and hedgerows. This countryside was idealized as idyllic, even though its creation was the product of the loss of small landholders, the closing of the commons and exploiting the resources of overseas colonial hinterlands. The landscape remains a means by which certain classes of people have signified themselves and their world through their imagined relationship with nature (Cosgrove 1998). In present-day post-colonial England, rural nature and the rural countryside symbolize English heritage, in contrast with the multicultural cities, and are increasingly attractive as a safe, rural idyll for the white, English middle class (Neal 2002).

The countryside is attractive as it appears to be closer to nature and the repository of traditional values and the 'true nation'. In the United States, a romantic strain of agrarianism which holds that the true wealth of the nation comes from the land, likewise privileges the rural countryside and the family farm, which are associated with traditional values such as self-reliance, simplicity and rural virtue. This agrarianism plays out in the anti-urbanism and anti-industrialism of the back-to-the-land movements (Bunce 1998), as well as in an environmental strain which sentimentalizes pre-industrial, peasant farming as a way of knowing and protecting nature (White 1996). This chapter examines the role of agricultural landscapes, farming traditions and the rural idyll in the construction of heritage and its use in tourism.

Agrarian heritage and rural livelihoods

Government policies in response to restructuring and the challenges facing agriculture including the impact of physical and human limits to production, cost-price squeezes, global competition and the increased mobility of capital and labor may favor the preservation of such agricultural landscapes through agritourism. To address agriculture's challenges, particularly in marginal areas, the European Union (EU) has moved from costly payments tied to agricultural overproduction to support based on a "multifunctional European Model of Agriculture" where farming provides collective benefits such as biodiversity and preservation of the social (agricultural) landscape. "Active farming", or a production system based on economic outcomes from producing food and fiber, is seen as the most sustainable way to protect cultural heritage and local traditional knowledge connected to pre-industrialized, pre-rationalized agriculture and landscape management (Daugstad et al. 2006). Under this system, the farmer would be a rural caretaker (Nilsson 2002). This multifunctional agriculture includes the development of tourism, particularly in much of Europe seen as marginal for intensive agriculture, but produces local food specialties. In one of those areas, the Veneto region of Italy, agritourism has been incorporated into small-scale farming operations where the average farm size is 4.5 hectares (about twelve acres), while emphasizing high-value local and regional foods. In return for economic incentives to producers and grants to remodel historic buildings to accommodate guests (e.g. a dairy barn into a cheese-making facility and sales area, or a restaurant with guest rooms), agritourism is heavily regulated, with participating licensed farmers required to have at least two years of farming experience and passing an exam following one hundred hours of training on law, farm management, financial accounting, hygiene and sanitation, transporting and processing food products and hospitality. In addition to selling locally produced food, wine and crafts, farmers can provide self-service snacks/light meals, full-service, sit-down meals or 'farm holidays' including meals, accommodation and recreational opportunities. For each level of service and for farm altitude, a varying percentage of the items purchased by tourists must be produced on the farm (Clemens 2004).

In large, advanced industrialized countries such as the United States, Canada and Australia, where agriculture still largely operates on the productivist model with mass industrial farming, further government support for agritourism on small to mid-sized farms that are unable to achieve economies of scale and/or produce crops such as fruits and vegetables and landscapes that have more appeal to tourists is needed. While compared to the Veneto example, these producers cannot draw on a long history of regional and local foods, rural Europe's relatively dense population and the EU's generous financial support for multifunctional agriculture and the shift to tourism; developing agritourism that ties locally produced foods to regional culture and traditions could provide improved returns in marginal production areas for a limited number of producers that would supply the produce, livestock and specialty foods for tourists (Clemens 2004). However, Clemens (2004) argues that even for a relatively small-scale change to occur, many US producers likely will require agricultural policies that provide greater incentives and less risk before they are willing to produce niche crops and specialty foods, participate in agritourism or provide products for other alternative markets.

For some farmers, this shift from conventional production methods and commodity markets to value adding and agritourism is occurring given market pressures and some smaller policy initiatives. In the United States, while large producers of major commodity crops such as corn, soybeans, wheat, cotton, sugar and rice receive billions of dollars under the Farm Bill's crop insurance and commodity programs, the most recent (2014) Farm Bill included some marketing and research support in the less than 1% of the 'Other' Farm Bill funding for producers of specialty crops (mainly fruits and vegetables) (McFerson 2014). These producers, while ineligible for commodity crop supports, have more potential for direct marketing and agritourism.

To keep land in agriculture as residential and commercial development pressures increase, small to medium-sized farms that cannot expand production due to fiscal or scale limitations have turned to agritourism. Agritourism day activities, which can include u-pick produce, hayrides, corn mazes, haunted houses, on-farm festivals, petting zoos, fish ponds and enjoying cider and donuts, appeal to consumers looking for cheaper produce, organic produce, specialty crops and/or a relaxing day in the countryside. Peri-urban agriculture, which is supported by US state and federal marketing grants, largely serves the retail and entertainment market rather than the less profitable wholesale one (McGehee and Kim 2004; Tew and Barbieri 2012; Veeck et al. 2006).

As in the United States, Australian agritourism also draws on diversified, not large commodity crop, farms that while large by European standards, are small in the Australian context, with an average property size around sixty hectares (Ecker et al. 2010). This Australian agritourism also focuses predominantly on day visits, rather than the European-style farmstays. For instance, in the rapidly urbanizing Hawkesbury food bowl on the edge of Sydney, Farm Gate Trail maps feature 'Taste, Buy and Learn' experiences at farms, as well as at complimentary arts and crafts and hospitality businesses and tours and galleries/museums that can create memorable tourism experiences.

While farmers generally do not see themselves as part of the tourism industry, they benefit from it as they access more profitable retail consumers (Knowd 2006). Likewise, agriculture and food experiences have the potential of drawing tourists in Cairns and the Great Barrier Reef to the nearby Atherton Tablelands (Getz 1999;

Turnour et al. 2013). One guided food and wine bus tour visits a coffee plantation; a tropical fruit winery featuring exotic mango, lychee, jaboticaba, passion fruit and bush cherry wines; a macadamia nut plantation; a historic teahouse; and a dairy that makes award-winning cheeses developed in response to deregulation and the need to value add. Food tourists who do not want to go on guided tours can access a Tropical North Queensland 'Taste Paradise' app to get information on food trails and on local restaurants, markets and producers (Che et al. 2013; Timothy and Boyd 2015). While the activities differ on the farms and in the regional areas, agritourism, which the University of California Small Farms Program (2011: n.p.) defines as "a commercial enterprise at a working farm, ranch, or agricultural plant conducted for the enjoyment of visitors that generates supplemental income for the owner", can encompass the farmstays that are common in Europe and New Zealand, as well as the day visits that are common in peri-urban North America and Australia.

Agritourism benefits from the desire of urbanities to affirm their identity by visiting places associated with the past, which may draw on selective memory or nostalgia of older visitors' childhood (McIntosh and Prentice 1999; Timothy and Ron 2013). In agritourism, the farm of the past is desired – a family-operated, pre-industrial, diverse crop farm, not an extensive, industrial monocrop one. Traditional, not modern, farms and a bucolic countryside that refers to an almost extinct way of farming are considered attractive to tourists in advanced industrialized countries (Daugstad et al. 2006; Fisher 2006; LaPan and Barbieri 2014).

However, in Longxian village, Zhejiang Province, China, the ecological, economic and social benefits of the ancient and still practiced Rice-Fish Agricultural Heritage System based on local 'inherited' knowledge and evolving experience is being recognized for its value for tourism, as well as agricultural production, farmland preservation, cultural preservation and community identity formation. This system in which 'Rice Field-fish' (carp) provide fertilizer and eat larvae and weeds in rice paddies and ponds that in turn provide shade and food for fish dates back to the Hongwu Period of the Ming Dynasty (1368–1398). In this area where conservation of the traditional rice fields is threatened by rural depopulation and outmigration, those highly connected with family members abroad appreciate the agricultural system's value as a heritage site (Sun, Jansen-Verbeke, Min and Shengkui 2011; Sun, Min, Shi and Jiang 2011).

However, the reach of such agricultural landscapes goes far beyond that of the family to include national and world rankings of heritage value, especially in countries such as the Philippines, China and Indonesia, where centuries-old rice paddies are preserved, and in some cases (e.g. the Rice Terraces of the Philippine Cordilleras) branded as a UNESCO World Heritage Site. Agricultural landscapes are among the most important ways in which farming and agriculture are valued as cultural heritage. These rural heritagescapes tell striking stories of people's struggles with nature, the effects of environmental determinism, family and ethnic histories, dietary values and culinary traditions (Harlan 1995; Setten 2005). These underlying heritage narratives imbued within all agricultural landscapes are appreciated by agrarian communities not only for the sustenance they afford but also the communal chronicles they disclose. Tourists value them for their aesthetic appeal, and they are often the substance of travelers' dreams of the 'extraordinary' (Sznajder et al. 2009; Timothy 2005) (Figure 6.1).

Given the importance of built and natural heritage assets in cultural landscapes and agritourism (Chen et al. 2010; Fisher 2006; Gao et al. 2014; Timothy 2005), many farmers interested in agritourism have preserved their tangible heritage. LaPan and Barbieri (2014) found over one-third of surveyed Missouri (United States) farms preserved tangible heritage on their lands. Of these farmers, the majority maintained historic buildings such as barns and mills or antique equipment such as tractors or tools. There are efforts in many parts of the world to begin saving the vernacular agricultural heritage, including farm buildings, fences and other such remnants of material culture (Derrett and St Vincent Welch 2008).

While intrinsic motivations such as preserving American rural heritage or preserving their own personal or family heritage were most cited in the Missouri study, economic reasons such as repurposing buildings for use in tourism or increasing the tourist appeal of the farm were important too. Additionally, on-farm revenue was positively associated with tangible heritage preservation whereas off-farm employment and farm size (corporatization) had a negative association. This finding may point to the importance of agritourism and its revenues that can help preserve family farms and rural heritage (LaPan and Barbieri 2014), although restoring and repurposing historic buildings that are unique and desired by agritourists can be a financial burden for the farmers (Gao et al. 2014) (Figure 6.2).

Figure 6.1 This example of an 'extraordinary' agricultural landscape in Myanmar is an important part of the rural experience (Photo: Dallen J. Timothy)

Figure 6.2 Rural heritage schoolhouse repurposed for agritourism in Washington Township, Michigan (United States) (Photo: Deborah Che)

Nonetheless, beyond the financial aspects associated with tourism, agricultural heritage is important to preserve for its educative, aesthetic and scientific values.

The activities that agritourism provides attract urban and suburban baby boomers and seniors who may be a few generations removed from the farm, who hold nostalgic and romanticized views of rural, agricultural areas, and who have their own family-oriented farm traditions such as farm visits (Timothy and Ron 2009). Farms that have had on-site retail and activities for decades appeal to parents who want their children to experience the same farms and farm activities they visited as children. Successful agritourism operators sell rural or small-town virtues such as simplicity, hospitality and personal service and relationship building, as well as connections with the farmer in selling produce and experiences that help explain the success of rural agritourism businesses given large retailers' cheaper, commoditized products (Che et al. 2005). According to Nilsson (2002: 8), to urbanities the countryside "may be regarded as an incarnation of calm and reflection, with a trait of backwardness and a lifestyle, that has developed from an environment once dominated by peasants in an old idealized picture of the farmer that has not totally disappeared". This can be reassuring in a fast-changing era of globalization, but the visited, nostalgic past is one with the pain removed (McIntosh and Prentice 1999). White (1996) writes that the way many feel closest to nature is through play that mimics work, which in a wilderness setting, could be backpacking temporarily, mimicking the early nineteenth-century Lewis and Clark trek across North America or treks of other early European explorers. In the farm tourism setting, the activity that most mimics work would be on self-service farms, such as pick-your-own, or u-pick, establishments where visitors harvest their own fruit (Gale 1997; Heimlich and Barnard 1992; Stephenson and Lev 2004) – a pleasurable way of knowing nature, as long as it hearkens to nostalgia for the past, not the hard, painful present reality of migrant fruit pickers.

Agritourism and the countryside also represent the intersection of food (e.g. past farmhouse cooking) with place, memory and identity (Duruz 1999). Given the gulf between many urban residents' diets and traditional eating habits and knowledge of how to prepare traditional foods, nostalgia is manifested in the desire to go 'back to nature' and for travel to rural idylls for regional and so-called traditional food. As with landscapes, culinary heritage is also strongly linked to peasant identities and practices (Bessière 1998, 2013). In travels, through food one experiences the local, rural farmer/producer and expresses a desire for common roots with the farming world, which can help explain the popularity of local markets and roadside fruit stands. Through food one can also discover place. Bessière and Tibere (2013) found that *terroir*, broadly understood, was one of the reasons tourists cited for purchasing rural products. For tourists, products only need to be seen as 'local' and authentic through labeling, associated with a producer and information provided about the product's manufacture and processing.

In England's Lake District, Sims (2009) found that 60% of the tourists interviewed had deliberately chosen to consume and take home as souvenirs foods or drinks they considered 'local' (i.e. traditionally English, home cooked), in part to get a sense of the region's culture, place and people. However, producers in the area held differing views on the relative importance of local ingredients and local manufacture, as well as an objective understanding of authenticity, with some approving local production uses of imported ingredients that would still support local food manufacturing and employment. Others felt only onsite production with local ingredients qualified as 'local'. For tourists, heritage and a constructed understanding of authenticity were relevant as local foods were valued not only because they were presumed to be local but also because they were seen to be 'traditional' products with a long history of being made in that location (Sims 2009).

In New World settler countries where non-indigenous culinary traditions are much more recent, local food and drink may be viewed differently than in Old World settings. Immigrant traditions may be celebrated as heritage, as in the case of olive agritourism producers in Australia, who are directly marketing their products and promoting their ancestors' food and their own Mediterranean culinary culture through tastings and on-site sales (Alonso and Krajsic 2013). Additionally, in these settler nations, the use of fresh, local produce utilized in innovative ways may be celebrated. In western Michigan's resort towns, restaurants showcase local wines, specialty fruits and vegetables from nearby farms (farm to table), and fresh whitefish from Native American fishers in regional and seasonally focused cuisine (Che 2006, 2010). A Tropical North Queensland farmer utilizes Australian native fruits from the family farm, as well as local organic meats, wild caught local seafood and other traditional ingredients in Lao/Thai, Indonesian, Middle Eastern, Vietnamese, Mediterranean and Malaysian cooking classes that she offers to expand the region's agritourism offerings (Che et al. 2013).

Motivations for engaging in agritourism and food tourism vary. Agritourism can generate the additional income needed to compensate for the fluctuations in agriculture and to continue farming and financially facilitate the lifestyle changes of urban and suburban families who move to rural locations (Ecker et al. 2010; McGehee and Kim 2004). In Cornwall, a region of England with distinct food traditions, culinary tourism has played an important role in assisting struggling dairy farmers who have problems with milk quotas by generating demand for traditional cheeses, Cornish butter, ice cream and cream (Everett and Aitchison 2008). However, motivations for participating in agritourism are not solely economic but are also socio-cultural as well. Enhancing quality of life and educating visitors about the rural and agricultural landscape, and educating the next generation of farmers and value-added food producers about agricultural and culinary heritage are also strong motivations (Ecker et al. 2010; Everett and Aitchison 2008; Tew and Barbieri 2012).

Conclusion

Since humans began domesticating plants and animals and cultivating the earth approximately 12,000 years ago, agricultural landscapes have gradually replaced the earth's pristine environments in many areas. This evolution changed the appearance and function of the land. Cultivation and animal husbandry replaced hunting and gathering, climatic conditions permitting. In most cases, this resulted in permanent changes from a natural ambit to an anthropic landscape where fields, orchards and animal shelters began to emerge. Later, distinctive land-use patterns and land tenure systems appeared with their accompanying paddies, pastures, subsistence smallholdings, farm buildings, support structures and eventually plantations, large-scale ranches and commercial farms.

Age-old agricultural landscapes are crucibles of meaning, identity, continuity and change. The same is true of functioning farms today. They reveal much about farming methods, humankind's need to subdue nature to survive, human-earth intercourse and people's gastronomic preferences through the ages. Indigenous peoples and rural residents throughout the world, particularly in less developed regions, consider themselves inseparable from the soil they cultivate. This evolutionary history and people's deep-seated bonds to the earth render agriculture and its associated landscapes vital cultural heritage wherever it is found – personal heritage for farmers and villagers, interesting agricultural heritage for tourists and global heritage for anyone who eats.

The functions and spatial manifestations of agriculture are constantly changing. Someday, the large, mechanized farms and plantations of the twenty-first century will be ancient heritage and will appeal to the cultural tourists of tomorrow. Today, however, the tourism machine generally relies on smallholdings, ranches, fruit farms, rural farmscapes and vintage agricultural relics for their heritage value. Agricultural heritage-based tourism distinctively invokes some degree of subjective nostalgia, or at least genuine curiosity. Day visits to the countryside to soak in the beauties of human-created cultural landscapes or to participate in harvesting fresh fruit, vegetables or eggs for their own consumption helps satiate people's desire to experience the romanticized charms of rural living. Likewise, spending extended holidays on a dude ranch or farmstay satisfies some people's need for a slower pace of life in the idyllic heritage 'spaces' of yesteryear.

References

Alonso, A.D. and Krajsic, V. (2013) Food heritage down under: olive growers as Mediterranean 'food ambassadors'. *Journal of Heritage Tourism*, 8(2/3): 158–171.

Bessière, J. (1998) Local development and heritage: traditional food and cuisine as tourist attractions in rural areas. *Sociologia Ruralis*, 38(1): 21–34.

Bessière, J. (2013) 'Heritagisation', a challenge for tourism promotion and regional development: an example of food heritage. *Journal of Heritage Tourism*, 8(4): 275–291.

Bessière, J. and Tibere, L. (2013) Traditional food and tourism: French tourist experience and food heritage in rural spaces. *Journal of the Science of Food and Agriculture*, 93(14): 3420–3425.

Bunce, M. (1998) Thirty years of farmland preservation in North America: discourses and ideologies of a movement. *Journal of Rural Studies*, 14: 233–247.

Che, D. (2006) Select Michigan: local food production, food safety, culinary heritage, and branding in Michigan agritourism. *Tourism Review International*, 9(4): 349–363.

Che, D. (2010) *Value-added agricultural products and entertainment in Michigan's Fruit Belt.* In G. Halseth, S. Markey and D. Bruce (eds) *The Next Rural Economies: Constructing Rural Place in a Global Economy*, pp. 102–114. Wallingford: CAB International.

Che, D., Veeck, G. and Veeck, A. (2005) Agritourism and the selling of local food production, family, and rural American traditions to maintain family farming heritage. In S. Essex, A. Gilg, R. Yarwood, J. Smithers and R. Wilson (eds) *Rural Change and Sustainability: Agriculture, the Environment and Communities*, pp. 108–122. Wallingford: CAB International.

Che, D., Wright, R. and Rae, R. (2013) Taste Paradise: Tropical North Queensland as a gastronomic tourism destination. *Papers in Applied Geography*, 36: 415–422.

Chen, J. S., Chang, L. and Cheng, J. (2010) Exploring the market segments of farm tourism in Taiwan. *Journal of Hospitality Marketing & Management*, 19(4): 309–325.

Clemens, R. (2004) Keeping farmers on the land: agritourism in the European Union. *Iowa Ag Review*, 10(3): 8–9.

Cosgrove, D.E. (1998) *Social Formation and Symbolic Landscape*. Madison, WI: University of Wisconsin Press.

Daugstad, K., Rønningen, K. and Skar, B. (2006) Agriculture as an upholder of cultural heritage? Conceptualizations and value judgements – A Norwegian perspective in an international context. *Journal of Rural Studies*, 22: 67–81.

Derrett, R. and St Vincent Welch, J. (2008) 40 sheds and 40 kilometers: agricultural sheds as heritage tourism opportunities. In B. Prideaux, D.J. Timothy and K. Chon (eds) *Cultural and Heritage Tourism in Asia and the Pacific*, pp. 73–83. London: Routledge.

Duruz, J. (1999) Cuisine Nostalgie? Tourism's romance with 'the Rural'. *Communal/Plural*, 7(1): 97–109.

Ecker, S., Clarke, R., Cartwright, S., Kancans, R., Please, P. and Binks, B. (2010) *Drivers of Regional Agritourism and Food Tourism in Australia*. Canberra: Australian Bureau of Agricultural and Resource Economics, Bureau of Rural Sciences.

Everett, S. and Aitchison, C. (2008) The role of food tourism in sustaining regional identity: a case study of Cornwall, South West England. *Journal of Sustainable Tourism*, 16(2): 150–167.

Fisher, D.G. (2006) The potential for rural heritage tourism in the Clarence Valley of Northern New South Wales. *Australian Geographer*, 37(3): 411–424.

Gale, F. (1997) Direct farm marketing as a rural development tool. *Rural Development Perspectives*, 12(2): 19–25.

Gao, J., Barbieri, C. and Valdivia, C. (2014) Agricultural landscape preferences: implications for agritourism development. *Journal of Travel Research*, 53(3): 366–379.

Getz, D. (1999) Resort-centered tours and development of the rural hinterland: the case of Cairns and the Atherton Tablelands. *Journal of Tourism Studies*, 10(2): 23–34.

Harlan, J.R. (1995) *The Living Fields: Our Agriculture Heritage*. Cambridge: Cambridge University Press.

Heimlich, R.E. and Barnard, C.H. (1992) Agricultural adaptation to urbanization: farm types in northeast metropolitan areas. *Northeastern Journal of Agricultural and Resource Economics*, 21(1): 50–60.

Knowd, I. (2006) Tourism as a mechanism for farm survival. *Journal of Sustainable Tourism*, 14(1): 24–42.

LaPan, C. and Barbieri, C. (2014) The role of agritourism in heritage preservation. *Current Issues in Tourism*, 17(8): 666–673.

Lowenthal, D. (1991) British national identity and the English landscape. *Rural History*, 2(2): 205–230.

McFerson, J. (2014) The climate of weather and politics. *American/Western Fruit Grower*, 134(4): 60–61.

McGehee, N.G. and Kim, K. (2004) Motivation for agri-tourism entrepreneurship. *Journal of Travel Research*, 43: 161–170.

McIntosh, A.J. and Prentice, R.C. (1999) Affirming authenticity: consuming cultural heritage. *Annals of Tourism Research*, 26(3): 589–612.

Neal, S. (2002) Rural landscapes, representations and racism: examining multicultural citizenship and policy-making in the English countryside. *Ethnic and Rural Studies*, 25(3): 442–461.

Nilsson, P.Å. (2002) Staying on farms: an ideological background. *Annals of Tourism Research*, 29(1): 7–24.

Setten, G. (2005) Farming the heritage: on the production and construction of a personal and practised landscape heritage. *International Journal of Heritage Studies*, 11(1): 67–79.

Sims, R. (2009) Food, place and authenticity: local food and the sustainable tourism experience. *Journal of Sustainable Tourism*, 17(3): 321–336.

Stephenson, G. and Lev, L. (2004) Common support for local agriculture in two contrasting Oregon communities. *Renewable Agriculture and Food Systems*, 19(4): 210–217.

Sun, Y., Jansen-Verbeke, M., Min, Q. and Shengkui, C. (2011) Tourism potential of agricultural heritage systems. *Tourism Geographies*, 13(1): 112–128.

Sun, Y., Min, Q., Shi, J. and Jiang, Y. (2011) Terraced landscapes as a cultural and natural heritage resource. *Tourism Geographies*, 13(2): 328–331.

Sznajder, M., Przezbórska, L. and Scrimgeour, F. (2009) *Agritourism*. Wallingford: CAB International.

Tew, C. and Barbieri, C. (2012) The perceived benefits of agritourism: the provider's perspective. *Tourism Management*, 33(1): 215–224.

Timothy, D.J. (2005) Rural tourism business: a North American overview. In D. Hall, I. Kirkpatrick and M. Mitchell (eds) *Rural Tourism and Sustainable Business*, pp. 41–62. Clevedon: Channel View Publications.

Timothy, D.J. and Boyd, S.W. (2015) *Tourism and Trails: Cultural, Ecological and Management Issues*. Bristol: Channel View Publications.

Timothy, D.J. and Ron, A.S. (2009) Farmers for a day: agricultural heritage and nostalgia in rural Israel. Paper presented at the annual conference of the Association of American Geographers, Las Vegas, Nevada, March 26.

Timothy, D.J. and Ron, A.S. (2013) Heritage cuisines, regional identity and sustainable tourism. In C.M. Hall and S. Gössling (eds) *Sustainable Culinary Systems: Local Foods, Innovation, Tourism and Hospitality*, pp. 275–290. London: Routledge.

The University of California Small Farms Program (2011) What Is Agritourism? Available online at http://sfp.ucdavis.edu/agritourism Accessed January 20, 2015.

Turnour, J., McShane, C., Thompson, M., Dale, A., Prideaux, B. and Atkinson, M. (2013) *Accounting for Agriculture in Place-Based Frameworks for Regional Development*. Cairns: James Cook University, Cairns Institute.

Veeck, G., Che, D. and Veeck, A.M. (2006) America's changing farmscape: a study of agricultural tourism in Michigan. *Professional Geographer*, 58(3): 235–248.

White, R. (1996) Are you an environmentalist or do you work for a living? Work and nature. In W. Cronon (ed) *Uncommon Ground: Rethinking the Human Place in Nature*, pp. 171–185. New York: W.W. Norton.

Williams, R. (1973) *The Country and the City*. New York: Oxford University Press.

7 Heirloom products in heritage places

Farmers' markets, local food and food diversity

C. Michael Hall

Introduction

Farmers' markets are one of most well-recognised elements of the local food economy that has undergone significant revival in the developed world since the 1990s. Farmers' markets are, of course, nothing new. In many parts of the world markets remain one of the main means of food purchase. In developed countries farmers' markets maintained an important position in food retailing after the industrial revolution and the advent of the railway and the steamship. It was only with the advent of the shopping mall and car-based travel and the related rise of the supermarket that farmers' markets went into major decline.

Farmers' markets have had substantial growth since they were (re)introduced in the United States, Canada, the United Kingdom, Australia and New Zealand (Brown 2001, 2002; Hall and Sharples 2008; Hall 2013). In the United States there were 1,755 farmers' markets operating nationwide in 1994, just under 4,500 by 2006 and 8,268 in 2014 (Hamilton 2002; United States Department of Agriculture [USDA] 2014). According to the USDA (2012), farmers' markets sales in the United States are estimated at being slightly over $1 billion annually, and more than 25 percent of vendors at surveyed markets derived their sole source of farm income from farmers' markets. In roughly the same period in Canada the number increased from 70 to more than 260 (Hall 2013).

In the United Kingdom the first of the modern farmers' markets was (re)established in 1997 in Bath, which followed many of the elements of the most successful US markets (Holloway and Kneafsey 2000). This number has now increased to more than 550 markets offering produce during the summer. Australian and New Zealand farmers' markets were similarly reestablished in the late 1990s. In Australia there were more than 110 in 2009 and more than 160 by early 2012 (Australian Farmers' Market Association 2009; Woodburn 2014). The first modern farmers' market in New Zealand was established at Whangerei in 1998 (Guthrie et al. 2006) with 50 farmers' markets in New Zealand by October 2009 (Hall et al. 2008), although there were only 44 markets that were members of Farmers' Markets New Zealand (FMNZ) in 2011 (Farmers' Markets NZ Inc 2012a) and 29 being listed on the FMNZ website as of June 2015. Yet the New Zealand situation highlights broader issues in defining a farmers' market, as Hall (2013) noted that, in New Zealand, if 'unofficial' farmers' markets were added, then it is likely that the total number of operating markets could exceed 70.

This chapter discusses the role of farmers' markets in the food and heritage relationship. The chapters argues that farmers' markets are significant for heritage in two different tangible ways. First is through the role of markets in occupying built heritage and/or helping to revitalise heritage spaces and districts, and second, by acting as a means to promote and sell heritage (also referred to as heirloom or landrace) fruit, vegetable and animal food products. This last heritage role is therefore extremely significant for the conservation of food and genetic diversity. These two heritage functions are integrated in the focus of farmers' markets on food localism and local food systems. Therefore, before discussing the heritage dimensions of farmers' markets in more detail, this chapter will next examine issues of defining farmers' markets and identifying the essential role of food localism.

Authentic and local: defining farmers' markets

The definition of what constitutes a farmers' market has long been problematic. As Pyle (1971: 167) recognised, "[E]verything that is called a farmers' market may not be one, and other names are given to meeting that have the form and function of a farmers' market". Other names for similar types of markets in North America include swap meets, flea markets, tailgate markets and farm stands (Brown 2001), although many of these are best understood as other forms of direct marketing from producer to consumer. Nevertheless, many markets will advertise themselves as farmers' markets even though they are technically not in the sense of all products available being a direct purchase from the grower of the produce. Furthermore, the different terms used for farmers' markets reflect retail change over time and different regional food supply and distribution channels (Hall 2013). Nevertheless, the core of 'official' definitions of farmers' markets reflects the notion that farmers' markets are "recurrent markets at fixed locations where farm products are sold by farmers themselves … at a true farmers market some, if not all, of the vendors must be producers who sell their own products" (Brown 2001: 658).

As Hall (2013: 101) has argued, "[T]he issue of definition is not just academic but also reflects broader concerns of consumers and producers that the farmers' market and its produce be regarded as a space in which consumers can trust the 'authentic' and 'local' qualities of what is being offered". Indeed, the local dimension remains a long-time recurring theme in international studies of farmers' markets (e.g. Payne 2002; Feagan et al. 2004; Selfa and Qazi 2005; Hall et al. 2008; Conner et al. 2009; Feagan and Morris 2009; Carey et al. 2011). The issue of definition is also subject to the regulatory environment in which they operate. For example, California's more than 600 farmers' markets have been certified under state legislation since 1977, while the Province of Alberta in Canada has run an Alberta Approved Farmers' Market Program since 1973, which includes more than 125 markets (Hall 2013). Nevertheless, the importance of localism in defining farmers' markets is reflected in definitions of several national and regional farmers' market organisations (Table 7.1), where terms such as 'local', 'fresh' (which implies that food has only travelled a short distance from its origin) and 'direct to consumer' or other terms that imply that the goods are vendor produced are frequently used (Feagan 2007; Hall 2013).

The modern agri-food system, along with the tourist system, particularly as it exists in the developed countries, or North, has provided consumers with an

Table 7.1 Examples of definitions of farmers' market

Country	*Organisation*	*Definition*
Australia	Australian Farmers' Market Association	'... a predominantly fresh food market that operates regularly within a community, at a focal public location that provides a suitable environment for farmers and food producers to sell farm-origin and associated value-added processed food products directly to customers'.
Australia – Victoria	Victorian Farmers' Market Association	'... a predominantly local fresh food and produce market that operates regularly at a public location which provides a suitable environment for farmers and food producers to sell their farm origin product and their associated value added primary products directly to customers'.
Canada – Alberta	Alberta Farmers' Market Association under the Alberta Approved Farmers' Market Program Guidelines	'Markets must maintain an annual average vendor split of 80/20 where 80% of the vendors are Albertans selling Alberta products which they, an immediate family member, a staff member or a member of a producer-owned cooperative or their staff have made, baked or grown. The remaining 20% of the vendors can be made up of out-of-province vendors, resellers or vendors selling commercially available products. Markets operating outside the 80/20 requirement will be granted conditional approval. Approval status will be revoked for any markets that have been conditional for two years without improvement.... Preference must be granted to Alberta producers who make, bake, or grow their products'.
Canada – British Columbia	BC Association of Farmers' Markets	'Only the farmer and/or the family are permitted to sell at a member market. Re-sellers are not permitted. At member markets, our focus is on selling locally grown or processed farm-fresh foods, so only a limited number of crafters can be found at our markets. You won't find any imported products. Most of our foods travel from less than 300 kilometres away'.
Canada – Ontario	Farmers' Markets Ontario	'... is a seasonal, multi-vendor, community-driven (not private) organization selling agricultural, food, art and craft products including home-grown produce, home-made crafts and value-added products where the vendors are primary producers (including preserves, baked goods, meat, fish, dairy products, etc.)'.

Country	Organisation	Definition
New Zealand	New Zealand Farmers' Market Association	'… a food market where local growers, farmers and artisan food producers sell their wares directly to consumers. Vendors may only sell what they grow, farm, pickle, preserve, bake, smoke or catch themselves from within a defined local area. The market takes place at a public location on a regular basis'.
United Kingdom	National Farmers' Retail & Markets Association (FARMA)	'… a market in which farmers, growers or producers from a defined local area are present in person to sell their own produce, direct to the public. All products sold should have been grown, reared, caught, brewed, pickled, baked, smoked or processed by the stallholder'.
United States	Farmers' Market Coalition	'A farmers market operates multiple times per year and is organized for the purpose of facilitating personal connections that create mutual benefits for local farmers, shoppers and communities. To fulfill that objective farmers markets define the term local, regularly communicate that definition to the public, and implement rules/guidelines of operation that ensure that the farmers market consists principally of farms selling directly to the public products that the farms have produced'.
United States – California	California Farmers' Markets Association (CFMA)	'The Certified Farmers' Markets (CFM) are diversified markets offering both certifiable and non-certifiable goods for sale.The CFM provides producers with the opportunity to sell their fresh, local products directly to the consumers without the intervention of a middleman.Each CFM is operated in accordance with regulations established in the *California Administrative Code* (Title 3, Chapter 3, Group 4, Article 6.5, Section 1392) pertaining to Direct Marketing. Each market is certified by the County Agricultural Commissioner as a direct marketing outlet for producers to sell their crops directly to consumers without meeting the usual size, standard pack and container requirements for such products. However, all produce must meet minimum quality standards.The non-certifiable goods add variety and enhance the festive ambiance of the Farmers' Market. Although the State Direct Marketing regulations require the producers of fresh fruit, nuts, vegetables, flowers, honey, eggs, nursery stock, and plants be required to be certified, the same producer-to-consumer philosophy applies for all items sold at the Market. The resale of products is prohibited'.

Sources: Alberta Agriculture and Forestry 2015; Australian Farmers' Market Association 2009; BC Association of Farmers' Markets 2011; California Farmers' Markets Association 2006: 1; Farmers' Market Coalition 2008; Farmers' Markets Ontario 2007; National Farmers' Retail and Markets Association 2009; New Zealand Farmers' Market Association 2007; Victorian Farmers' Market Association 2011.

unparalled range of products, available virtually all year round, and at prices that account for historically unprecedented minor shares of household budgets (Sage 2012). However, this has come at a significant environmental, economic and social cost (Lang 2010; Gössling and Hall 2013), with losses in traditional farming systems and products and food diversity, and an increase of food insecurity in many locations as a result of lower local production and dependence on food supply chains stretching thousands of miles. This has meant increased dependence on fossil fuel and growing emissions from agricultural production and supply at a time of growing concern over climate change (Gössling and Hall 2013). In addition, food production in the modern agri-food system also affects environment and biodiversity as a result of changed farming methods and practices, such as the increased use of biocides, chemical fertilisers, deep ploughing and hedgerow and natural vegetation clearance. Sage (2012: 100) also highlights that the superstructure of the global food system, built upon rather limited genetic foundations, is "narrowing further as a result of agricultural modernisation and intensification".

The genetic base of commercial livestock and plant seed supply is far smaller than the traditional pre-agro-food-system farming base. Commercial seed supply is geared towards the availability of increased farming technologies, high water and energy inputs, chemical fertilisers and biocides and a high degree of mechanisation. The top five transnational seed companies control 47 percent of global commercial seed sales (Sage 2012: 103). In contrast, traditional agriculture tends to be highly diverse and marked by multifunctional operations and based on a much wider range of seed supplies. Such traditional farming strategies served at least two major functions. First, they minimised risk: "practices such as polycultures, intercropping, staggered planting times and so on had the advantages of reducing total crop losses, spreading labour demands, diversifying food sources and ensuring some degree of food security over the year. Second, different varieties were cultivated for different culinary and cultural purposes" (Sage 2012: 100–101).

Food safety, concerns over supply and security and associated risk reduction strategies have therefore become highly significant issues with respect to consumer purchasing and the food supply chain overall (Sage 2012; Turner and Hope 2014). Furthermore, food and encouraging local products and their consumption have also become an important part of many economic development and urban regeneration strategies (Hall and Gössling 2013: 27). The enthusiasm for farmers' and public markets, therefore, perhaps reflects Teil and Hennion's (2004: 25) observation: "Different people in different situations bring into play a collective knowledge, of which taste is a result. In other words, taste is a way of building relationships, with things and with people; it is not simply a property of goods, nor is it a competence of people". Nevertheless, the growing taste for local food systems in some locations is having considerable implications for heritage as some communities seek to (re)embrace more traditional food consumption and production relationships.

Local food systems are "deliberate formed food systems that are characterized by a close producer-consumer relationship within a designated place or local area" (Gössling and Hall 2013: 27). Local food systems support long-term connections; meet economic, social, health and environmental needs; link producers and markets via locally focused infrastructure; promote environmental health; and provide a competitive advantage to local food businesses (Food System Economic Partnership 2006; Buck et al. 2007; Hall and Sharples 2008; Silkes 2012; Turner and Hope 2014). Buck et al. (2007: 3) argue that the potential benefits of such a system include strengthening "the local economy by growing the agricultural sector, creating jobs, providing more choices for consumers, contributing to the local tax base, and reinvesting local money exchanged for food back into local farms and businesses".

Figure 7.1 outlines elements of a local food system for a tourism destination. In such a system, producers and consumers are linked via infrastructures, including farmers' markets, direct marketing and short supply chains, which can provide a competitive advantage for local farmers, processors, distributors, retailers and consumers alike, meaning that farmers receive a greater return for their produce as there are fewer intermediaries. "By sharing the risks and rewards of food production, processing, distribution, and retail with other local partners, farmers and businesses can explore opportunities to produce new varieties of foods or expand existing ventures to meet a local or regional need" (Buck et al. 2007: 3). Similarly, though in perhaps a more overt response to the agro-food system, Anderson and Cook (2000: 237) argue that the major advantage of localising food systems "is that this process reworks power and knowledge relationships in food supply

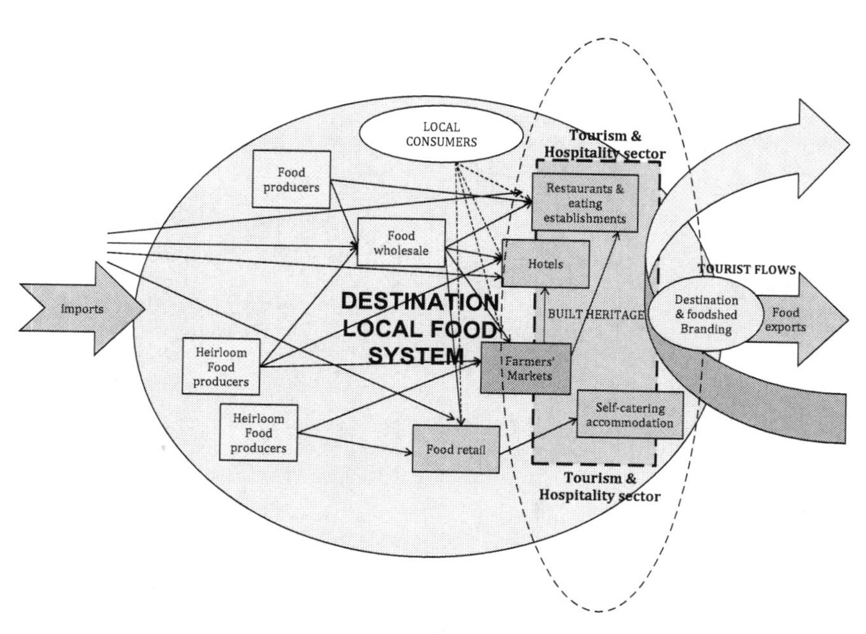

Figure 7.1 Destination Local Food System

systems that have become distorted by increasing distance (physical, social, and metaphorical) between producers and consumers . . . [and] gives priority to local and environmental integrity before corporate profit-making". Indeed, the political dimensions of heritage are at the forefront of both the market movement as well as the conservation of food diversity. The next section discusses some of these issues with respect to farmers' markets and heritage.

Farmers' markets and built heritage

As suggested in the previous section, farmers' markets may take a variety of forms. Table 7.2 illustrates some of these relationships which differ according to the location of the market, especially as to whether there is a purpose-built building or not, and the period over which the market is run. Clearly, many markets are seasonal because of both supply and weather conditions, while there is a strong tradition of harvest and Christmas festivals in parts of Europe. Many of these markets, as with some farmers' markets, have been running in various forms for decades if not centuries and may have received formal heritage status. For example, the Cambridge Farmers' Market in Canada has been operating for more

Table 7.2 A typology of farmers' markets and heritage

Heritage context	*Permanent (open most days of week)*	*Year round (open less than half of the week)*	*Seasonal*
Market held inside a designated market space (i.e. a public market) in a heritage area	Byward Market, Ottawa, OntarioPike Place Market, Seattle	St. Jacobs Market, Ontario	Special Christmas markets are often held in market spaces in Germany and the Nordic countries
Market held inside a reused heritage building	Reading Terminal Market, Philadelphia	Fremantle Market, Western Australia	Ottawa farmers' market operates inside a different building over winter weekends in the Aberdeen Pavilion at Lansdowne
Market held outside in a heritage district as a continuing use of space (historical continuity)	Market Square, Cambridge	New Maxwell Street Market, Chicago	Covent Garden outdoor farmers' market, London
New market held in a new space in a heritage location	Granville Island Market, British Columbia	Danes County Farmers' Market, Madison, Wisconsin	Lyttleton Market, Lyttleton, New Zealand

than 100 years. It occupies a historic building and adjacent lot in the city core and enjoys the status of a designated heritage property (Smithers et al. 2008) (Figure 7.2). Nevertheless, the development of new market infrastructure and space in heritage precincts can be extremely controversial for both socio-economic and architectural and aesthetic reasons (Tunbridge 2000, 2001). Indeed the Ontario Heritage Foundation noted the challenge of the need for sensitive infill buildings where heritage landscapes have critical gaps or when existing buildings need to be demolished for aesthetic, safety or appropriate economic reasons. From an integrated approach, new work should be clearly distinguishable from old (Fram 1992). The opposite approach is to contrast with adjacent buildings, for example by creating a structure for an activity that may be of limited duration, such as a farmers' or public market, as in the case in Ottawa.

Although a number of farmers' markets have operated in the same purpose-built space for long periods of time, such as the Toronto and Halifax public markets in Canada or the Pike Place Markets in Seattle, urban redevelopment often places substantial pressures on market spaces as city governments and property owners seek higher returns, sometimes forcing them to move (Xu et al. 2014). For example, the Maxwell Street Market in Chicago has had to move several times. Its location "remains impermanent, as new commercial development raises land values in the area" (Morales 2006: 1).

Figure 7.2 The Fremantle Market is representative of an established historic market (Photo: C. Michael Hall)

The Maxwell Street Market began as a collection of small street markets in poor immigrant neighbourhoods south and west of the Loop in Chicago in the 1880s. In 1912, the Chicago City Council passed an ordinance designating the Maxwell Street Market an official marketplace for the city's people. In the 1950s, the city cleared the market area east of Union Street, pushing the market farther to the west, in a large redevelopment that opened a path for the Dan Ryan expressway. The market remained in the Maxwell/Halsted area until 1994, when it was relocated five blocks east to Canal Street as a result of the South Campus expansion of the University of Illinois at Chicago. In September 1994, the city opened the New Maxwell Street Market along Canal Street, where it gradually moved to concentrate on both sides of Roosevelt Road, from Taylor Street to the railroad viaduct at 16th Street. In 2007, the city relocated the market three blocks west to Des Plaines Street. Importantly, the market provided a focus for heritage preservation. "During the 1990s, MSF led efforts to create a National Historic District in the Maxwell/Halsted area. Thanks in part to its efforts, some of the original commercial buildings and distinctive façades were preserved during the area's redevelopment" (Morales 2006: 3).

Indeed, one of the most important attributes of farmers' markets, whether permanent or seasonal, is that they help enliven public space (Morales et al. 1995; Çela et al. 2007). Farmers' markets have therefore become an important urban regeneration tool and are often proposed as part of economic revitalisation and redevelopment projects (Soward et al. 2008; Caruso et al. 2013; Pride et al. 2013). The concept of regeneration includes both physical, i.e. concerned with material architecture and image, physical plant and infrastructure, urban design and form, and social/immaterial dimensions, which are concerned with improving the quality of life of those who already live in areas targeted for regeneration and/or attracting new permanent and temporary migrants. These concerns have been particularly applied to regeneration of heritage precincts and cultural quarters. A cultural quarter is defined by Roadhouse (2010: 24) as "a geographical area of a large town or city which acts as a focus for cultural and artistic activities through the presence of a group of buildings devoted to housing a range of such activities, and purpose designed or adapted spaces to create a sense of identity, providing an environment to facilitate and encourage the provision of cultural and artistic services and activities".

From a policy perspective, cultural quarters and heritage precincts are regarded by governments as serving several significant roles as development catalysts within the broader field of 'culture-led' regeneration (Evans 2005). Cultural industries, including cultural and heritage tourism, are widely regarded as economically significant initiatives for the development of creative, innovative and more diversified economies. The social and environmental aspects of quartering are also regarded as having social benefits such as providing a sense of collective belonging or enhanced local identity and sense of social inclusion (Bell and Jayne 2004), which may provide a basis for more sustainable urban development (Darlow 1996). These are the very same social benefits that many also ascribe to the development of farmers' markets (Hall et al. 2008). Although, as McCarthy (2005:

298) stresses, "perhaps of greater urgency", cultural quarters are regarded as "a means to enhance image via branding or re-branding in order to attract mobile capital and visitor income in the context of globalising forces and city competition". From this perspective, farmers' markets not only serve to enliven space and create 'atmosphere' for locals and visitors alike, but also, by emphasising local food systems and community relations, they serve as attractions for tourists who wish to experience the local (Timothy 2005).

The wide range of policy objectives for heritage precincts and cultural quarters, and the role of farmers' markets within them, can nevertheless lead to significant implementation and assessment issues as some of the aims are potentially contradictory, creating what Mommaas (2004: 530) termed, an "ad hoc blending of arguments and opportunities", and confusion over even basic concepts (McCarthy 2005). Furthermore, the focus on cultural quarters for economic development and regeneration purposes also presents something of a paradox, as such serial reproduction of regeneration strategies may potentially reduce the very heterogeneity that is meant to be their unique selling proposition (Malecki 2004; González 2011). For example, Eaton (2008) questions whether the focus on farmers' markets and local food in the Niagara region of Canada has shifted from retaining and conserving heritage and encouraging sustainable food to being more concerned with attracting tourists and consequently leading to the commodification of place. Kohn (2009) is even harsher in his criticism and writes of 'dreamworlds of deindustrialisation' with reference to the Distillery District, a 13-acre industrial heritage site located on the edge of downtown Toronto, Canada. He argues that the Distillery District's combination of industrial ruin with "[r]etail shops selling handmade contemporary furniture, Swedish beds, Italian kitchen fixtures, wearable art, artisanal cheese, and gold jewellery" (Kohn 2009: n.p.), as well as a Summer Sunday market, illustrates many of the forces that are reconfiguring cities: commodification, gentrification, the city as theme park and spectacle, post-industrialism and the consumer preferences of the creative class. Similarly, with reference to 'local' food and drink in the same location, Mathews and Picton (2014: 337) argue that "craft beer works as a vehicle in the manufacture of new spaces of cultural consumption. Specifically, craft beer production and consumption are used to aestheticize the industrial past and pacify resistance to central-city gentrification".

> Yet there is something disturbing about the conversion of abandoned industrial spaces into high end cultural venues. Whereas most critics have faulted such projects for their nostalgic character, I ask whether nostalgia must always have a depoliticizing effect. When read in a certain way, the Distillery District makes the economic transformation from Fordism to post-Fordism visible. It brazenly exposes dynamics of gentrification and commodification of culture that are remaking other parts of the city in a more piecemeal fashion.... [T]he Distillery District both conceals and reveals the social forces remaking contemporary urban life.
>
> (Kohn 2009: ii)

Nevertheless, the redevelopment of urban heritage need not be over-commodified, and spaces of community rather than commercial imperatives can be developed, for example, as debate about the transformation of Lansdowne Park in Ottawa, a multipurpose city-run open space that is home to heritage buildings, an arena and stadium as well as several weekly and annual community events, including the city's farmers' markets, indicates. Lansdowne Live!, a proposal in 2009 by a group of local business owners to build a large-scale hotel and shopping centre at the park became a lightning rod for debate about the park's 'potential' and 'real' contributions to the livability of the city, the quality of life of its inhabitants and the experiential environment for visitors (Donohoe et al. 2011). Indeed such activism, which in the long run led to the Ottawa farmers' markets being permanently located at Lansdowne, is also reflected in growing interest in the role of markets as a focal point of urban agriculture (Nasr and Komisar 2012; Hardman and Larkham 2014).

Heirloom heritage

The extremely significant role of farmers' markets with respect to urban built heritage as part of local food systems, as well as the seeming contradictions that arise from the increased commodification of heritage, also apply to fruit and vegetables. As noted above, the local food system concept and the localism of farmers' markets serve to favour local varieties of fruit and vegetables, in the same way that the agro-food system favours product that can be shipped around the world to supermarkets, and is therefore reasonably homogenous in presentation and is able to keep for extended periods of time. As Donati et al. (2013) noted in the case of farmers' markets and community gardens in Melbourne, Australia, the fragility of many heirloom vegetables means they are unsuited to long transport, while retail and wholesale markets also impose aesthetic and dimensional specifications they may fail to meet.

Heirloom vegetable varieties are defined as being at least 50 years old (Watson 1996) and have usually been preserved by regional, ethnic or family groups in part because of their taste and contribution to identity (Veteto 2008; Shields 2015), but extremely importantly because they are usually not suited to the demands of supermarkets and modern food retailing whether because of their appearance or because of their lack of longevity. As Table 7.1 indicated, farmers' markets associations and regulations reinforce the provision of local varieties and thereby help create retail space and a market for varieties that might otherwise not be commercially viable. The socio-technical practices of farmers' markets, therefore, provide a means to help conserve food diversity and, because of positive feedback along the supply chain, conserve fruit, vegetable and animal varieties that might otherwise be lost because of a lack of a commercial market (Hultine et al. 2007; Conner et al. 2009; Tchoukaleyska, 2013).

In Norway, for example, such is the significance of locally oriented food systems that they have become recognised within their national strategy for conserving plant genetic resources for food and agriculture (Asdal 2008). Farmers' markets and direct marketing to local consumers also provide positive benefits for seed-saving networks that utilise local varieties that have developed over time to suit local growing conditions (Volkening 2006), while similar benefits also apply to livestock varieties (Negri et al. 2009).

Nevertheless, heirloom varieties, like farmers' markets and the spaces they occupy, may also become subject to commodification. The heirloom fruit and vegetable may become a cultural object and commodity (Jordan 2007; Rath 2014) rather than something inherently prized for its taste. Indeed, heirloom varieties may become sought after for their 'authenticity' (Stiles et al. 2011) and for their integral role in cuisine (Shields 2015). At an economic level such shifts in taste may become helpful to some producers, but in the long run only serve to encourage the mobility of taste for the other rather than the local.

Conclusions

This chapter has examined the way in which farmers' markets and heirloom foods are enmeshed within local food systems and the tangible and intangible dimensions of heritage. In doing so it has highlighted the manner in which food heritage is caught within broader debates over sustainability, commoditisation and changing urban form.

Farmers' markets have shown enormous growth in developed countries in recent years as many consumers, as well as producers, have sought to embrace short supply chains. The desire to develop local food systems, of which farmers' markets are a focal point, reflects a range of economic, social, political and environmental goals. However, at the same time that farmers' markets serve to reinforce certain aspects of regional identity and heritage, they may simultaneously also reinforce some of the same global forces that the local food system is trying to respond to. This may mean that while food heritage, from a narrow perspective where taste and variety are concerned, other aspects both tangible, i.e. built environment, and intangible, i.e. senses of community and place, may be lost. This chapter therefore reflects the essentially contested nature of much heritage, whether it be industrial heritage or a tomato, and how it can be used by different sets of stakeholders for their own means.

The reification of food to a form of cultural capital nevertheless creates a range of issues for the conservation of food heritage. Farmers' markets do provide great opportunities for enlivening heritage spaces and may in themselves be heritage attractions and integral to their community's sense of place. The challenge for markets, though, is to be able to retain such linkages so that they remain lived heritage rather than a stage show for the tourists to come look at the locals and what they think they eat.

References

Alberta Agriculture and Forestry (2015) Alberta Approved Farmers' Market Program Guidelines. Available online at http://www1.agric.gov.ab.ca/$Department/deptdocs.nsf/all/apa2577 Accessed April 1, 2015.

Anderson, M.D. and Cook, J.T. (2000) Does food security require local food systems? In J.M. Harris (ed) *Rethinking Sustainability: Power, Knowledge and Institutions*, pp. 228–248. Ann Arbor: University of Michigan Press.

Australian Farmers' Market Association (2009) About. Available online at http://www.farmersmarkets.org.au/ Accessed October 1, 2009.

Asdal, Å. (2008). *State of Plant Genetic Resources for Food and Agriculture in Norway. Second Norwegian National Report on Conservation and Sustainable Utilisation of Plant Genetic Resources for Food and Agriculture, Commissioned Report from Skog og landskap*. Oslo: Norwegian Ministry for Agriculture and Food.

BC Association of Farmers' Markets (2011) About us. Available online at http://www.bcfarmersmarket.org/about.htm Accessed March, 26 2012.

Bell, D. and Jayne, M. (2004) *City of Quarters: Urban Villages in the Contemporary City*. Aldershot: Ashgate.

Brown, A. (2001) Counting farmers markets. *Geographical Review*, 91: 655–674.

Brown, A. (2002) Farmers' market research 1940–2000: an inventory and review. *American Journal of Alternative Agriculture*, 17(4): 167–176.

Buck, K., Kaminski, L.E., Stockmann, D.P. and Vail, A.J. (2007) *Investigating Opportunities to Strengthen the Local Food System in Southeastern Michigan, Executive Summary*. Ann Arbor: University of Michigan, School of Natural Resources and Environment.

California Farmers' Markets Association (2006) *California Farmers' Markets Association Rules and Regulations for Certified Farmers' Markets*. Walnut Creek: California Farmers' Markets Association.

Carey, L., Bell, P., Duff, A., Sheridan, M. and Shields, M. (2011) Farmers' market consumers: a Scottish perspective. *International Journal of Consumer Studies*, 35(3): 300–306.

Caruso, N., Fredericks, A., Merritt, C., Pitt, S., Wilson, K. and Robinson, A. (2013) *Revitalizing Woonsocket: A Main St. Implementation Plan. Historic Preservation*. Roger Williams University. Available online at http://docs.rwu.edu/cpc_preservation/4 Accessed April 1, 2015.

Conner, D.S., Montria, A.D., Montria, D.N. and Hamm, M.W. (2009) Consumer demand for local produce at extended season farmers' markets: guiding farmer marketing strategies. *Renewable Agriculture and Food Systems*, 24: 251–259.

Çela, A., Knowles-Lankford, J. and Lankford, S. (2007) Local food festivals in Northeast Iowa communities: a visitor and economic impact study. *Managing Leisure*, 12(2/3): 171–186.

Darlow, A. (1996) Cultural policy and urban sustainability: making a missing link? *Planning Practice and Research*, 11: 291–301.

Donati, K., Taylor, C. and Pearson, C.J. (2013) Local food and dietary diversity: farmers markets and community gardens in Melbourne, Australia. In J. Fanzo, D. Hunter, T. Borelli and F. Mattei (eds) *Diversifying Food and Diets: Using Agricultural Biodiversity to Improve Nutrition and Health*, pp. 326–335. London: Earthscan.

Donohoe, H.M., Salo, B., Gilmore, T.C., Valentine, S., Aslamzada, M., Byrd, C., Dawar, H., Evans, A., Latkowcer, J., Macedow, L, Rubacha, S. and Sutherland, C. (2011) A youth perspective on leisure, livability, and Ottawa's Lansdowne Park. *Loisir et Société/Society and Leisure*, 34(2): 43–74.

Eaton, E. (2008) From feeding the locals to selling the locale: adapting local sustainable food projects in Niagara to neocommunitarianism and neoliberalism. *Geoforum*, 39(2): 994–1006.

Evans, G. (2005) Measure for measure: evaluating the evidence of culture's contribution to regeneration. *Urban Studies*, 42(5/6): 959–983.

Farmers' Market Coalition (2008) Welcome to the FMC. Available online at http://farmersmarketcoalition.org/ Accessed March 26, 2012.

Farmers' Markets NZ Inc (2012) History of the Farmers' Market Movement. Available online at http://www.farmersmarkets.org.nz/ Accessed March 26, 2012.

Farmers' Markets Ontario (FMO) (2007) Membership Information. Available online at http://www.farmersmarketsontario.com/MembershipInfo.cfm Accessed October 1, 2007.

Feagan, R. (2007) The place of food: mapping out the "local" in local food systems. *Progress in Human Geography*, 31(1): 23–42.

Feagan, R. and Morris, D. (2009) Consumer quest for embeddedness: a case study of the Brantford Farmers' Market. *International Journal of Consumer Studies*, 33(3): 235–243.

Feagan, R., Morris, D. and Krug, K. (2004) Niagara region farmers' markets: local food systems and sustainability considerations. *Local Environment*, 9(3): 235–54.

Food System Economic Partnership (2006) *Alternative Regional Food System Models: Successes and Lessons Learned: A Preliminary Literature Review*. Ann Arbor, MI: Food System Economic Partnership.

Fram, M. (1992) *Well Preserved: The Ontario Heritage Foundation's Manual of Principles and Practice for Architectural Conservation*, Rev. Edn. Toronto: Stoddart.

González, S. (2011) Bilbao and Barcelona 'in motion': how urban regeneration 'models' travel and mutate in the global flows of policy tourism. *Urban Studies*, 48(7): 1397–1418.

Gössling, S. and Hall, C.M. (2013) Sustainable culinary systems: an introduction. In C.M. Hall and S. Gössling (eds) *Sustainable Culinary Systems: Local Foods, Innovation, and Tourism & Hospitality*, pp. 3–44. London: Routledge.

Guthrie, J., Guthrie, A., Lawson, R. and Cameron, A. (2006) Farmers' markets: the small business counter-revolution in food production and retailing. *British Food Journal*, 108: 560–573.

Hall, C.M. (2013) The local in farmers' markets in New Zealand. In C.M. Hall and S. Gössling (eds), *Sustainable Culinary Systems: Local Foods, Innovation, and Tourism & Hospitality*, pp. 99–121. London: Routledge.

Hall, C.M. and Gössling, S. (eds) (2013) *Sustainable Culinary Systems: Local Foods, Innovation, and Tourism & Hospitality*. London: Routledge.

Hall, C.M., Mitchell, R., Scott, D. and Sharples, L. (2008) The authentic market experiences of farmers' markets. In C.M. Hall and L. Sharples (eds) *Food and Wine Festivals and Events around the World: Development, Management and Markets*, pp. 197–231. Oxford: Butterworth Heinemann.

Hall, C.M. and Sharples, L. (eds) (2008) *Food and Wine Festivals and Events around the World: Development, Management and Markets*. Oxford: Butterworth Heinemann.

Hamilton, L.M. (2002) The American farmers market. *Gastronomica*, 2(3): 73–77.

Hardman, M. and Larkham, P.J. (2014) The rise of the 'food charter': a mechanism to increase urban agriculture. *Land Use Policy*, 39: 400–402.

Holloway, L. and Kneafsey, M. (2000) Reading the space of the farmers' market: a preliminary investigation from the UK. *Sociologia Ruralis*, 40: 285–299.

Hultine, S.A., Cooperband, L.R., Curry, M. and Gasteyer, S. (2007) Linking small farms to rural communities with local food: A case study of the local food project in Fairbury, Illinois. *Community Development*, 38(3): 61–76.

Jordan, J.A. (2007) The heirloom tomato as cultural object: investigating taste and space. *Sociologia Ruralis*, 47(1): 20–41.

Kohn, M. (2009) Dreamworlds of deindustrialization. *Theory & Event*, 12(4): n.p. (online). Available at: http://muse.jhu.edu/login?auth=0&type=summary&url=/journals/theory_and_event/v012/12.4.kohn.html

Lang, T. (2010) From "value-for-money" to "values-for-money"? Ethical food and policy in Europe. *Environment and Planning A*, 42: 1814–1832.

Malecki, E.J. (2004) Jockeying for position: what it means and why it matters to regional development policy when places compete. *Regional Studies*, 38(9): 1101–1120.

Mathews, V. and Picton, R.M. (2014) Intoxifying gentrification: brew pubs and the geography of post-industrial heritage. *Urban Geography*, 35(3): 337–356.

McCarthy, J. (2005) Cultural quarters and regeneration: the case of Wolverhampton. *Planning, Practice & Research*, 20(3): 297–311.

Mommaas, H. (2004) Cultural clusters and the post-industrial city: towards the remapping of urban cultural policy. *Urban Studies*, 41(3): 507–532.

Morales, A. (2006) *New Maxwell Street Market Its Present and Future*. Evanston, IL: Maxwell Street Foundation.

Morales, A., Balkin, S. and Persky, J. (1995) The value of benefits of a public street market: the case of Maxwell Street. *Economic Development Quarterly*, 9(4): 304–320.

Nasr, J. and Komisar, J. (2012) The integration of food and agriculture into urban planning and design practices. In A. Viljoen and J. Wiskerke (eds) *Sustainable Food Planning: Evolving Theory and* Practice, pp. 47–60. Wageningen: Wageningen Academic Publishers.

National Farmers' Retail and Markets Association (FARMA) (2009) Certified Farmers' Markets. Find a Farmers' Market. Available online at http://www.farmersmarkets.org.uk/findafmkt.htm Accessed April 1, 2012.

Negri, V., Maxted, N. and Veteläinen, M. (2009) European landrace conservation: an introduction. In M. Veteläinen, V. Negri, and N. Maxted (eds) *European Landraces On-farm Conservation, Management and Use. Bioversity Technical Bulletin 15*, pp. 1–22. Rome: Biodiversity International.

New Zealand Farmers' Market Association (2007) *Fresh Market Locations*. Available online at http://www.farmersmarket.org.nz/locations.htm Accessed October 1, 2007.

Payne, T. (2002) *U.S. Farmers Markets – 2000: A Study of Emerging Trends*, Washington, DC: Agricultural Marketing Service, USDA.

Pride, M., Frye, S., Barney, J., Childs, M., Isaac, C. and Wilson, C. (2013) *Reviving Mainstreet 2012: Doña Ana+ Las Cruces Communitites*. Las Cruces: Design and Planning Assistance Center, University of New Mexico.

Pyle, J. (1971) Farmers' markets in United States: functional anachronisms? *Geographical Review*, 61: 167–197.

Rath, E.C. (2014) New meanings for old vegetables in Kyoto. *Food, Culture & Society*, 17(2): 203–223.

Roadhouse, S. (ed) (2010) *Cultural Qu4rters: Principles and Practice*, 2nd Edn. Bristol: Intellect.

Sage, C. (2012) *Environment and Food*. London: Routledge.

Sánchez, I.A., Lassaletta, L., McCollin, D. and Bunce, R.G.H. (2010) The effect of hedgerow loss on microclimate in the Mediterranean region: an investigation in central Spain. *Agroforestry Systems*, 78(1): 13–25.

Selfa, T. and Qazi, J. (2005) 'Place, taste, or face-to-face? Understanding producer–consumer networks in "local" food systems in Washington State. *Agriculture and Human Values*, 22: 451–464.

Shields, D.S. (2015) *Southern Provisions: The Creation and Revival of a Cuisine*. Chicago: University of Chicago Press.

Silkes, C.A. (2012) Farmers' markets: a case for culinary tourism. *Journal of Culinary Science & Technology*, 10(4): 326–336.

Smithers, J., Lamarche, J. and Joseph, A.E. (2008) Unpacking the terms of engagement with local food at the farmers' market: Insights from Ontario. *Journal of Rural Studies*, 24(3): 337–350.

Soward, R., Warzecha, M. and MacKay, K. (2008) *The Hydrostone: Neighbourhood Futures Report*. Halifax: Dalhousie University.

Stiles, K., Altıok, Ö. and Bell, M.M. (2011) The ghosts of taste: food and the cultural politics of authenticity. *Agriculture and Human Values*, 28(2): 225–236.

Tchoukaleyska, R. (2013) Regulating the farmers' market: Paysan expertise, quality production and local food. *Geoforum*, 45: 211–218.

Teil, G. and Hennion, A. (2004) Discovering quality or performing taste? A sociology of the amateur. In M. Harvey, A. McMeekin and A. Warde (eds) *Qualities of Food*, pp. 19–37. Manchester: Manchester University Press.

Timothy, D.J. (2005) *Shopping Tourism, Retailing and Leisure*. Bristol: Channel View Publications.

Tunbridge, J.E. (2000) Heritage momentum or maelstrom? The case of Ottawa's Byward Market. *International Journal of Heritage Studies*, 6(3): 269–291.

Tunbridge, J.E. (2001) Ottawa's Byward Market: a festive bone of contention? *The Canadian Geographer*, 45(3): 356–370.

Turner, B. and Hope, C. (2014) Ecological connections: reimagining the role of farmers' markets. *Rural Society*, 23(2): 175–187.

United States Department of Agriculture (USDA), Agricultural Marketing Service (2012) *Farmers Market Services*. Washington, DC: Marketing Services Division, USDA Agricultural Marketing Service.

United States Department of Agriculture (USDA), Agricultural Marketing Service (2014) *National Count of Farmers Market Directory Listing Graph: 1994–2014*. Washington, DC: Marketing Services Division, USDA Agricultural Marketing Service.

Veteto, J.R. (2008) The history and survival of traditional heirloom vegetable varieties in the southern Appalachian Mountains of western North Carolina. *Agriculture and Human Values*, 25(1): 121–134.

Victorian Farmers' Market Association (2011) About the VFMA. Available online at http://www.vicfarmersmarkets.org.au/content/about-vfma Accessed March 25, 2012.

Volkening, T. (2006) Seed Savers Exchange. *Journal of Agricultural & Food Information*, 7(2/3): 3–15.

Watson, B. (1996) *Taylor's Guide to Heirloom Vegetables*. New York: Houghton Mifflin Harcourt.

Woodburn, V. (2014) *Understanding the Characteristics of Australian Farmers' Markets*. Barton: Rural Industries Research and Development Corporation.

Xu, H., Wan, X. and Fan, X. (2014) Rethinking authenticity in the implementation of China's heritage conservation: the case of Hongcun Village. *Tourism Geographies*, 16(5): 799–811.

8 Religious heritage, spiritual aliment and food for the soul

Dallen J. Timothy and Amos S. Ron

Introduction

Almost all religious and spiritual practices have direct or indirect connections to food. Many of today's culinary delights and food-related practices derive from religious customs or spiritual traditions, and aliment is deemed sacred in many religions (Civitello 2004; Denker 2003; Laudan 2013; Roth-Haillote 2006; Sahu 2015; Wirzba 2011; Yoshizawa 1999). Food "is central to religion – as symbol, as subject of prayers, as marker of sharing and unsharing, and as communion" (Anderson 2014: 189). The roots of Thanksgiving in the United States and Canada, for example, those countries' most celebrated annual feast, are not only in the commemoration of successful harvests but also in demonstrating gratitude to God for his bounteous blessings. While Thanksgiving has become more secularized in its celebratory elements, its origins come from the faith of North America's earliest European settlers (Pleck 1999). America's beloved cheesecake is also said to have had Jewish celebratory origins (Denker 2003).

This chapter is based on the view that religion is one of the most important manifestations of human culture. The beliefs, practices, ceremonies, doctrine, languages, social mores and morals of the world's faiths are among the most penetrating constituents of human heritage (Timothy and Olsen 2006). Food and religion are in many ways inseparable. Food and drink form part of the physical manifestation of beliefs and spiritual traditions, and food is frequently the center of people's spiritual universe. This chapter first examines the multifarious relationships between religion and cuisine, followed by a synopsis of prescribed and proscribed foods and gastronomic practices among some of the world's main religions. Finally, it describes the ways in which service providers and tourism destinations are beginning to cater to the food-based religious requirements of the traveling public.

Religion, food and heritage

Religion is one of the most salient manifestations of heritage in the world today. Religion and spirituality are heritage from at least two perspectives. First, religion provides much by way of tangible culture. Religious buildings, sacred sites and material culture are clear physical manifestations of faith as part of the cultural landscapes of places. Secondly, the beliefs, rites, rituals, commandments, music and ceremonies associated with all faith traditions are important, albeit intangible, elements of cultural heritage passed down from generation to generation through family, faith organizations and social alliances. Both types of religious heritage are associated with food. Food of many types is an important part of worship. It plays a central role in offerings, sacraments, celebrations, ceremonies and scriptures. Most holy writ includes many allusions to aliment and drink of many varieties, forming the foundations for the treatment of comestibles and their preparation methods. For instance, the Bible tells many stories of food-related miracles and events, such as the manna from heaven, the miraculous quails, turning the water to wine, the Last Supper and Christ's feeding of the five thousand. Temples, churches and other religious buildings provide venues for food-centered ordinances and observances, and some of the material culture of faith is directly connect to, or derived from, food and drink.

To illustrate the primary linkages between religious tourism and food, Ron and Timothy (2013: 236–237) described nine relationships. While their model focuses specifically on pilgrimage/religious tourism, it applies equally beyond the context of tourism to religion and food in general. Thus, Figure 8.1 depicts the main heritage relationships between religion/faith and food. The first relationship is alms. Utilizing food in almsgiving is customary in many different faiths. Instead of offering money to beggars and the homeless, many religionists choose to offer food items as alms for the poor. Second, offerings to the gods frequently consist of fresh food items: fruits, rice, sweets, vegetables or prepared items such as soups

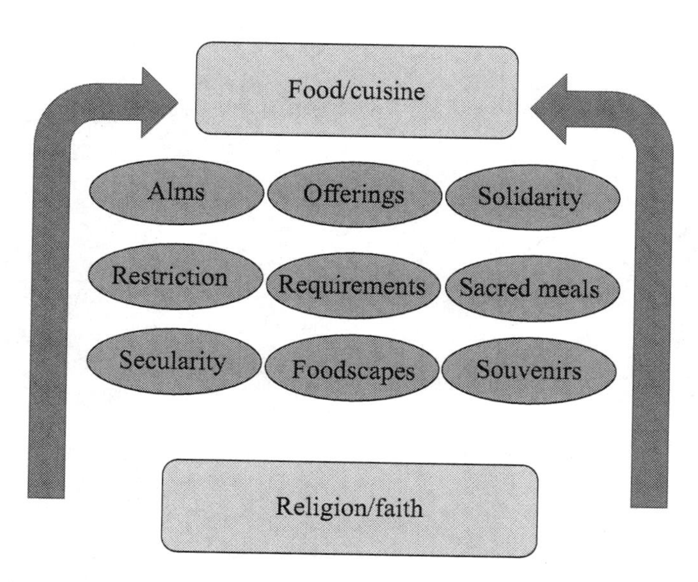

Figure 8.1 Relationships between religion and food (modified after Ron and Timothy 2013)

(Avieli 2012; LeCount 2001) (Figure 8.2). In much of Asia, rice is deemed sacred because of its life-giving properties (Norman 2012; Yoshizawa 1999), which is why it is a staple temple offering throughout Asia. Food-based supplication of the divine for blessings and forgiveness has a long history, particularly in South Asian and East Asian faith societies.

The third relationship is how cuisine can encourage solidarity among adherents of a religious group. Even if the aliment itself is not spiritual in origin, the socialization process of dining with co-religionists while undertaking a pilgrimage or at home in a congregational setting can help build fealty, faith and testimony. Food serves to "distinguish believers within defined communities and to cement this social bond through common ritualized practice" (Albala 2011: 7).

Fourth, dietary taboos or restrictions (discussed at greater length later in the chapter) require many of the faithful to refrain from partaking of certain foods, slaughtering techniques or cooking methods (Norman 2012; Sopher 1967). By the same token, food laws encourage religious adherents to eat and enjoy the bounties from God. While some faiths have no official doctrines, policies or statements regarding food, consuming fruits, vegetables and grains is encouraged by almost all religions, with a few exceptions of prohibitions against certain grains and certain times of the year. The fifth relationship relates to the fourth, but in this case, religious adherents are required to consume certain victuals, especially during holidays and celebratory times of the year, pilgrimages or religious services.

Figure 8.2 Worshippers' offerings at a temple in Taipei, Taiwan (Photo: Dallen J. Timothy)

Sixth, eating religious gastronomy or holy meals is thought by some to bring one closer to deity. These meals often commemorate sacred events, such as Passover or Easter, and may enhance one's spirituality. Some Christian groups in Europe and North America celebrate Jewish sacred meals, such as Passover, because of their shared belief in the miracles of the Old Testament. Some Jewish and many Christian groups demonstrate considerable interest in eating biblical food. As a result, various institutions in Israel and the United States offer lectures on foods of the Bible and biblical meals for tour groups (Ron and Timothy 2013). Although these run the risk of becoming overly simplistic and 'condensed interpretations' of a very complex set of religions meanings and practices from the Jewish vantage point (Graburn 1982; Harrison 1997), for the pilgrims themselves, such meals can leave a lasting impression.

Secularity is the seventh relationship. While this tends more toward some sort of spirituality or self-fulfillment rather than any organized religion per se, extreme food enthusiasts have been known to travel the world in search of the most exotic or most sensuous culinary experiences of all. This may be likened to secular pilgrimages, wherein devout fans or serious hobbyists travel to sites and events associated with the object of their interest. For instance, some people undertake pilgrimage-like journeys to the home football stadium of their favorite team or more devotedly follow the team throughout the season. Others aspire to visit the gravesite of their favorite musician or movie star (Alderman 2002; Liutikas 2014; Reader and Walter 1992). In the case of sport pilgrimages, eating hot dogs and popcorn in a revered stadium is as much a part of the 'spiritual' heritage as the game itself.

The eighth connection is evident in the cultural landscapes of places that are frequented by pilgrims or other religious tourists. In these situations, food may be a prominent part of the religious landscape. Visual imagery (e.g. food-related souvenirs, signs and advertisements) embraces the gastronomic characteristics of an area's religious heritage and is a prominent part of the local tourismscape. Signs and symbols of loaves and fishes, alluding to the miracles of Jesus, are pervasive throughout Israel on signs and souvenirs, as are printed references to the 'Land of Milk and Honey' (Ron and Timothy 2013). In the village of Cana, most tourist souvenirs are wine related, alluding to Jesus's miracle of turning water to wine at this locale. These sacred foodscapes may be intentionally designed to attract the faithful, or they develop organically. Either way, they can enhance the place-bound pilgrim experience.

Finally, cuisine-related souvenirs are an important takeaway from a visit to a sacred site. For devotees, food souvenirs become tastier and more meaningful when purchased from a sacred locale (e.g. olive oil and wine from the Holy Land or certain 'Buddhist' kimchis from Korea), and they can help extend the spatial reach of the sacred experience to the home front.

Prescribed and proscribed foods and gastronomic practices

Most organized religions have some form of taboo regarding the consumption of food (Bonnekessen 2010; Sopher 1967). In fact, "food is the major object of religious taboo across all cultures: what you can eat is usually as regulated as whom you can marry" (Cunha et al. 2008: 747–748). These alimentary restrictions are all divinely inspired, but they are based on various concepts of self-mastery, penance or the body as a temple of God – cleanliness, healthfulness and addiction avoidance. Food prohibitions "purify the body and soul through abstinence" (Albala 2011: 7).

Hinduism has a long history of restricting certain foods. Hinduism strongly encourages a vegetarian lifestyle because harming animals is considered iniquitous. The strictest Hindus abstain from eating any animal products, including eggs or dairy, as well as garlic, onions, turnips or mushrooms (Brown 2015; Ganeri 1998; Kilara and Iya 1992). Others practice lacto-ovo vegetarianism but avoid animal flesh. Many Hindus, however, eat fish, chicken and other meats, almost always with the exception of beef. While cows are not worshipped in Hinduism, they are respected as a source of food (dairy only) and a symbol of life (Brown 2015). The types of meat consumed and how much or how often varies from family to family. Besides foodstuffs, Hinduism stipulates specific preparation and eating practices; some have spiritual foundations, while others are cultural practices associated with India or other Hindu-dominant regions.

Traditional Hinduism, particularly in rural areas of South Asia, embraces the caste system, which determines what social class a person is born into. While the caste system is becoming less relevant to contemporary generations, it is still alive and well in India. Caste determines the kinds of food that can be consumed and the processes involved. Some castes, for example, can eat meat, while others are strict vegetarians. Members of the Dalit (untouchable) caste are not permitted to touch food or drink at events where mixed castes are present (Laudan 2013). Food should only be consumed when prepared by someone of the same caste. Mixed caste dining used to be forbidden, but in most areas it is now becoming more acceptable. Ritual washings of hands, feet and mouth are common before each meal, and eating is done with the fingers of the right hand (Dugan 1994; Ganeri 1998).

Orthodox Jews adhere to a set of food laws known as *kashruth*, which is based on ancient scripture from the books of Leviticus and Deuteronomy. These kosher dietetic laws hinge on three principles: kosher foods (including certain animals) can be eaten, blood cannot be consumed and meat and milk products cannot be served together in the same dish or even during the same meal (Anderson 2014; Brown 2015; Dugan 1994; Ioannides and Ioannides 2006; Regenstein et al. 2003). In addition to the kosher animals and preparation methods of the kashruth, glatt kosher additionally includes eating meat only from animals with smooth or defect-free lungs. However, today glatt kosher is commonly used as a generic term for an even stricter code of kashruth. Kosher and glatt kosher regulations guide many elements of the daily life of the Hassidic Jewish community (Shatenstein et al. 1993). Split-hooved ruminants (e.g. cows, goats and sheep), most domestic fowl and scaled fish are generally kosher. Pork, carnivores or birds of prey, non-scaled fish, and shellfish are not kosher and cannot be consumed or cooked in a kosher kitchen. A prominent theory is that pork was originally banned not because pigs are dirty or diseased but because pigs eat everything – animals, blood and carrion – and are therefore not herbivores and not kosher (Beardsworth and Keil 1997; Hunn 1979, cited in Anderson 2014). For similar reasons, some religious societies do not eat chicken because it is a scavenging animal. Jewish law also requires that all blood must be removed, and the slaughtering of animals must be done by an authorized religious authority (Brown 2015). There are many prohibited and permitted food items and cooking methods in Judaism, but for non-specialists, Jewish foodways can seem complicated.

Certain feasts, holidays and other celebrations in Judaism also call for special foods to be prepared and eaten. During the eight days of Passover, unleavened bread is the only grain product that can be eaten, to commemorate the ancient exodus from Egypt, during which time the Jews' bread did not even have time to rise (Brown 2015). Rosh Hashanah, Succoth, Yom Kippur and Hanukkah are important celebrations that are commemorated with special meals. Fried foods, such as latkes (potato pancakes) and sufganiot (Hannukah donuts) are usually consumed during Hannukah in memory of the miracle of the single long-burning cruse of oil which kept the second temple illuminated (Ganeri 1998; Muhammad et al. 2009).

Buddhism encourages a vegetarian lifestyle, although many adherents eat meat, as long as the animal is slaughtered by someone else. Whether or not a Buddhist eats meat depends on the country where he/she lives, a personal choice and which sect of Buddhism he/she belongs to (Brown 2015; Norman 2012; Sopher 1967). Many traditional Buddhists and most monks in East Asia also avoid the 'pungent' foods: garlic, onions, shallots, leeks and chives (Dugan 1994; Son and Xu 2013), and the use of unnatural or added flavors (e.g. salt, chili peppers and certain spices) is strongly discouraged. Despite their prohibition by monks, nuns and other strict adherents, these pungent and flavorful ingredients are extremely popular today in the gastronomy of many predominantly Buddhist societies, such as the widespread use of hot chilies and garlic in Thai cuisine.

An emphasis on vegetarianism, healthy foods, freshness and spirituality has resulted in the widespread popularity of 'Buddhist cuisine' or 'temple food', a gastronomic craze chiefly popular in East and Southeast Asia (Anderson 2014; Moon 2008; Son and Xu 2013). This vegan or vegetarian movement stirred by the strict diets of Buddhist monks and nuns and the principles of 'nonviolence', freshness, simplicity and naturalness has inspired the proliferation of Buddhist restaurants in countries such as China, Singapore, Vietnam, Malaysia, Taiwan, Japan, South Korea and Thailand. Since the 1990s, Buddhist food has taken center stage in much of Asia owing to people's concerns about their health, as well as a growing consciousness about food heritage and tradition (Son and Xu 2013).

Many Christian churches encourage their members to avoid excessive amounts of alcohol and to remain sober, although this varies by denomination and by individuals' own choices or level of commitment to the faith. Some Christian sects have specific dietary restrictions or strong recommendations against certain consumables. For example, members of the Church of Jesus Christ of Latter-day Saints (Mormons) in good standing adhere to prohibitions outlined in the 'Word of Wisdom' on the consumption of alcohol, tobacco, coffee and caffeinated tea, and they are advised to avoid excessive meat consumption (Brown 2015; Hoskisson 2012). Seventh-day Adventists place a high value on healthy eating. The use of alcohol and tobacco is strongly discouraged. The church encourages a vegetarian or vegan diet, and many Adventists are vegetarian. Adventists who do choose to eat meat follow the kosher laws set forth in Leviticus, avoiding pork, shellfish and other 'unclean' animal flesh (Brown 2015; Dugan 1994). Until the 1960s, meat (except fish) was proscribed food for Roman Catholics on Fridays as propitiation for sins and as a symbolic sacrificial gesture for gratitude for the sacrifice of Jesus (Albala 2011). Since the 1960s, Friday abstinence from meat is limited to Lent, although many traditionalists still refrain from eating meat on Fridays, instead consuming only fish. Many restaurants in countries with large Catholic populations continue to offer 'fish Friday' specials (Dugan 1994). Fish became the symbol of devotion for Catholics because Jesus prepared fish for his apostles following his resurrection, most of his apostles were fishermen and his followers became 'fishers of Men' in the Kingdom (Villarrubia 2010).

For Muslims, foods are either *halal* (allowed) or *haram* (forbidden). The Quran establishes the culinary rules for Muslims, which include not consuming blood; kosher or halal animal flesh is permitted; proper slaughtering methods are required; carrion is not allowed; and alcoholic beverages or items containing alcohol, such as vanilla or wine vinegar, are not permitted (Brown 2015; Dugan 1994; Regenstein et al. 2003). Halal meat comes from approved animals that have been butchered in accordance with Islamic procedures (Riaz 1998). Pork, carnivorous animals, birds of prey, reptiles and amphibians, certain sea animals (e.g. sharks) and certain gelatins are haram (Anderson 2014; Brown 2015). Many of the same foods prohibited in Judaism are also forbidden in Islam with one notable exception being shellfish, which Muslims can enjoy freely.

Immigration and multiculturalism are affecting the availability of halal foods in non-Islamic countries and the availability of haram foods in Muslim states. With increased Islamic migration to Europe, Australia and North America, the halal food industry in the West is expanding rapidly. It is now quite easy for Muslims to locate and purchase halal meats and other permissible aliment (Ahmed 2008; Riaz and Chaudry 2004). Anyone visiting or living in a Muslim-majority country is free to eat halal foods (Aziz and Chok 2013), but given increasing numbers of non-Muslim expatriates in certain countries, even forbidden foods are slowly becoming available. For example, alcohol and pork are now obtainable at large supermarkets in countries such as the United Arab Emirates. These items are generally sold in special, obscure rooms that are off-limits to Muslims and staffed by expatriate workers (Figure 8.3).

Fasting is another crucial food-related custom of many of the world's religions. In some faiths, fasting is an elective activity that can be done whenever one feels the need. Living without aliment or drink for a designated period of time is believed to strengthen the spirit, humble the soul and thereby make the person become more receptive to spiritual promptings or more penitent for sins. Some fasts are prescribed or required. Muslims fast from dawn to dusk during the month of Ramadan to commemorate the revelation of the Quran to the prophet

Figure 8.3 The 'pork room' of a large supermarket in the United Arab Emirates (Photo: Dallen J. Timothy)

Mohammed (Brown 2015). Daytime fasting during the month of Ramadan is a pillar of Islam and required of those who are able. Many restaurants in Muslim-majority countries close during the holy month's daylight hours. A similar month-long fast is observed by members of the Bahá'í faith.

In Judaism, fasting from sunset to dusk on the following day is essential on Yom Kippur and Tisha B'av. Buddhist monks do not eat after the midday meal, and adherents to Jainism, Hinduism and other Asian religions also observe certain fasts at certain times. Fasting in Christianity varies church by church, with some requiring fasting during specified days of the month, before designated rituals and ceremonies, refraining only from certain foods at certain times of the year, with other sects stipulating a set period of time for fasting (Smith 2011).

Meeting the faith-based dietary needs of travelers

There has been a lot of discussion in the tourism, hospitality and food services industries about the importance of catering to the religious requirements of customers (Dugan 1994; Hassan and Hall 2003; Weidenfeld and Ron 2008). Facilitating the comestible requirements of Muslim, Jewish, Hindu, Buddhist and certain Christian tourists is good business, just as it is for international companies to adapt to local conditions where they are represented. Some multinational fast-food corporations have made a concerted effort to be sensitive to the religious needs of resident consumers. McDonald's, for example, for the most part honors local religious values. In Indonesia and other Muslim countries, menus usually offer beef burgers rather than hamburgers, owing to the connotations of pork in relation to 'ham'. In India, beef products are not sold at McDonald's, but fish and chicken sandwiches are. In Israel, just less than one third of McDonald's restaurants follow the kosher code of not serving meat and dairy together; in these restaurants there are no cheeseburgers on the menu.

Although the majority of livestock (sheep and cattle) in New Zealand is slaughtered according to Islamic sharia practices for export to the Middle East, it is relatively difficult for Muslim travelers to find halal restaurants and other tourism service providers (Hassan and Awang 2009; Hassan and Hall 2003). Many observant Jews also have difficulty finding certified kosher catering establishments (Ioannides and Ioannides 2006). While some travelers relax their adherence to halal and kosher laws while traveling, owing to a lack of compliant restaurants and markets, many devout Jewish and Muslim tourists carry dried and tinned food with them in their suitcases to enable them to prepare their own meals, especially in areas where they know kosher or halal foods will not be available (Cohen and Avieli 2004). More lenient Jews or Muslims may choose to eat only fish or vegetarian meals while traveling (Ioannides and Ioannides 2006).

It should be noted here that there is a difference between pilgrims/religious tourists and general or leisure tourists who happen to belong to a specific religion. Obviously, places that are major pilgrimage destinations already have well-established kosher and halal operations and services. However, general-interest destinations in the Western world generally have fewer food and lodging operations compatible with the beliefs of members of certain faiths.

Many entrepreneurial restaurateurs have started to appreciate the needs of Jewish consumers. The proliferation of kosher Thai, Japanese, Italian, Indian and French restaurants in the United States, for example, attests to an increasing religious awareness within the business community (Jochnowitz 2004; Rotkovitz 2004). Some tour operators are aware of the lucrative Jewish and Muslim markets. Jewish tour organizers offer kosher experiences even in some unlikely places. One company offers African bush tours to practicing Jews, which allow them to have "a truly exciting and comfortable African experience without the hassle of looking for kosher food in the bush … this company caters to a wide segment of the market including student travelers and luxury-oriented individuals" (Ioannides and Ioannides 2006: 161). Blumenhotels established a 'kosher village' resort near Zell am See, Austria. It offers hotels and rentable apartments, kosher restaurants and cafes, a mikveh for men and gender-segregated swimming pools, childcare and Sabbath services (Ioannides and Ioannides 2006). Kosher and glatt kosher cruises, ski holiday packages and mountain treks to Machu Picchu and Mt Everest are becoming more commonplace, making it possible for observant Jews to travel to places many had heretofore felt unable to visit without compromising their dietary obligations.

There are at present approximately 1.5 billion Muslims living in a multitude of countries. Increased standards of living in the largest Islam-dominated developing countries, such as Indonesia, Malaysia and Pakistan, and growing wealth in the Middle East, means that mounting numbers of Muslims are able to travel internationally. In many cases, they choose to spend their holidays in other Muslim nations because of the ease of finding halal foods and staying in sharia-compliant hotels (Gaffar et al. 2015; Henderson 2003; Stephenson 2014; Zamani-Farahani and Henderson 2010; Zulkharnain and Jamal 2012). "For devout Muslims, hotels that offer gender segregated swimming and recreation facilities … prayer rooms or that are located near mosques are more desirable, and restaurants must offer halal foods prepared in a suitable manner for Muslim consumption" (Timothy and Iverson 2006: 198). Muslim-majority countries, such as Malaysia, Indonesia and Turkey, have labored tirelessly in recent years to promote themselves as 'Muslim-friendly destinations', and their efforts are paying off as arrivals to these countries from Middle Eastern states and other Islamic nations have increased substantially in the past ten years (Gaffar et al. 2015). Non-Muslim countries also have recently started to realize that Muslims from the Middle East and Asia are a valuable travel cohort that should be encouraged to visit.

Much like the general star rating system used throughout the world, there are regular kashrut or glatt kosher ratings systems for hotels, restaurants and other tourism service providers in Israel and abroad, which cater to the varying travel and hospitality needs of observant Jews. A couple of rating systems have also been devised recently to provide potential Muslim tourists a way of determining the level of a restaurant or hotel's compliance to Islamic law. These rating systems are especially popular in Islamic countries, which already largely conform to sharia regulations, but they are growing in importance in non-Muslim destinations as well, at least in places that desire to attract the lucrative Muslim market.

The first of these is the Islamic Quality Standard for Hotels (IQS) (Othman and Othman 2013). A collaborative effort between Universiti Teknologi Mara and the Universal Crescent Standard Center in Malaysia, the IQS was formulated to show how well a hotel conforms to Islamic principles. Not having alcoholic beverages on the premises and serving only halal foods are the basic requirements for a lodging or food service provider to be an IQS candidate. Other features factor into the ranking, including separate swimming pools (or different pool open hours for men and women) and spas for men and women, Muslim prayer facilities, posted prayer schedules, qiblat (Mecca directional marker) in the rooms, in-room prayer rugs, a Quran in each room and other related amenities. Level of conformance, together with degree of luxury and services results in a property's being ranked on a scale of IQS One Crescent to IQS Seven Crescent, with IQS1 being basic and IQS7 being Super Excellent Luxury. These guidelines help food and accommodations providers become Muslim-friendly facilities (Othman and Othman 2013).

A similar evaluation system, Crescent Rating, is based in Singapore. It also uses a seven-level ranking scheme for hotels, which resembles that of the IQS program. Its restaurant rankings are unique, however. Restaurant or café Muslim-friendliness is scored as AAA, AA, A, B and C, with AAA being best. The criteria Crescent Rating uses are as follows:

- Is the restaurant served only by a halal-certified kitchen?
- Is the restaurant served only by a kitchen assured halal by the manager?
- Is the kitchen managed by a Muslim staff?
- Is all meat used from halal-certified suppliers?
- Is there alcohol on the menu?
- Does the restaurant serve vegetarian or seafood only?
- Does the restaurant serve any non-halal meats?

If an establishment serves any haram meats, it cannot be rated in this classification system. AAA providers must be serviced only by a certified halal kitchen, serve no alcohol and provide no non-halal meats. A C-ranked restaurant, the least sharia-compliant, may include businesses that serve only seafood or vegetarian meals, and those whose managers assure the kitchen is halal (Crescent Rating 2015). Both of these two rating systems provide assessments for lodging and food service providers around the world, who desire to make their properties more attractive to the burgeoning Muslim travel market.

Conclusion

Food and eating practices are laden with spiritual meaning, and religion is often at the cusp of emergent foodways and gastronomic adaptations. Most major scriptural texts refer frequently to food and drink, either part of the daily narrative of the ancients or as referents in stories of miracles and God's dealings with humankind. Religiously influenced cuisine and foodways derive largely from commandments or taboos, native foods in areas where a given religion began, harvest celebrations, holiday festivities or commemorations of blessings and sacred life events. People's religious background and the ways in which their faith determines culinary behavior is an important part of personal heritage. Just as culinary avoidances, such as insects, dog meat or horse meat on American menus, are socially conditioned, religious gustatory restrictions or allowances can have long-term implications for subsequent generations, even if they choose not to practice the faith of their forebears (Sheikh and Thomas 1994). In this sense, then, "religious foodways … can be explained either on the basis of ecological sense or on the basis of religious and ritual logic. They are not blind immemorial but pragmatic adaptations to community life" (Anderson 2014: 198).

Food is used in various religious ways. Ancient religious practices continue daily to shape how billions of people grow, harvest or slaughter, prepare and consume everyday aliment. For example, adherents to some faiths are required to avoid certain meats, while others are strongly encouraged to avoid meat altogether. Even the ways in which fruits and vegetables are prepared and eaten may be dictated by holy writ or otherworldly traditions. Many of these edicts have both temporal and spatial characteristics. Religious calendars dictate that specific foods may only be allowed at certain times of the day, week, month or year. During periods of fasting, food and drink are restricted or prohibited entirely. There might even be a geographical element, wherein certain foods may only be eaten and culinary rituals exercised at precise locations. An ancient example of this that continues today can be found among the Samaritans, who still practice animal sacrifice and consume the meat only on Mt Gerizim.

Finally, one of the biggest consumers of cultural heritage – tourism – is inseparable from religious food traditions. This is especially the case today as people from many walks of life have the means to travel outside their homelands or beyond their religiously bounded social domains. For decades, and even centuries, people of faith have avoided traveling away from the halal or kosher security of home, anticipating the difficulty of remaining faithful to alimentary obligations. Some adventured to the margins but carried their own food with them, while others elected to holiday in domestic destinations or in faraway places where their faith also predominated (e.g. Israeli or European Hassidic Jews visiting Brooklyn, New York, or Saudis vacationing in Indonesia). Good business sense prevailed, however, and today, tour companies, travel intermediaries and service providers (e.g. airlines, hotels and restaurants) are consciously serving the everyday needs of disparate market segments, including Buddhists, Hindus, Jews and Muslims. Through globalization processes, the widespread availability of religiously permissible foods, activities and spaces has extended the range of human leisure mobility far beyond its traditional limits.

References

Ahmed, A. (2008) Marketing of halal meat in the United Kingdom: supermarkets versus local shops. *British Food Journal*, 110(7): 655–670.

Albala, K. (2011) Historical background to food and Christianity. In K. Albala and T. Eden (eds) *Food and Faith in Christian Culture*, pp. 7–19. New York: Columbia University Press.

Alderman, D.H. (2002) Writing on the Graceland wall: on the importance of authorship in pilgrimage landscapes. *Tourism Recreation Research*, 27(2): 27–33.

Anderson, E.N. (2014) *Everyone Eats: Understanding Food and Culture*, 2nd Edn. New York: New York University Press.

Avieli, N. (2012) *Rice Talks: Food and Community in a Vietnamese Town*. Bloomington, IN: Indiana University Press.
Aziz, Y.A. and Chok, N.V. (2013) The role of halal awareness, halal certification, and marketing components in determining halal purchase intention among non-Muslims in Malaysia: a structural equation modeling approach. *Journal of International Food & Agribusiness Marketing*, 25(1): 1–23.
Beardsworth, A. and Keil, T. (1997) *Sociology on the Menu: An Invitation to the Study of Food and Society*. London: Routledge.
Bonnekessen, B. (2010) Food is good to teach: an exploration of the cultural meanings of food. *Food, Culture & Society*, 13(2): 279–295.
Brown, A. (2015) *Understanding Food Principles and Preparation*. Stamford, CT: Cengage.
Civitello, L. (2004) *Cuisine and Culture: A History of Food & People*. Hoboken, NJ: Wiley.
Cohen, E. and Avieli, N. (2004) Food in tourism: attraction and impediment. *Annals of Tourism Research*, 31(4): 755–778.
Cunha, M., Cabral-Cardoso, C. and Clegg, S. (2008) Manna from heaven: the exuberance of food as a topic for research in management and organization. *Human Relations*, 61(7): 935–963.
Denker, J. (2003) *The World on a Plate: A Tour through the History of America's Ethnic Cuisines*. Boulder, CO: Westview Press.
Dugan, B. (1994) Religion and food service. *The Cornell Hotel and Restaurant Administration Quarterly*, 35(6): 80–85.
Gaffar, V., Othman, N. and Setiyorini, H.P.D. (2015) Comparative study of Islamic Quality Standard for Hotel in Malaysia and Indonesia. Paper presented at the World Halal Summit, Kuala Lumpur, April 2, 2015.
Ganeri, A. (1998) *Religious Food*. Austin: Raintree.
Graburn, N. (1982) Tourism, leisure and museums. Paper presented at the Annual Conference of the Canadian Museums Association, Halifax, Nova Scotia.
Harrison, J. (1997) Museums and touristic expectations. *Annals of Tourism Research*, 24(1): 23–40.
Hassan, W.M.W. and Awang, K.W. (2009) Halal food in New Zealand restaurants: an exploratory study. *International Journal of Economics and Management*, 3(2): 385–402.
Hassan, M.W. and Hall, C.M. (2003) The demand for halal food among Muslim travellers in New Zealand. In C.M. Hall, L. Sharples, R. Mitchell, B. Cambourne and N. Macionis (eds) *Food Tourism around the World: Development, Management and Markets*, pp. 81–101. Oxford: Butterworth Heinemann.
Henderson, J.C. (2003) Managing tourism and Islam in peninsular Malaysia. *Tourism Management*, 24(4): 447–456.
Hoskisson, P.Y. (2012) The Word of Wisdom in its first decade. *Journal of Mormon History*, 38(1): 131–200.
Hunn, E. (1979) The abominations of Leviticus revisited. In R. Ellen and D. Pearson (eds) *Classifications in the Social Context*, pp. 103–118. New York: Academic Press.
Ioannides, M.C. and Ioannides, D. (2006) Global Jewish tourism: pilgrimages and remembrance. In D.J. Timothy and D.H. Olsen (eds) *Tourism, Religion and Spiritual Journeys*, pp. 156–171. London: Routledge.
Jochnowitz, E. (2004) Flavors of memory: Jewish food as culinary tourism in Poland. In L.M. Long (ed.) *Culinary Tourism*, pp. 97–113. Lexington: University Press of Kentucky.
Kilara, A. and Iya, K.K. (1992) Food and dietary habits of the Hindu. *Food Technology*, 46(10): 94–104.

Laudan, R. (2013) *Cuisine and Empire: Cooking in World History*. Berkeley: University of California Press.

LeCount, L.J. (2001) Like water for chocolate: feasting and political ritual among the Late Classic Maya at Xunantunich, Belize. *American Anthropologist*, 103(4): 935–953.

Liutikas, D. (2014) Lithuanian valuistic journeys: traditional and secular pilgrimage. *Journal of Heritage Tourism*, 9(4): 299–316.

Moon, S.S. (2008) Buddhist temple food in South Korea: interests and agency in the reinvention of tradition in the age of globalization. *Korea Journal*, 48: 147–180.

Muhammad, R., Zahari, M.S.M., Othman, Z., Jamaluddin, M.R. and Rashdi, M.O. (2009) Modernization and ethnic festival food. In *Proceedings of the International Conference of Business and Economics*, pp. 1–14. Kuching, Malaysia.

Norman, C.E. (2012) Food and religion. In J.M. Pilcher (ed) *The Oxford Handbook of Food History*, pp. 409–426. Oxford: Oxford University Press.

Othman, N. and Othman, S. (2013) *Islamic Quality Standard for Hotel*. Shah Alam, Malaysia: Universiti Teknologi Mara & the Universal Crescent Standard Center.

Pleck, E. (1999) The making of the domestic occasion: the history of Thanksgiving in the United States. *Journal of Social History*, 32(4): 773–789.

Reader, I. and Walter, T. (eds) (1992) *Pilgrimage in Popular Culture*. London: MacMillan.

Regenstein, J.M., Chaudry, M.M. and Regenstein, C.E. (2003) The kosher and halal food laws. *Comprehensive Reviews in Food Science and Food Safety*, 2(3): 111–127.

Riaz, M.N. (1998) Halal food: an insight into a growing food industry segment. *International Food Marketing and Technology*, 12(6): 6–9.

Riaz, M.N. and Chaudry, M.M. (2004) *Halal Food Production*. Boca Raton, FL: CRC Press.

Ron, A.S. and Timothy, D.J. (2013) The Land of Milk and Honey: Biblical foods, heritage and Holy Land tourism. *Journal of Heritage Tourism*, 8(2/3): 234–247.

Roth-Haillote, R. (2006) Les nourritures substantielles du corps et de l'Espirit. *Anthropology of Food*, 5: n.p. (online). Available at: https://aof.revues.org/71

Rotkovitz, M. (2004) Kashering the melting pot: Oreos, sushi restaurants, "Kosher Treif," and the observant American Jew. In L.M. Long (ed) *Culinary Tourism*, pp. 157–185. Lexington: University Press of Kentucky.

Sahu, C.K. (2015) Makar Festival of Mayurbhanj: at a glance. *International Journal of Research in Social Sciences*, 5(1): 163–172.

Shatenstein, B., Ghadirian, P. and Lambert, J. (1993) Influence of the Jewish religion and Jewish laws (*Kashruth*) on family food habits in an ultra-orthodox population in Montreal. *Ecology of Food and Nutrition*, 31(1): 27–44.

Sheikh, N. and Thomas, J. (1994) Factors influencing food choice among ethnic minority adolescents. *Nutrition and Food Science*, 94(5): 29–35.

Smith, K. (2011) *Food and Religion: Fasting, Religious Diets and More*. Charleston, SC: Bibliobazaar.

Son, A. and Xu, H. (2013) Religious food as a tourism attraction: the roles of Buddhist temple food in Western tourist experience. *Journal of Heritage Tourism*, 8(2/3): 248–258.

Sopher, D.E. (1967) *Geography of Religions*. London: Prentice Hall.

Stephenson, M.L. (2014) Deciphering 'Islamic hospitality': developments, challenges and opportunities. *Tourism Management*, 40: 155–164.

Timothy, D.J. and Iverson, T. (2006) Tourism and Islam: considerations of culture and duty. In D.J. Timothy and D.H. Olsen (eds) *Tourism, Religion and Spiritual Journeys*, pp. 186–205. London: Routledge.

Timothy, D.J. and Olsen, D.H. (eds) (2006) *Tourism, Religion and Spiritual Journeys*. London: Routledge.

Villarrubia, E. (2010) Why do Catholics eat fish on Friday? *Catholicism.org*, February 26. Available online at http://catholicism.org/why-do-catholics-eat-fish-on-friday-2.html Accessed June 20, 2015.

Weidenfeld, A. and Ron, A. (2008) Religious needs in the tourism industry. *Anatolia*, 19(2): 357–361.

Wirzba, N. (2011) *Food and Faith: A Theology of Eating*. New York: Cambridge University Press.

Yoshizawa, K. (1999) Sake: production and flavor. *Food Reviews International*, 15(1): 83–107.

Zamani-Farahani, H. and Henderson, J.C. (2010) Islamic tourism and managing tourism development in Islamic societies: the cases of Iran and Saudi Arabia. *International Journal of Tourism Research*, 12(1): 79–89.

Zulkharnain, A. and Jamal, S.A. (2012) Muslim guest perceptions of value towards Syariah concept hotel. In A. Zainal, S.M. Radzi, R. Hashim, C.T. Chik and R. Abu (eds) *Current Issues in Hospitality and Tourism: Research and Innovations*, pp. 337–340. Leiden: CRC Press.

9 Iconic cuisines, marketing and place promotion

Sally Everett

Introduction

This chapter looks at how food and drink narratives are utilised to promote and create place identities. By exploring the concepts of heritage branding and constructed historical narratives, it illustrates how iconic cuisines are being employed to promote place and attract consumers. It argues that the marketing process is more than utilising established aspects of heritage cuisines and historical truths, as it is often about creating narratives to meet the evolving needs of destinations and its producers. Heritage and its tangible manifestations are being adopted to create brands, food iconography and gastronomic narratives of place which do not always have an established or notable history to draw upon. As Lowenthal (1998) has argued, heritage has an ability to make the past relevant for contemporary contexts and purposes and provides existential anchors. Increasingly, promotional campaigns are adopting these anchors and narratives of food heritage to offer a kind of certainty in a world of uncertainty. Certainly it is suggested that finding ways to unlock the hidden value of a brand's heritage can harness past and present to safeguard the future.

This chapter presents and evaluates promotional activities related to different market segmentations for food and drink and focuses on how iconic cuisines are being used as promotional vehicles and heritage brands. It offers critical reflections which explore the agglomeration of functions as part of its discussions around destination marketing and cumulative attractiveness of place. By drawing on culinary examples from around the world it illustrates the complexity of creating place and what it is to be 'iconic', suggesting it is not just the promotion of something pre-existing, but something far more contemporary, creative and strategic. Numerous marketing approaches and interpretation methods are used in place promotion through food and drink, including the explosion of social media channels, events, cookery schools and reinvention of place, and it is important to look at how these mechanisms seek to target distinct types of people and market segments. Increasingly we are seeing local and regional agencies adopting food and drink histories and heritage branding strategies to attract visitors, promote political agendas and develop destinations. Further, it is also possible to find examples of national and regional marketing strategies and social media vehicles using food offers to attract additional inward investment. It is clear, despite its contested nature, that 'heritage' is good for place promotion and good for business.

A history of heritage-inspired place promotion

The word 'heritage' is contested, but it works as a carrier of historical values from the past and is therefore relevant to describe the way food as a cultural object is passed down through the generations via folklore, recipes and human processes. Since the dawn of time, food has reflected the culture of a country and its people, making it the ideal product to offer as an attraction in a destination with many possibilities as a powerful marketing tool (du Rand and Heath 2006). Certainly, in the last ten years, we can see the growth of work and research which examines how people experience new cultures and places and how this contributes to their continuation and retention (Everett 2009; Fields 2002). It is also apparent that this attention is supporting the growth and recognition of 'iconic cuisines'. The DailyMeal.com suggests iconic cuisines are dishes that say more about a place than just what foods are eaten there: "If you look a little closer, they reveal an inside truth about who they nourish and can be an up-close lens on a place's history. These foods draw influence from a country's politics, geography, climate, a people's makeup, and its culture. They've stood the test of time – whether derived from a colonist's cuisine or in spite of it, and whether they've been updated for modern palates or kept in traditional form" (DailyMeal, 16/01/15: n.p.). However, the concept 'iconic' is also not without controversy and debate. Stephen Fry, actor and novelist, tweeted on 20/1/15, "How would it be if there were a media-wide moratorium on the use of the word 'iconic' for the next ten years?", suggesting that the term 'iconic' may be overused and potentially meaningless in the dilution of its image and relevance. One might ask what makes a cuisine or foodstuff iconic. History or clever marketing? Perhaps a mixture of both. Definitions of 'iconic' include being 'widely recognised and well-established', or 'widely known and acknowledged especially for distinctive excellence', and it is this concept of being 'well established' which lends itself to historic narratives and the need to establish a heritage, or story. Certainly travel books encourage a person to eat pizza in Naples, fish curry in Goa, dim sum in Hong Kong, lamb kofta in Istanbul and sushi in Tokyo.

Balmer (2011) claims heritage has been the focus of attention in marketing and management in the fields of heritage marketing, heritage tourism and the nascent area of corporate heritage brands for quite some time. Despite this, Tikkanen (2007) argues that only relatively recently have governments and agencies utilised food and culinary products in destination promotion and putting the development of food at the centre of product offerings. Furthermore, the intersections between heritage and consumption have largely been ignored by marketing and branding academics (Otnes and Maclaren 2007). Du Rand and Heath (2006) also note that food has been a relatively underdeveloped part of studies that explore the marketing mix or strategy of a region despite research showing that food and drink are key tangible and intangible goods and services within a place's portfolio (Okumus et al. 2007).

To attract the discerning consumer, producers and retailers often adopt strategies that exploit stories and traditions behind regional and local food, for example using phrases such as 'where the meat pie was born' and 'the original recipe chicken'. Food in the right packaging of cultural and social heritage narratives has the potential to attract consumers and can serve as tools for the reproduction and reinforcement of social relations and status (Cohen and Avieli 2004). In their study of London restaurants, Cook and Crang (1996) argue that regional cuisines are invented traditions, where food and drink represent cultural artefacts that are adopted as tangible emblems and signifiers of identity. Such concepts should be considered when discussing culinary heritage and the continuation of traditional foods within regions (Everett and Aitchison 2008). Business signs that display words such as 'original' and 'established in 1981' seek to attract consumers by reassuring them of the product's authenticity and provenance.

As the association between place, promotion and food becomes ever more potent in the minds of consumers and in the marketing armoury of those responsible for destination promotion, we increasingly see heritage images of everyday foods explicitly linked to their place of origin, or associated with an image that conveys an appropriate feel or message. Marketing campaigns are increasingly adopting messages that relay this nostalgic rhetoric and hark back to small-scale, cottage and rural production. For example, the UK retailer Marks & Spencer's employs images of country cottages on biscuit tins to convey a sense of tradition and home baking. It is increasingly apparent that emotional and symbolic attachment between a brand and a consumer is stronger and more effective when brands connect heritage and authenticity to their image (Ballantyne et al. 2006). Hakala et al. (2011: 448) state, "In turbulent times consumers become less confident in the future, wishing to protect themselves from the harsh, unpredictable realities of the outside world and seeking reassurance from the products they buy". Further, longevity, core values, use of symbols, history and tradition are key dimensions of corporate heritage brands such as Hovis bread, Patek Philippe and Fortnum & Mason.

Identity formation and the symbolism of nostalgia

The link between food and identity is born out in manufacturing approaches where product packaging is increasingly featuring farmers and historic backgrounds and using faded images to give a sense of the 'homemade' and a simpler life. Bell and Valentine (1997: 34) suggested that foodstuffs are culturally embedded symbols, where "regional identity becomes enshrined in bottles of wine and hunks of cheese", and certainly heritage identities have multiple institutional role identities that are utilised in various contexts and for a variety of purposes to sustain and strengthen. As well as providing sensory pleasures, food provides the anchor for narratives of cultural expression -– whether through rituals or festivals, they all have visitor appeal. Perhaps more intriguing are the places where there are no obvious flagship attractions, iconic cuisines or notable social history to draw on. In some instances developing an iconic cuisine can be regarded less as a reflection of reality (or history) and more as a marketing exercise of creativity, imagination and ingenuity. Increasingly, local and regional foods are part of a packaged commodity, a vehicle of identity development and recognition which draws on concepts of identity linked with notions of a 'sense of place' through emotional place attachment. Moginon et al. (2012) found these approaches in the context of indigenous food promotion in South Africa, which invested $1.8 million into a project that produced a cookbook of indigenous foodstuffs for visitors: "Ever tried samp, African ground nuts, mealies or sorghum? Or, if you have, how about potele, isithwalaphishi, ditlhakwana, mutuku or inkobe?" (SciDev.net 28/6/04: n.p.). This project aimed to promote indigenous foods to visitors, sell it as souvenirs and raise the profile of South Africa as a destination, becoming an effective marketing and promotion tool for this destination's cultural and political development.

Places are often branded with stereotypes of food, meals and traditions, and advertising often distills a wide variety of regional difference in ingredients, style and approach into a digestible simplified package of symbols and images. Traditional foods have strong symbolic value and have become expressions of local communities, signifiers of identities and artefacts of nostalgic resurrection. The concept behind the South African project was to ensure visitors had a memento and souvenir of the country, encouraging the returning visitor to continue to purchase that product or seek out that cuisine back in their hometown or country. In the United Kingdom, a project in the county of Hampshire was developed which drew on heritage to promote place identity and community. Leaflets with old images, recipes and people's tales effectively created an iconic cuisine through careful presentation of the past. Similarly, in Israel, Ron and Timothy (2013) found that Biblical food had been reinvented as a heritage cuisine for religious tourists in Jerusalem and the broader Holy Land.

The manifestation of heritage and nationalistic narratives in the promotion of food and wine

Balmer's (2011) corporate heritage identity framework places the heritage identity construct vis-à-vis other related constructs such as nostalgia, tradition and custom. This useful model outlines the concept of relative invariance, which seeks to explain the seemingly contradictory position of why heritage identities can remain the same by adapting to change, claiming "corporate heritage identities and brands are invested with special qualities in that they are a melding of identity continuity, identity change and are also invested with the identities of time (times past, present and future)" (Balmer 2011: 1380). Certainly, food heritage identities are an accretion of various identities, which are linked to institutions, places, cultures and time frames. Balmer ponders on the concept that if we want things to stay the same, things will have to change and links this to identity change, continuance and time. The constructs presented in his work provide a useful list of how food is used in promotional heritage narratives (i.e. tradition, custom, nostalgia, melancholia, iconic branding, retro branding, heritage marketing, heritage tourism, corporate heritage identities and corporate heritage brands). When it comes to finding the best example of an iconic cuisine that illustrates these constructs, there is a plentiful choice with examples such as a smartphone app created to find iconic street food in Penang and an official 'trail' in Canada for finding the best butter tarts.

The profile of iconic cuisines is further strengthened through heritage events. Holding regional festivals is essential for promoting the destination branding of regions, where food-themed special events or festivals can play an important role not only in regional development but also in destination branding (Hall and Sharples 2008). The growth of oyster festivals in Ireland; garlic festivals in the Isle of Wight and California; and asparagus, beer and generic food festivals across the globe, find heritage tightly woven into the premise for the event. For example, The Great Aussie Pie Contest was created to find the best everyday commercially produced meat pie in Australia, to promote the higher quality pie production as well as attempting to increase media attention upon the foodstuff, but the iconic meat pie became dwarfed by the omnipresent advertising of fast-food chains. Although some regional food festivals are organised mainly for community celebration, such events are also adopted for destination marketing and branding purposes: a basic step for building destination branding (Lee and Arcodia 2011).

Wine is another fascinating example of employing past and current narratives to promote visitation of places. Wine labelling increasingly draws on the concept of *terroir* and heritage which serve to forge a 'vintage' identity, often masking the youth of some wine regions (Harvey et al. 2014). In well-known wine regions such as Bordeaux, La Rioja and Piedmont, vines have been an iconic part of the landscape for centuries, and time integrates vines into the regions' culture and tradition, progressively becoming place references (Banks et al. 2007), where the iconic nature of some wines helps identify the wine-producing region. Alonso and Northcote (2009) explore strategies of regions that lack a traditional background in wine making – how do new wines overcome the absence of established traditions that lend themselves to regional branding for 'Old World' heritage? A lack of a traditional heritage of wine making offers challenges in terms of origin branding, but a heritage is therefore created and winery operators in emerging wine-producing regions are using alternative means for 'origin branding' that emphasise heritage and landscape characteristics centring on the wider 'rural idyll'. For example, in California the heavy Italian influence is used to build an identity and a theme dubbed 'Cal-Ital landscapes'.

Phillips (2000) suggests that wine is the most historically charged and culturally symbolic of the foods and beverages. Certainly the lack of a traditional heritage of wine making in Australia presents special challenges in terms of origin branding. The case of Barossa Valley, Australia, is an example where wine, food and the region's German heritage contribute to its growing popularity as a tourist destination, and where the heritage of wine plays a fundamental role in the region's tourism strategy. Alonso and Northcote (2009) find "wineries are acting as ambassadors in their regions, educating visitors, helping create a wine culture that 'connects' their region with the outside world, advertising and marketing their region in the process" (p. 1256). In the absence of 'Old World' wine heritages, producers are constructing new heritages that link wine making with other vintage industries and rural landscapes, forging a new local identity that has importance as a cultural marker, not just a marketing device.

Aside from creating new identities, iconic foods are also being harnessed to advance social and political agendas, affording insights into a destination's culture and future. Many countries aspire to have an identifiable and appealing cuisine comprising signature dishes that can be nation-building tools and generators of civic pride (Cusack 2000). For example, preference for Russian ingredients and products has been read as a statement of nationalist sentiment in the post-socialist years (Caldwell 2002). In nation building, fostering demand for the 'iconic' is more problematic when food histories are absent. It is, however, possible, as we see in full national campaigns such as the promotion of Malaysia and the use of food images connected with heritage and creation of place identity. Chaney and Ryan (2012) and Henderson's (2014) work on Singapore finds that food is a critical dimension of ethnic and national identity, arguing food heritage helps promote it as a destination while meeting local development and economic needs, yet questions whether a uniquely Singaporean cuisine actually exists at all. The Tourism Board promises a "world of flavours" emanating from a "rich multicultural heritage" (Singapore Tourist Board 2012: n.p.), but there is ambiguity about the existence of a national cuisine. Food has become a contentious marker of ethnic identity in a mixed society and a vehicle of political and religious tension; for example, Islamic strictures about food and utensils may make it difficult for Muslims and non-Muslims to share meals in Singapore. Ownership of an iconic cuisine can be highly political as illustrated by public debates over the origin of chicken rice between Malaysia and Singapore. Pratt (2007: 285) summarises this situation more generally, stating that food histories are constructed "within a romantic discourse of the local, the traditional and the authentic" and are often fictional and obscure the convergence between mass and small-scale operations.

Building supply and demand of iconic cuisines

The production of place through food and its eventual consumption is a virtuous circle, where production and consumption are not dichotomous entities but work together (Everett 2009). Increasingly, hybrid spaces are being developed where consumer needs have to vie for position with production requirements. Producers are adopting and adapting new spaces of consumptive leisure to accommodate touristic interests, manipulating their identities and patterns of traditional production to facilitate growing consumptive demands. In generating demand and consumer interest, food producers are increasingly adopting and creating destination advertising and a rhetoric of authenticity through products and packaging (Scarpato and Daniele 2003). It is the importance of imagery through well-produced materials that informs understandings to build demand and fuel supply. Certainly food can be the driving force that motivates people to visit places we see as gastronomic destinations, such as Italy and France, but certainly less culinary established destinations, such as Australia and Switzerland, are now responding, and spend on marketing and promoting is increasing. Destinations are creating new narratives, compensating and inventing heritage traditions to capitalise on the demand for special interest tourism. For instance, the World Heritage town of Hoi An in Vietnam is an example where one just has to walk through its pedestrianised areas to see rows of new cookery schools, a backdrop to tourists enjoying its colourful and buzzing market; certainly visitors enjoy culinary offerings to rival any top culinary destination (see Figures 9.1 and 9.2). Avieli (2013) suggests that Hoi

Figure 9.1 The iconic Vietnamese 'coolie' hats and food on display in Hoi An, Vietnam (Photo: Sally Everett 2014)

Figure 9.2 A restaurant promotes its cooking classes, Hoi An, Vietnam (Photo: Sally Everett 2014)

An has purposely developed an invented culinary heritage in the context of modern tourism which drives its promotional activity, but it is telling that local people struggle to identify with this reinvented image. The adoption of heritage narratives is clearly working to attract visitors, but once again we see heritage as a created entity, rather than an organised one that constructs a 'new' history for places.

There is much to suggest a link between the growth of food tourism and the regeneration of rural areas and communities. There is significant convergence between food tourism and rural tourism literature, and there has been growing recognition that rural businesses must embrace integrated development and diversification and supply attractive heritage narratives of food and production to survive (Hall and Roberts 2001). Rural development literature critically evaluates how culinary activities and growing demand for 'authentic' food experiences can assist in sustaining rural communities and livelihoods. From festivals promoting local produce to wine tourism and farmstays, the connections to food and drink tourism are made obvious, seeking to encourage economic partnership and increase consumer demand. Indeed, origin and production methods have become important, as consumers increasingly associate better quality with traditional products and nostalgia. It is increasingly accepted that national cuisines are often more invented than real, although foods with a close connection to a particular locale may assist in articulating a sense of place identity amongst residents (Guerrero et al. 2009). Regardless of how slippery the concept of authenticity is, there remains an appreciation that food has a heritage (whether actual or illusory) which merits conservation.

There is a sense that food is becoming increasingly globalised through universal conformity and standardisation, although globalisation should not be regarded as the destroyer of all, as there are opportunities for coexistence and conjugation (Mak et al. 2012). It appears that the forces driving globalisation can act to strengthen specific food cultures. One initiative to secure such histories is the growth of externally approved designations, such as the EU Protection of Geographical Indications and Designations of Origin, which support destination marketing campaigns by focusing on protecting foods produced, processed and prepared in a given geographical area using recognised know-how and food linked to the geographical area. Gellynck et al.'s (2012) study of EU traditional food products illustrates this powerful link and allure; when food is formally recognised and linked to particular geographic areas, such designations take on a significant role in the market and are increasingly requested by consumers seeking 'a return to traditions'. In the United States, the 'Santa Cruz Valley Harvest' Heritage Food Brand Program (2015) also assists local producers, restaurants and grocers by allowing them to use a recognisable logo that consumers associate with the strapline, "Heritage foods of the Santa Cruz Valley: locally produced foods tied to the region's history and cultural identity". Coordinated by the Heritage Alliance, the food 'brand' promotes locally grown food and supports traditional farming with references to the local and traditional.

One recent phenomenon dominating promotional avenues and marketing is certainly the rapid growth of social media channels, online promotion vehicles and web-based marketing campaigns. This has meant traditional approaches to place promotion have been challenged, giving way to instantaneous and informal approaches to place promotion including consumer-authored reviews and suggestions through sites such as Trip Advisor. One growth area is blogs, where social media is providing relevant, fluid iconic culinary commentary. Blogging has become a powerful marketing approach, examples include the iconic food of Taiwan (http://artofadventuring.com/chinese-cuisine-five-iconic-taiwan-foods/) or Singapore (http://sethlui.com/best-local-famous-foods-to-eat-singapore/) with titles such as '10 Iconic Foods of New York City, and Where To Find Them' and 'Sarawak Top 10 Iconic Food'. With magazines, websites, television and Twitter feeds dedicated to food, stories are given new life and traditions are transformed to fit new fashions. With advanced web technologies, destinations are establishing real and online spatial and social zones, based upon a cultural tradition and its food, where food trails and packaged journeys bring together iconic cuisines, producers and foodstuffs into a much larger and enticing offer.

Heritage branding

We perhaps naively consider that history must be a prerequisite of heritage branding, but it is of course more fluid than this. The idea of a heritage brand is widely recognised to be a future priority and focus in branding research (Hakala et al.

2011), with analysis of a brand's strength, emotional effect and place in the heart (Ballantyne et al. 2006). This idea of employing 'heritage branding' as a way to tell a story that builds an emotional connection with consumers is a powerful one when used well, even when there is little historic fact behind its offer. For example, Heritage Foods (India) Ltd is one of the largest private-sector dairy enterprises in southern India and expanded to grocery retailing under the brand 'Heritage Fresh', but little is obviously historic. The brand is said to have become one of the few resources to provide a long-term competitive advantage (Lindemann 2003). For example, Jack Daniel's whisky is often cited as an example of a brand that makes the most of its heritage as the United States's oldest (registered) whisky distiller. The company's advertising consistently focuses on the craftsmanship that goes into the whisky's production, and the design of their label draws on images and typography from the past. This iconic whisky is an illustration that a brand's success is based on its saliency, differentiability and intensity, and on the trust attached to the associations. It is proposed by Hakala et al. (2011: 454) that "brand heritage is a composite concept incorporating the history of the brand in numbers of years of operation and the power of the brand story over time, as well as the consistency and continuity of the core values, the product brands and the visual symbols".

Furthermore, many iconic brands such as Heinz, Kellogg's and Guinness use aspects of their heritage to drive sales and the imagery of tradition, and simple production is recognisable across the globe. The power of the Guinness brand transcends continents, luring people to visit St James's Gate in Dublin, Ireland, as the 'spiritual' home of the 'black stuff'. As suggested by Urde et al. (2007: 449), "a heritage brand is recognisable from the following characteristics: a track record, longevity, core values, history, and the use of symbols", and Guinness has arguably developed an established heritage that speaks to consumers through a plethora of symbols, graphics, nostalgia, packaging and advertising. Taking an historical perspective, heritage identities, such as that of Guinness, acquire new identities over the passage of time and thus take on board new meanings and greater relevance as they become associated with places, cultures and with time frames. It is a clever creation of a brand history linked to a sense of cultural continuity and communal tradition which provides a sense of ubiquitous presence. Another example is Coca-Cola whose name and logo are discernible virtually everywhere, and the vast majority of people alive today can recognise it (Beasley and Danesi 2002). Another example is Bacardi Rum's New Marketing Campaign, which celebrates 'Rich Cuban Heritage', pulling on its origins in Cuba and its founder Don Facundo Bacardí Massó and his dramatic historical narrative about bringing change to the rum industry (Barcardi 2014).

Summary and conclusion

This chapter has provided an illustrated summary of the narratives and approaches that are being used as part of the romanticisation and commodification of food heritages, destination promotion and brand differentiation. As Henderson

(2014: 913) has stated, "Food is a link with the past, representing continuity and familiarity, and inspires a yearning for what are perceived to be authentic tastes and experiences on the part of residents". Certainly, food has a central and iconic role in society and carries significant cultural, historic and social significance in terms of identity construction. Dishes like the street food of Penang, Malaysia, are endowed with iconic status, and food heritage is believed to be worthy of celebration and conservation, and even if it is less established in the case of Singapore, it carries powerful messages that attract consumers but may also underpin long-standing political agendas.

Effective destination marketing is the mechanism by which consumer expectations are managed and constructed. Marketing approaches are making intrinsic links between an area's history, its cultural heritage and food. Regional products, dishes and culinary stories are now providing destinations with powerful virtual and iconographic narratives of the culture of a place, a people and history. Place promotion poses the challenge of increasing visitor numbers whilst ensuring a destination retains its original attractiveness. References to pure, sustaining heritage by supporting traditional industries encapsulate the idea of locally embedded symbols and sense of place deriving from agricultural traditions. Messages are about sustaining cultures and ways of life. For example, this chapter suggests iconic food can be used to shed light on the history of a country, its geography and contemporary society as well as link powerfully to its political and economic systems. Heritage cuisines have been presented here as powerful marketing tools and iconic symbols of place, but must be regarded as fluid, evolving and powerful narratives that are not necessarily supported by historical fact or strict authentic narratives. Likewise, what makes a food 'iconic' is perhaps more about the imagery and the reach of those signs and messages than any sustained presence in history. Food is regularly developed into something iconic, which can be central to identity at an ethnic and national level, where the adoption of heritage identities is powerful because they meet customer and stakeholder needs by encapsulating emotions and needs and building identity. In looking at more recent perspectives such as Balmer's (2011), these approaches differ from that of Lowenthal (1998) by suggesting that heritage has a tripartite temporal dynamic in that it is meaningful to the past, present and prospective future, thereby suggesting there is a lot to be said for the future of iconic cuisines to be utilised in future destination promotion.

References

Alonso, A.D. and Northcote, J. (2009) Wine, history, landscape: origin branding in Western Australia. *British Food Journal*, 111(11): 1248–1259.

Avieli, N. (2013) What is 'Local Food?' Dynamic culinary heritage in the World Heritage Site of Hoi An, Vietnam. *Journal of Heritage Tourism*, 8(2/3): 120–132.

Bacardi (2014) Available online at http://fandbnews.com/bacardi-rums-new-marketing-campaign-celebrates-rich-cuban-heritage/ Accessed December 12, 2014.

Ballantyne, R., Warren, A. and Nobbs, K. (2006) The evolution of brand choice. *Brand Management*, 13(4/5): 339–352.

Balmer, J. (2011) Corporate heritage identities, corporate heritage brands and the multiple heritage identities of the British Monarchy. *European Journal of Marketing*, 45(9/10): 1380–1398.

Banks, G., Kelly, S., Lewis, N. and Sharpe, S. (2007) Place 'From One Glance': the use of place in the marketing of New Zealand and Australian wines. *Australian Geographer*, 38(1): 15–35.

Beasley, R. and Danesi, M. (2002) *Persuasive Signs: The Semiotics of Advertising, Volume 4*. Berlin: Walter de Gruyter.

Bell, D. and Valentine, G. (1997) *Consuming Geographies: We Are Where We Eat*. London: Routledge.

Caldwell, M.L. (2002) The taste of nationalism: food politics in postsocialist Moscow. *Ethnos*, 67(3): 295–319.

Chaney, S. and Ryan, C. (2012) Analysing the evolution of Singapore's World Gourmet Summit: an example of gastronomic tourism. *International Journal of Hospitality Management*, 31(2): 309–318.

Cohen, E. and Avieli, N., (2004) Food in tourism – attraction and impediment. *Annals of Tourism Research*, 31 (4), pp. 755–778.

Cook, I. and Crang, P. (1996). The world on a plate: culinary culture, displacement and geographical knowledge. *Journal of Material Culture*, 1(1): 131–154.

Cusack, I. (2000) African cuisines: recipes for nationbuilding? *Journal of African Cultural Studies*, 13(2): 207–225.

Daily Meal (2015) Available online at http://www.thedailymeal.com/food-travel-150-iconic-dishes-around-world Accessed February 12, 2014.

Du Rand, G.E. and Heath, E. (2006) Towards a framework for food tourism as an element of destination marketing. *Current Issues in Tourism*, 9(3): 206–234.

Everett, S. (2009) Beyond the visual gaze? The pursuit of an embodied experience through food tourism. *Tourist Studies*, 8(3): 337–358.

Everett, S. and Aitchison, C. (2008) The role of food tourism in sustaining regional identity: a case study of Cornwall, South West England. *Journal of Sustainable Tourism*, 16(2): 150–167.

Fields, K. (2002) Demand for the gastronomy tourism product: motivational factors. In A.M. Hjalager and G. Richards (eds) *Tourism and Gastronomy*, pp. 36–50. London: Routledge.

Gellynck, X., Banterle, A., Kühne, B., Carraresi, L. and Stranieri, S. (2012) Market orientation and marketing management of traditional food producers in the EU. *British Food Journal*, 114(4): 481–499.

Guerrero, L., Guàrdia, M.D., Xicola, J., Verbeke, W., Vanhonacker, F., Zakowska-Biemans, S. and Hersleth, M. (2009) Consumer-driven definition of traditional food products and innovation in traditional foods: a qualitative cross-cultural study. *Appetite*, 52(2): 345–354.

Hakala, U., Lätti, S. and Sandberg, B. (2011). Operationalising brand heritage and cultural heritage. *Journal of Product & Brand Management*, 20(6): 447–456.

Hall, C.M. and Sharples, L. (eds) (2008) *Food and Wine Festivals and Events around the World: Development, Management and Markets*. London: Routledge.

Hall, D. and Roberts, L. (eds) (2001) *Rural Tourism and Recreation: Principles to Practice*. Wallingford: CAB International.

Harvey, M., White, L. and Frost, W. (2014) *Wine and Identity: Branding, Heritage, Terroir.* London: Routledge.

Henderson, J. (2014) Food and culture: in search of a Singapore cuisine. *British Food Journal*, 116(6): 904–917.

Lee, I. and Arcodia, C. (2011) The role of regional food festivals for destination branding. *International Journal of Tourism Research*, 13(4): 355–367.

Lindemann, J. (2003) *Brand Valuation: The Economy of Brands*. London: Palgrave Macmillan.

Lowenthal, D. (1998) *The Heritage Crusade and the Spoils of History*. Cambridge: Cambridge University Press.

Mak, A., Lumbers, M. and Eves, A. (2012) Globalisation and food consumption in tourism. *Annals of Tourism Research*, 39(1): 171–196.

Moginon, D.F., Toh, P.S. and Saad, M. (2012) Indigenous food and destination marketing. In A. Zainal, S.M. Radzi, R. Hashim, C.T. Chik and R. Abu (eds) *Current Issues in Hospitality and Tourism: Research and Innovations*, pp. 355–358. London: Taylor and Francis.

Okumus, B., Okumus, F. and McKercher, B. (2007) Incorporating local and international cuisines in the marketing of tourism destinations: the cases of Hong Kong and Turkey. *Tourism Management*, 28(1): 253–261.

Otnes, C.C. and Maclaren, P. (2007) The consumption of cultural heritage among a British Royal Family brand tribe. In R. Kozinets, B. Cova, and A. Shanker (eds) *Consumer Tribes: Theory, Practice, and Prospects*, pp. 51–66. London: Elsevier/Butterworth Heinemann.

Phillips, R. (2000) *A Short History of Wine*. London: Allen Lane Penguin Press.

Pratt, J. (2007) Food values: the local and the authentic. *Critique of Anthropology*, 27(3): 285–300.

Ron, A.S. and Timothy, D.J. (2013) The Land of Milk and Honey: Biblical foods, heritage and Holy Land tourism. *Journal of Heritage Tourism*, 8(2/3): 234–247.

Santa Cruz Valley Harvest (2005) Available online at http://www.santacruzheritage.org/home Accessed May 15, 2015.

Scarpato, R. and Daniele, R. (2003) New global cuisine: tourism, authenticity and sense of place in modern gastronomy. In C.M. Hall, L. Sharples, R. Mitchell, N. Macionis and B. Cambourne (eds) *Food Tourism around the World: Development, Management and Markets*, pp. 296–313. Oxford: Butterworth Heinemann.

SciDev.net (2004, June 28) Available online at http://www.scidev.net/sub-saharan-africa/indigenous/news/south-africa-builds-market-for-traditional-foods-ssa.html Accessed November 25, 2014.

Singapore Tourist Board (STB) (2012) Available online at https://www.stb.gov.sg/ Accessed January 13, 2014.

Tikkanen, I. (2007) Maslow's hierarchy and food tourism in Finland: five cases. *British Food Journal*, 109(9): 721–734.

Urde, M., Greyser, S.A. and Balmer, J.M.T. (2007) Corporate brands with a heritage. *The Journal of Brand Management*, 15(1): 4–19.

10 Culinary trails

Atsuko Hashimoto and David J. Telfer

Explore the back roads and country inns. Do something you've never done before, like dine in a greenhouse. Talk to local farmers and indulge your curiosity about local produce and ingredients. Connect with local chefs who only use farm fresh products and chat with local winemakers and brewmasters, whose passion and family history are evident in every sip.

(Southwest Ontario Tourism Corporation 2015: 4)

Introduction

Heritage culinary trails not only preserve ancient foodways and cultural identity for future generations, they also represent opportunities for marketing culinary heritage through destination branding, thereby generating regional development. Culinary trails link farmers, roadside markets, farmers markets, restaurants, breweries, wineries, food festivals and the tourism industry, all highlighting local heritage cuisines. As Timothy and Ron (2013: 99) suggest, heritage cuisines are a mix of the "tangible (e.g. ingredients and cooking accoutrements) and intangible (e.g. tastes, smells, recipes and eating traditions) elements that contribute to the cultural values and characteristics of places". In some nations – for instance, Japan – heritage cuisine is more vigorously defined in order to distinguish 'heritage' cuisine and contemporary 'local' cuisine, which can incorporate the same tangible and intangible characteristics. Yet culinary trails often encompass both heritage cuisine (ancient foodways), as well as local cuisine, which may have evolved from traditional foodways. In some cases, culinary trails also include more modern and innovative food products and practices – for instance, the Scottish chocolate trails, which accompany more traditional culinary products.

Richards and Wilson (2007) argue that destinations are replacing culture-led development with creative development. The development of new innovative culinary products linked to thematic culinary routes is an indication of such. In a world economy where places compete against each other for economic advantage (Kotler et al. 1993) cuisine trails have become important features in destination branding. "Places are indeed products whose identities and values must be designed and marketed" (Kotler et al. 1993: 10), and culinary heritage, as an historical resource provides the real and imagined attraction for culinary enthusiasts. Anderson and Law (2012: 284) suggest that as "rural food producers continue to explore opportunities for product diversification, food trails continue to be proposed as a strategy for rural tourism development". This chapter explores the evolution of culinary routes, the links to identity and authenticity, as well as practices and trends along culinary routes using a variety of international examples.

Evolution of culinary trails

Wall (1997) classified tourism attractions into points, lines and areas. Culinary trails link heritage cuisine assets into linear attractions. By linking attractions, culinary trails highlight local food, local producers and their production techniques, preserving and promoting culinary heritage while also generating partnerships, stimulating new investment, generating place marketing and promoting local development. Heritage and cultural trails exist in almost every country, and Timothy and Boyd (2015) highlight two main types of cultural heritage trails illustrating different paths in their historical evolution. The first is organically evolved cultural routes which follow the track of an original historic trail or a more recent intentional corridor. Many of these are based on traditional indigenous hunting and migration routes and are cultural in origin. Over time the original track becomes a developed track or route where areas of interest evolve into intervening opportunities. Organic tourist trails include long-distance routes that were part of an original trade route such as the Silk Road, explorer or settler routes like the Cabot Trail, ancient pilgrimage routes such as the Camino de Santiago and human-created linear courses, including railways, highways, canals and political borders.

The Cabot Trail mentioned above is in the province of Nova Scotia, Canada, and named after the Italian explorer John Cabot, who encountered the indigenous Mi'kmaq people and explored this part of Canada in the late fifteenth and early sixteenth centuries. The trail was completed in 1932 connecting major communities with French, Irish and Scottish cultural backgrounds. While the trail has a primarily recreational purpose, its location and the communities along it have developed heritage cuisines and cultural festivals that are important components of the trail experience. The Cabot Trail is also referred to as a "300 kilometre Seafood Trail" where fresh lobster and crab are key dining elements along the way (Government of Nova Scotia 2015).

Greenways are another example of organically evolved cultural routes around the world. They are typically disused railway lines, waterways or ancient trade routes that have been made over into non-motorised trails. The well-known *Vias Verde* (Greenways) project in Spain (Vias Verde 2015), the transnational Prague-Vienna Greenways (Friends of Czech Greenways 2013), as well as various bicycle routes or non-motorised routes have been adopted in other countries. As part of the *Vias Verde* project, the *Via Verde del Aceite*, or the Olive Oil Greenway, takes travellers on a culinary adventure through sloping olive groves "featuring some of the most magnificent vestiges of the three cultures that left their legacy here: Christian, Jewish and Islamic" (van Wijck 2015: n.p.). The Trans Canada Trail established in 1992 is a non-motorised greenway running 17,000 kilometres, linking the Atlantic, Pacific and Arctic coasts, running through or near 1,000 communities. It is the world's longest multiuse recreational trail, combining land trails and water trails. Managed as a charitable organisation, one of the benefits of the Trans Canada Trail is it provides a "deepening awareness of Canada's history, culture and natural heritage" (Trans Canada Trail 2015: n.p.). In some places, the trail is divided into sections such as the Confederation Trail (Prince Edward Island), which is marketed in association with the culinary heritage of the area.

The second main type of cultural heritage trail is the purposive cultural route, or heritage trails that were not necessarily original paths or trails but have been intentionally developed and assembled for modern tourist and recreation use (Timothy and Boyd 2015). These designed routes are developed from a defined geographic area that has nodes of common thematic interest. These purposive routes are typically delineated not by historical association but rather by thematic content to link sites, establishments and communities that share similar pasts and products that appeal to comparable demand cohorts. Such routes include maritime routes; urban heritage trails; literary, film and music trails; industrial trails; agriculture trails; food and wine routes; beer and whisky trails; food trails; and religious trails. The attractions along the routes and trails may not have been initially connected; however, connecting the new and/or evolving thematic points of interest is what instigated the creation of the trails. For example, Visit Scotland promotes food and drink trails with suggested travel itineraries. The Scottish whisky distilleries may have been operating for centuries, but the formalised trails that connect the distilleries mainly for tourism or recreational purposes are relatively new. The Malt Whisky Trail began to attract tourists in the early 1990s. In 2005, Visit Scotland launched EastScotland in part to campaign for food and drink experiences under Scottish hospitality (Klepp and Hosea 2008). Similarly, the Scottish Cheese Trail, the Chocolate Trail and farms and shops that are widespread across Scotland are now incorporated into suggested food-and-drink itineraries.

The Council of Europe designates Cultural Routes, and in 2005, The Routes of the Olive Tree were designated, incorporating the following countries: Albania, Algeria, Bosnia and Herzegovina, Cyprus, Croatia, Egypt, France, Greece, Italy, Jordan, Lebanon, Libya, Malta, Morocco, Portugal, Serbia, Slovenia, Spain, Syria, Tunisia and Turkey. The importance of the Mediterranean Basin's culinary heritage is evident in the description statement of the route that highlights the importance of the olive tree, which reads:

> The presence of the olive tree has marked not only the landscape but also the everyday lives of the Mediterranean peoples. A mythical and sacred tree, it is associated with their rites and customs and has influenced their ways of life, creating a specific ancient civilisation, the 'olive tree civilisation'.
>
> (Council of Europe 2015: n.p.)

The Southwest Ontario Tourism Corporation is a provincially mandated regional tourism organisation in the province of Ontario, Canada. A recent marketing initiative has been to develop a number of culinary itineraries including Rural Routes, Homegrown Treasures, Country Comfort and the Bounty Trail (Figure 10.1). The opening message of the campaign is "Take the road less travelled for an authentic culinary experience. Unleash your taste for adventure and join us on a special journey to discover the unique food and drink experiences of Ontario's Southwest" (Southwest Ontario Tourism Corporation 2015: n.p.).

Purposive routes can be of varying scales. For instance, the Niagara Wine Route focuses on the Niagara region of Canada, while Tastes of Nova Scotia covers an entire province. In contrast, a small section of a city may be included in a specific trail. The town of Paal, in the Western Cape province of South Africa, is known for its wine route (Paal Tourism 2015; South African Tourism 2015). However, the Spice Route has been developed to promote "a selection of hand picked artisanal producers" (Spice Route 2015: n.p.), including beer brewing companies, wineries, cured meat makers, distilleries, restaurants and cafes, and all of these are contained in a small village.

Whether culinary trails are organic in evolution or are purposively created routes, they have the potential to increase the connection between heritage and other cultural components, and thus increase the duration of visitors' length of stay and level of exposure to an area's heritage components. From a regional

Figure 10.1 Signs directing tourists along a rural agricultural/food route and to farm sellers in the Niagara Region of Canada (Photo: Atsuko Hashimoto)

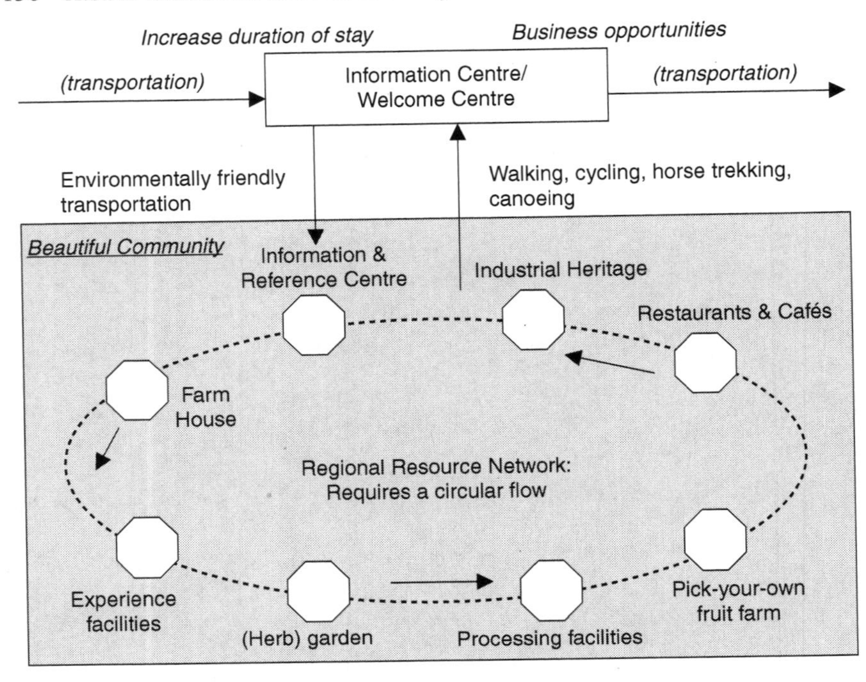

Figure 10.2 The creation of culinary heritage routes (Modified from Ihara 2003)

development perspective (Telfer 2015), the creation of food routes or taste trails means strengthening cultural identity, traditional social practices, environmental protection and also the creation of business opportunities. Figure 10.2 illustrates the creation of a culinary heritage route as the various components of the route (e.g. farms, restaurants, distilleries) come together in a regional resources network increasing visitors' length of stay and generating business opportunities.

Identity, authenticity and promoting culinary heritage through trails

Culinary heritage and the identity of people who consume specific foodstuffs are invariably linked to the past. Food availability in a specific area is often limited by environmental, physiological, geographical or technological limitations, which in turn shaped the food culture in the area. Different cultures and societies find different meanings and symbolism in foodstuffs. The interpretation, adoption or rejection of available foodstuffs based on people's "needs, means and intentions" (Scholliers 2001: 4) have led to the transformation and taming of natural foodstuffs into cultural products, including reinterpretation of naturalness of foodstuffs, table manners and eating habits (Atkinson 1983; Civitello 2004; Montanari 2004), and hence, artificial creation of 'culinary heritage' and associated 'identity' over time. According to Timothy and Ron (2013: 99), "foodways, cuisine, gastronomy, and epicurean delicacy are all elements of the broader system of cultural heritage". Food heritage and identity can also be created by, and associated with, social class, wealth discrepancy, gender distinction and in today's societies, food philosophies (Hall 1996; Pilcher 2006; Scholliers 2001).

In a similar train of thought, the concept of 'foodscape' is becoming more popular. Johnston and Baumann (2010: 3) defined foodscape as a "dynamic social construction that relates food to specific places, people and meanings". Adema's (2009: 5) definition of foodscape as "the multiple informative historic and contemporary personal, social, political, cultural and economic forces that inform how people think about and use (or eschew) food in various spaces they inhabit" resonates with the general understanding of 'culinary heritage'. Foodscapes not only shape the culinary heritage people are exposed to; they also influence people's behaviour and health (Mikkelsen 2011). With modern technology and media, 'mental foodscapes' have been created and imprinted in people's minds. Mental foodscapes are not necessarily an accurate reflection of local food heritage or culinary culture, but they are imaginary geographies and imageries of food (Bildtgård 2009), where people would like to go and consume certain type of food and drink.

In examining culinary heritage as a source of local initiatives and a factor in territorial identity construction, Bessière (1998: 29) refers to the work of Crozier and Friedberg (1977) and states that "establishing concrete initiatives in a given geographic area, is the dynamic process by which individual or collective actors with a shared memory promote a common heritage product". In Canada, culinary heritage is influenced by a long history of immigration, together with regional product availability. Chefs are combining these cultural traditions with local products, creating new styles and forms of cooking across the country (Hashimoto and Telfer 2006). As an example of regional diversification, the authors note as one example of many *La Route des Saveurs* (Flavour Trail) in the Charlevoix region of Quebec.

Peace (2011) documents how small-scale farmers, winegrowers and other entrepreneurs have idealised the Barossa landscape in Australia and have fabricated the heritage that is integral to the idea of a distinctive cuisine. Peace (2011) notes the cultural production of myths about an idyllic past in order to compound the value of contemporary food and drink. A strong component of culinary routes is their link to place, real or imagined. This has been picked up in marketing routes, as revealed in the line from the *Culinary Itineraries* magazine: "Just a short drive away but far from routine you'll find a delightful change of scenery and the road less travelled to local terroir, pastoral landscapes, postcard country scenes and bountiful breathing space" (Southwest Ontario Tourism Corporation 2015: 4).

Everett (2011) examined the relationship between food production, place and identity in bed and breakfasts in the area of the Viking Trail on Newfoundland's west coast in Canada. These lodging establishments offer local specialties emphasising home cooking, and the meals provide opportunities for the operators to perform local identities for their guests.

Food festivals are important celebrations in the annual life of a culinary trail. They often revolve around harvest time. The Niagara Icewine festival in January celebrates the production of sweet dessert wine produced from grapes that are harvested when still frozen on the vines. For 2015, an online Food Festival Calendar for the United Kingdom lists eighty-two food events from March to October (The Festival Calendar 2015). Japan boasts numerous food and drink festivals nationwide throughout the year typically linked to the harvest season of the main ingredients. The main culinary attractions are the regional heritage food or drink, which also promotes local traditions and festive events along the heritage routes (Hashimoto and Telfer 2008). Japan is also known for its 'One Village One Product' concept whereby individual villages are identified with, or known for, the production of specific agricultural products. These products appear on signs along village roadways and at train stations (Figure 10.3). Travellers can go from train station to train station encountering these signs and purchasing Japanese *bento* (lunch) boxes featuring the traditional ingredient from that particular area.

There are numerous regional cuisines, which evolved from local ingredients unique to these areas; however, the Ministry of Agriculture, Forestry and Fisheries organised a project to select and designate the Regional Heritage Food or Drinks of Japan in 2007 to differentiate regional heritage cuisine from contemporary local food (Rural Development Planning Commission 2007). While heritage

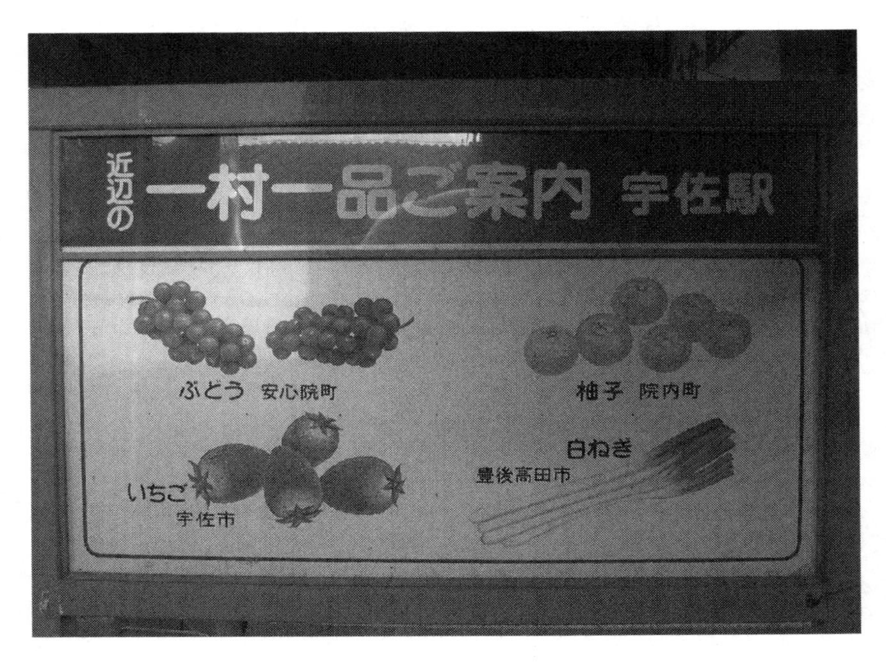

Figure 10.3 Railway station sign denoting a community's specialty agricultural products (Photo: Atsuko Hashimoto)

cuisine might mean recently created or reconstructed food and drink in the New World (e.g. icewine in Canada), the erosion of heritage cuisine can be a serious concern in the Old World. The case of Japan discussed earlier in this paragraph shows the rather extreme measure of the designation of regional heritage food and drinks in order to preserve an authentic form of heritage. In contrast, culinary heritage designations in the European Union stemmed from food security concerns, and in some cases these designations have evolved products into culinary routes. The European Union maintains three designation schemes:

- **Protected Designation of Origin – PDO**: covers agricultural products and foodstuffs that are produced, processed and prepared in a given geographical area using recognised techniques.
- **Protected Geographic Indication – PGI**: covers agricultural products and foodstuffs closely linked to the geographical area. At least one of the stages of production or preparation takes place in the area.
- **Traditional Specialty Guaranteed – TSG**: highlights traditional character, either in the composition or means of production (Europa 2015).

The most frequently discussed European designations are PDO and PGI. Parrott et al.'s (2002) study identified the distinctive differences in understanding and usage of these designations in northern and southern European nations. The awareness of regional food products and production techniques is much higher in southern Europe, except for Greece, and therefore consumer attitudes towards these designations are stronger, and people are more inclined to purchase designated products. The vast majority of PDO/PGI products are self evidently from rural areas, and more than 70% of PDO/PGI products come from agriculturally disadvantaged less favoured areas (LFA). Except for Greece and the United Kingdom, most PDO products are from LFAs (e.g. 100% of Austrian PDOs and nearly 90% of Spanish, French and Italian PDOs) (Parrott et al. 2002).

Although the PDO/PGI designation of regional food products does not seem to create immediate impacts on the creation of trails in northern Europe, the countries of southern Europe appear to have taken advantage of these designations for regional development. Regions that have historical gastronomic interests, such as Italy, have created food trails and routes for visitors. For instance, the Italian region of Emilia-Romagna, has a PDO Parma ham page on its travel website, suggesting "Routes of Ham" (Emilia Romagna Turismo 2013). Marescotti (2003), using the example of the PDO/PGI designation of the cherry of Lari, Italy, suggested networks could be built between local businesses and communities to provide new opportunities for agricultural and rural development. A couple of the expected positive outcomes of PDO recognition are "pull-effects on other local agricultural and craft products", "local culture and traditions would be strengthened by the protection of product reputation", "rural economy should be fostered" and "rural development dynamics would receive new inputs" (Marescotti 2003: n.p.). Nonetheless, the PDO/PGI designation of regional products is mainly used for cultural protection, environmental protection and an increase in international market sales. However, the designations can have beneficial effects for the creation of culinary heritage trails.

Practices and trends in culinary routes

As already noted, culinary trails have become important elements in regional development (Telfer 2015; Timothy and Boyd 2015). This section explores contemporary trends associated with culinary routes. Anderson and Law (2012) suggest the key themes for an advanced framework for food trail performance include overall product, trail product, communication, trail management, economic viability, future possibility and planning context. Culinary trails not only connect destinations on a linear route, they also connect clusters of associated businesses linked to the route. In culinary trail clusters of farms, farmers' markets, restaurants, tourism businesses and related destinations, marketing associations and governments form tourism clusters, which help link the route together. Telfer (2001a) examined the importance of strategic alliances along the Niagara Wine Route and found the importance of formal and informal agreements between wineries, tour operators and the food industry highlighting the significance of horizontal and vertical linkages. Porter (1998: 263–266) suggests that the common characteristics of successful cluster initiatives include:

- a shared understanding of competitiveness and the role of clusters in creating a competitive advantage
- a focus on removing obstacles and easing constraints to cluster upgrading
- a structure that embraces all clusters in a nation or state
- appropriate cluster boundaries
- wide involvement of cluster participants and associated interests
- private sector leadership
- close attention to personal relationships
- a bias towards action
- institutionalisation

The key to maximising benefits of food and wine tourism in local and regional development, according to Hall (2012: 57) is "understanding the role of the intangible economy in regional competitiveness". The intangibles include intellectual property of place, brand, new networks and relationships and intellectual capital. Networks and cluster relationships are also important in developing intangible capital (Hall 2012). The key factors developing successful food tourism clusters and networks are listed below and share some common elements with Porter's list above:

- innovative clusters
- government financing and policies
- skills and knowledge levels (human capital)
- technological capabilities (research and development activities)

- transport, information and communication infrastructure
- availability and expertise of capital financing in the region
- strong tax and regulatory environment
- skilled migrants and their associated capital
- spatial proximity of network members (co-location tends to enhance network development)
- clarity of public governance (the clearer the roles of various government agencies and departments in development, the greater the ease in successful network development)
- entrepreneurial and innovative champion(s)
- regular face-to-face meetings (to develop relationships and trust between parties (Hall 2012: 58).

Along the Niagara Wine Route in Ontario, Canada, are a series of embedded clusters (Telfer 2001b) ranging from a heritage wine tourism village with a winery, restaurants, hotel and shopping facilities to the entire Niagara Wine Route covering the Niagara region with more than ninety wineries. Telfer and Hashimoto (2013) proposed a continuum on wineries ranging from wine production to wine tourism. At one end of the continuum, the wineries mainly focus on the vineyards and wine production. At the other end of the scale the wineries have become a full tourist attraction with elaborate tasting bars, restaurants and cooking schools, and they collaborate with tour operators and other wineries to build wine tourism clusters as part of a culinary trail.

Destination management organisations, business associations and local governments are developing culinary tourism strategies that promote culinary trails such as *Ontario's Four-Year Culinary Tourism Strategy and Action Plan 2011–2015* and the *South Australian Food and Wine Tourism Strategy 2009–2014*, both of which stress collaboration. Despite the rapid expansion of culinary trails around the world, and their importance for preserving heritage cuisines and promoting regional development, there can be challenges in collaboration, and not all of them succeed. Plummer et al. (2006) found challenges in maintaining partnerships in a culinary trail over time, as different stakeholders with conflicting interests may not always align. Culinary trails also link the concepts of 'farm to table', 'slow food' and 'organic production', meeting current demands to experience local foods and also potentially promoting sustainable development.

The Internet has become an important avenue of marketing culinary routes. It is especially important for culinary trails with limited marketing budgets. Jacobs (2010) assembled a *Selected Internet Guide to Culinary Trails*, which covers sixteen different countries. The routes in the guide range from very formal trails that control and process memberships, brand the product through distinct labels and signage and then do the marketing through print maps and the Internet. Jacobs's second category is figurative routes consisting of a list of destinations with a complementary theme. In investigating the selected culinary routes on the Internet, Jacobs (2010) stresses the importance of friendliness of websites in terms of navigability and the ability for consumers to locate maps of participating operators.

In his sample of public tourism destination organisations from the Internet Jacobs (2010: 125) found the features of the best culinary trails include:

- a conscious commitment to educating the potential user about the historical, architectural and cultural context of the product
- a clear brand that uses simple and memorable symbols such as the growing agreement for the signage of wine routes
- an effective slogan or phrase that typifies the theme of the trail such as (savour the flavours)
- a high level of aesthetic appeal for several senses that uses quality photographs, artwork and video and audio clips
- a provision for modern communication through MP3 players, iPods, downloadable blogs and access to broadcasts
- strong linkages with complementary operations
- the inclusion of product information including a calendar of events and the posting of recipes
- hooks such as subscriptions that entitle members to the most topical information about the product and destination and instil a sense of partnership
- readily downloadable maps that can be taken, a problem with interactive maps if there is no provision for a print version
- a planning trip function and calculators
- a calendar of events
- an effective search engine to explore the site
- the creation of organized itineraries that suit the diverse needs of trail users
- the appeal of unique or unusual products such as tacos or ice cream (Jacobs 2010: 125).

In addition to having an effective website, mobile apps are being created for travellers to download to their mobile phones or other portable electronic devices. The Blue Mountains Apple Pie Trail in the Georgian Bay area of Canada has such a downloadable app, which includes a map, Apple Pie Trail stops, Apple Pie Trail Adventures, Apple Pie Tours, accommodation and a tool to enhance travellers' pictures with a souvenir frame so they can be uploaded to various platforms on the Internet (Apple Pie Trail 2015).

In addition to efforts by the operators of the culinary trails, there has been a tremendous expansion in tour operators running culinary tours along the trails. For example, *La Route des Gourmets* is a destination management company focusing on culinary tourism in France. They offer an "opportunity to discover French cuisine, wine and local 'terroir' products through a selection of the best Paris gourmet city tours, cooking schools in Paris, day-trips around the region and all inclusive excursions to some of France's famed culinary destinations" (La Routes des Gourmets 2015: n.p.). From Paris the tours leave for various regions including Normandy, Champagne, Alsace, Burgundy, Bordeaux, the Loire River Valley, Cognac and other culinary destinations.

Likewise, taking advantage of shifts in consumer demand towards the experience economy, the Tuscany Active Gourmet Walking Tour in Italy presented by Backroads Travel Company (2015: n.p.) offers the following highlights:

- walk through vineyards, woodlands and the Renaissance hill towns, getting to know our local *amici* (friends) along the way
- prepare local farm-to-table recipes passed through countless generations
- follow the *strade bianche* (white roads) of southern Tuscany's Val d'Orcia
- savour Chianti Classico and other superb Tuscan wines
- relish handmade cuisine from your first plate of *pici all'aglione* to your bowl-scraping spoonful of *tiramisu.*

Conclusion

Culinary routes connect food heritage assets or points along linear routes generating regional development in an area. In some cases, ancient foodways are being preserved and protected, while in other locations new food identities are being created, branded and marketed. The main challenge, as with any partnership, is participant commitment and longevity.

It is not easy to define clearly what 'authentic heritage cuisine' is in many nations in this era of globalisation. Particularly in the New World, where migrations of cultures and people form the basis of mixed cultural identities, so-called 'authentic' heritage cuisine may be using substituted ingredients or modernised cooking methods and equipment. This raises questions for some, that this could disqualify a dish from being authentic heritage cuisine. It is also important to note that foodways are dynamic and change over time. Europe's designation of Protected Designation of Origin (PDO) and Protected Geographic Indication (PGI) is a significant step to protect heritage cuisines, cultural identities and natural environments in a specific area, yet it raises the possibility of constraining innovation and the evolution of foodways. To maintain the PDO or PGI recognition, the farms, breweries and distilleries or processing factories cannot relocate from the site, for example, even to the other side of the river.

As discussed earlier in this chapter, heritage and cultural identities have been created, nurtured and established over time. The identification and designation of authentic heritage cuisine may be an attempt to stop time in order to preserve the past, yet it is undeniable that such recognitions allow the opportunity for the development of rural areas through culinary trails. The creation of food trails, especially when the main attractions are heritage cuisine and contemporary local gastronomy, will self-evidently promote traditional agriculture, land management and environmental protection, and encourage new business opportunities and collaborations, which in turn may lead to social and economic development. Using markers such as PDO and PGI, an area can entice tourists and attract global buyers of PDO- or PGI-labelled products.

For a food region to be attractive for visitors and buyers, area businesses must collaborate to create a welcoming environment and must market their culinary trail effectively (Stanley and Stanley 2015). The trail can be small in scale within the boundaries of a single community or a large-scale, cross-boundary trail that connects a number of communities, which together can offer a network of distinctive food and drink attractions. For example, the city of Dublin, Ireland, has a 2.5-hour 'Dublin Tasting Trail' (cultural tasting walk) (Fab Food Trails 2015), and many regions in Germany have wine routes (Die Deutsche Zentrale für Tourismus 2014), while a Hungary-Slovakia-Romania-Ukraine joint scheme hosts the cross-border Carpathian Culinary Heritage Network (JTS 2012). Trails such as Greenways in Europe and the Trans Canada Trail are not purposefully designed for culinary adventures, but trail users encounter gastronomic experiences and food heritage in each of the communities they stop in, adding additional value to their journeys.

As the culinary interests of visitors and buyers are heightened, global competition between gastronomic traditions has also become fierce. Culinary operators, tour operators, destination management organisations and local governments are responding to the increases in demand, forging new alliances and strategies along taste trails. Regions with PDO- or PGI-designated products, or similar kinds of heritage recognition, can use this to their advantage for marketing, promotion and branding. On the other hand, the New World or newly emerging nations that do not have officially distinguished culinary heritage traditions are relying on collaboration and associations of interested stakeholders to promote new gastronomic traditions and food trails. Some Old World countries are also now creating new food products and innovative dishes and drinks to form the substance of culinary routes. Most of North America's cities and provinces/states now have culinary trails. In Canada, for example, Taste of Nova Scotia is a joint marketing programme between the provincial government and the private sector. Prince Edward Island Flavours Culinary Trail is sponsored by the provincial government and the PEI Culinary Alliance, whereas Savour Ottawa is a collaborative initiative between Ottawa Tourism, the city of Ottawa and grassroots organisations. In some countries, culinary trails are becoming a means to preserve heritage foods and culinary practices and, in other nations, a primary means of attracting tourists and showcasing innovative epicurean products made from local ingredients.

References

Adema, P. (2009) *Garlic Capital of the World: Gilroy, Garlic, and the Making of a Festive Foodscape.* Jackson, MS: University Press of Mississippi.

Anderson, A. and Law, L. (2012) An advanced framework for food trail performance. *Journal of Vacation Marketing*, 18(4): 275–286.

Apple Pie Trail (2015) *Home Page: Welcome to Apple Pie Country.* Available online at http://www.applepietrail.ca Accessed February 25, 2015.

Atkinson, P. (1983) Eating virtue. In A. Murcott (ed) *The Sociology of Food and Eating*, pp. 9–17. Aldershot: Gower Publishing Company.

Backroads Travel Company (2015) Tuscany Active Gourmet Walking Tour. Available online at http://www.backroads.com/trips/WCTQ/tuscany-hiking-tour Accessed February 26, 2015.

Bessière, J. (1998) Local development and heritage: traditional food and cuisine as tourist attractions in rural areas. *Sociologia Ruralis*, 38(1): 21–34.

Bildtgåd, T. (2009) Mental foodscapes: where Swedes would go to eat well (and places they would avoid). *Food, Culture & Society*, 12: 497–523.

Civitello, L. (2004) *Cuisine and Culture: A History of Food and People*. Hoboken, NJ: Wiley.

Council of Europe (2015) The Routes of the Olive Tree. Available online at http://www.coe.int/t/dg4/cultureheritage/culture/Routes/olive_en.asp Accessed February 26, 2015.

Crozier, M. and Friedberg, E. (1977) *L'acteur et le système*. Paris: Seuil.

Die Deutsche Zentrale für Tourismus (2014) *Weinanbauregionen: Feine Tropfen aus gutem Grund*. Available online at http://www.germany.travel/de/staedte-kultur/gemuetlichkeit/weinland/weinanbauregionen/weinanbauregionen.html Accessed February 25, 2015.

Emilia Romagna Turismo (2013) *PDO Parma Ham*. Available online at http://www.emiliaromagnaturismo.com/en/flavours/gastronomic-products/pdo-parm-ham.html Accessed February 19, 2015.

Europa (2015) *Agriculture and Rural Development: Geographical indications and traditional specialties*. Available online at http://ec.europa.eu/agriculture/quality/schemes/index_en.htm Accessed January 23, 2015.

Everett, H. (2011) Newfoundland and Labrador on a plate: bed, breakfast and regional identity. *Cuizine: The Journal of Canadian Food Cultures* 3(1): n.p. (online). Available at: https://www.erudit.org/revue/cuizine/2011/v3/n1/1004728ar.html.

Fab Food Trails (2015) *Dublin Walking Tours: Dublin Tasting Trail*. Available online at http://www.fabfoodtrails.ie/dublin-tasting-trail/ Accessed February 25, 2015.

Festival Calendar, The (2015) Food Festivals 2015. Available online at http://www.thefestivalcalendar.co.uk/food-festivals-calendar.php?row=72 Accessed February 26, 2015.

Friends of Czech Greenways (2013) *Home Page: "The Prague-Vienna Greenways"*. Available online at http://www.pragueviennagreenways.org Accessed February 19, 2015.

Government of Nova Scotia (2015) *The Cabot Trail*. Available online at http://www.cabottrail.travel Accessed February 19, 2015.

Hall, C.M. (2012) Boosting food and tourism-related regional economic development. In *OECD Food and the Tourism Experience: The OECD-Korea Workshop*, pp. 49–62. OECD Publishing. (online). Available at: http://www.keepeek.com/Digital-Asset-Management/oecd/industry-and-services/food-and-the-tourism-experience_9789264171923-en#page59.

Hall, S. (1996) Introduction: who needs "identity"? In S. Hall and P. du Gay (eds) *Questions of Cultural Identity*, pp.1–17. London: Sage.

Hashimoto, A. and Telfer, D.J. (2006) Selling Canadian culinary tourism: branding the global and regional product. *Tourism Geographies*, 8(1): 31–55.

Hashimoto, A. and Telfer, D.J. (2008) From saké to sea urchin: food and drink festivals and regional identity in Japan. In C.M. Hall and L. Sharples (eds) *Food and Wine Festivals and Events around the World: Development, Management and Markets*, pp. 249–278. Oxford: Butterworth Heinemann.

Ihara, M. (2003) Ecomuseum ni yoru Saisei Machi-zukuri [Re-creation of communities through Ecomuseum]. In H. Yamada (ed) *Chiiki Saisei no Machi-zukuri, Mura-zukuri [Re-creation of Towns and Communities for Regional Rejuvenation]*, pp. 29–58. Tokyo: Gyosei.

Jacobs, H. (2010) *A Selected Internet Guide to Culinary Trails*. Available online at http://www.geography.ryerson.ca/geo509/A_Selected_Internet_Guide_to_Culinary_Trails.pdf Accessed January 30, 2015.

Johnston, J. and Baumann, S. (2010) *Foodies: Democracy and Distinction in the Gourmet Foodscape*. Abingdon: Routledge

JTS (Hungary-Slovakia-Romania-Ukraine ENPI Cross-border Cooperation Programme Joint Technical Secretariat) (2012) *Press Release: Carpathian Culinary Heritage Network Is Identified with the Logo*. Available online at http://www.huskrouacbc.net/uploads/editors/Press_release(logo_winner)_engl.pdf Accessed February 25, 2015.

JTS (Hungary-Slovakia-Romania-Ukraine ENPI Cross-border Cooperation Programme Joint Technical Secretariat) (2015) *Welcome to the Website of the Hungary-Slovakia-Romania-Ukraine ENPI Cross-border Cooperation Programme 2007–2013*. Available online at http://www.huskroua-cbc.net/en/project_idea_and_partner_search_form/8 Accessed February 25, 2015.

Klepp, I.A. and Hosea, J. (2008) Connecting local food to global consumers via the Internet. In G. Rusten and S. Skerratt (eds) *Information and Communication Technologies in Rural Society: Being Rural in a Digital Age*, pp. 63–82. Abingdon: Routledge.

Kotler, P., Haider, D. and Rein, I. (1993) *Marketing Places: Attracting Investment, Industry, and Tourism to Cities, and Nations*. New York: The Free Press.

La Routes des Gourmets (2015) *The French Specialist in Gourmet Wine and Food Tours*. Available online at http://www.laroutedesgourmets.fr/en/ Accessed February 26, 2015.

Marescotti, A. (2003) *Typical products and rural development: Who benefits from PDO/PGI recognition?* Paper (draft version) presented at the 83rd EAAE SEMINAR – Food Quality Products in the Advent of the 21st Century: Production, Demand and Public Policy, Chania, Greece, September.

Mikkelsen, B.E. (2011) Images of foodscapes: introduction to foodscape studies and their application in the study of healthy eating out-of-home environments. *Perspectives in Public Health*, 131(5): 209–216.

Montanari, M. (2004) *Food Is Culture* [A. Sonnenfeld trans. 2006]. New York: Columbia University Press.

Paal Tourism (2015) *Visit Paal Homepage*. Available online at http://www.paarlonline.com Accessed February 19, 2015.

Parrott, N., Wilson, N. and Murdoch, J. (2002) Spatializing quality: regional protection and the alternative geography of food. *European Urban and Regional Studies*, 9(3): 241–261.

Peace, A. (2011) Barossa dreaming: imaging place and constituting cuisine in contemporary Australia. *Anthropological Forum*, 21(1): 23–42.

Pilcher, J.M. (2006) *Food in World History*. Abingdon: Routledge.

Plummer, R., Telfer, D. and Hashimoto, A. (2006) The rise and fall of the Waterloo-Wellington Ale Trail: a study of collaboration within the tourism Industry. *Current Issues in Tourism*, 9(3): 191–205.

Porter, M. (1998) *On Competition: A Harvard Business Review Book*. Boston: Harvard Business School Publishing.

Richards, G. and Wilson, J. (2007) Tourism development trajectories from culture to creativity? In G. Richards and J. Wilson (eds) *Tourism, Creativity and Development*, pp. 1–33. London: Routledge.

Rural Development Planning Commission (2007) *Kyodo Ryori Hyaku*-sen [one hundred regional heritage food]. Available online at http://www.rdpc.or.jp/kyoudoryouri100/ Accessed February 19, 2015.

Scholliers, P. (2001) Meals, food narratives, and sentiments of belonging in past and present. In P. Sholliers (ed) *Food Drink and Identity: Cooking, Eating and Drinking in Europe since the Middle Ages*, pp. 3–22. Oxford: Berg.

Spice Route (2015) *Spice Route homepage*. Available online at http://www.spiceroute.co.za Accessed February 19, 2015.

South African Tourism (2015) *Paal, Western Cape*. Available online at http://www.southafrica.net/za/en/articles/entry/article-southafrica.net-paarl Accessed February 19, 2015.

Southwest Ontario Tourism Corporation (2015) Ontario's Southwest Culinary Itineraries. Available online at http://www.flippubs.com/publication/?i=203270 Accessed February 3, 2015.

Stanley, J. and Stanley, L. (2015) *Food Tourism: A Practical Marketing Guide*. Wallingford: CAB International.

Telfer, D.J. (2001a) Strategic alliances along the Niagara Wine Route. *Tourism Management*, 22(1): 21–30.

Telfer, D.J. (2001b) From a wine tourism village to a regional wine route: an investigation of the competitive advantage of embedded clusters in Niagara, Canada. *Tourism Recreation Research*, 26(2): 23–33.

Telfer, D.J. (2015) Tourism and regional development issues. In R. Sharpley and D.J. Telfer (eds) *Tourism and Development Concepts and Issues*, 2nd Edn, pp.140–177. Bristol: Channel View Publications.

Telfer, D.J. and Hashimoto, A. (2013) Wine and culinary tourism in Niagara. In M. Ripmeester, P. Mackintosh and C. Fullerton (eds) *The World of Niagara Wine*, pp. 281–299. Waterloo: Wilfred Laurier University Press.

Timothy, D.J. and Boyd, S.W. (2015) *Tourism and Trails: Cultural, Ecological and Management Issues*. Bristol: Channel View Publications.

Timothy, D.J. and Ron, A.S. (2013) Understanding heritage cuisines and tourism: identity, image, authenticity and change. *Journal of Heritage Tourism*, 8(2/3): 99–104.

Trans Canada Trail (2015) *Home Page*. Available online at http://tctrail.ca Accessed February 19, 2015.

van Wijck, A. (2015) Spain for foodies: conquering the heart of Spain, Olive Oil Greenway in Jaén. Food & Wines from Spain. Available online at http://www.foodswinesfromspain.com/spanishfoodwine/global/shop-travel-dine/spain-for-foodies/routes/4446007.html Accessed February 25, 2015.

Vias verde (2015) *Home Page*. Available online at http://www.viasverdes.com Accessed February 19, 2015.

Wall, G. (1997) Tourism attractions: points, lines, and areas. *Annals of Tourism Research*, 24(1): 249–243.

11 Food festivals and heritage awareness

Dallen J. Timothy and Miguel Pena

Introduction

As the first chapter in this book emphasized, heritage is an elusive concept, but lying at its core is an inheritance from the past. Many tangible or intangible elements are included in the broader scope of cultural heritage (Timothy 2014). Humans are celebratory animals. We like to rejoice in major life events, such as births, marriages and graduations, and we look for any excuse to celebrate – nature, culture, family and food. As an integral part of the human experience, food and foodways are also an important part of the heritage of humankind and something worthy of celebrating (Getz 2005; Hall and Sharples 2008b).

Culinary festivals and similar events venerate local cuisine and foodways, food-associated culture, eating customs, preparation practices and social relations. In short, gastronomic events celebrate communities and their comestible heritage. Even non-food festivals are satiated with references to food and culinary delights. If not always healthy, celebratory food is tasty and awash with social codes and cultural meanings. Sporting events, carnivals, music festivities and ethnic celebrations of many sorts feature food as a prominent component of every festivalscape (Getz 2005). Culinary festivals occur all over the world. Every region has at least one food item of which it is proudest and which it desires to share with the outside world (Hall and Sharples 2008b).

This chapter examines the role of culinary celebrations or food festivals as purveyors of local heritage. It describes the primary markets for food festivals and provides a typology of event types from a heritage perspective. Of particular importance is an ideographic model that shows how these different types of events support and define the principles and characteristics of cultural heritage.

Food festivals and events

There are countless food events throughout the world. They commemorate many things, including impactful occurrences, famous people, immigrant heritage, bounteous harvests, gastronomical patrimony, environmental conditions and agricultural traditions (Hashimoto and Telfer 2008; Sharples 2008; Timothy 2011). Getz and Robinson (2014) identified several types of gustatory events, including farmers' markets/fish markets, ethnic festivals where food is a prominent component, wine and food tastings, dining in an expensive restaurant, banquets, food trade fairs, food competitions/cook-offs, culinary shows, seminars or conferences about food, special events at a restaurant, lessons on food or wine pairing, professional cooking classes, indigenous/bush food experiences and food festivals. Of primary importance in this chapter are food festivals and similar events where comestibles and the cultural heritage associated with them are the primary focus of the occasion.

Food festivals can be seen broadly and from the perspective of their genesis and present manifestation from two different perspectives. The first perspective relates to events that develop organically from native celebrations of life, such as births, initiations, harvests, marriages or other of life's important events (Muhammad et al. 2009). They may be religious or secular in nature, but they were originally not designed to attract outsiders; they were instead already existing or traditional celebrations of health, gratitude and happiness that have through time, and usually intentionally, been modified and commercialized for economic purposes (Hashimoto and Telfer 2008). Udell and Wilson (1978, cited in Lewis 1997: 76) dubbed this type "commercialized indigenous" festivals. The second type resembles what Lewis (1997: 73–74) labeled "rationally constructed food festivals", or invented, commercially developed events that celebrate a particular food item and connect it to a specific location. These are recent inventions designed to increase tourist expenditures and develop a brand image (Rotherham 2008). Occasionally the alimentary item(s) celebrated did not exist locally until a decision was made to highlight it for an event.

Like many other planned events, culinary festivals fulfill a variety of purposes. First, they are instruments for stimulating local economic development by providing jobs and encouraging spending by local residents, visitors and out-of-town vendors (Hall and Sharples 2008b; Sharples and Lyons 2008). They also help stimulate entrepreneurial activity as residents become involved in cottage industries, such as making handicrafts, jams and jellies, honey, herbs, nuts and candies (Hall and Sharples 2008a) and other money-making ventures, such as offering parking on private property, selling bottled water or washing cars.

Many food festivals and related events are organized, sponsored and financed by local governments, volunteer community organizations or business alliances (e.g. chambers of commerce) to stimulate local expenditures (Hede 2008). Some culinary events are planned and underwritten by corporations that use the opportunity to promote their products, enhance their brand or improve relations with the community.

Culinary festivals can directly increase local food production and sales at supermarkets, roadside stands, restaurants, wineries and breweries and farmers' markets as attendees consume large volumes of comestibles over the course of the fair (Çela et al. 2007; Einarsen and Mykletun 2012; Hall and Sharples 2008a; Wargenau and Che 2006). Much of the public today desires to know the source of the food they eat. "Traceability is increasingly important" (Haven-Tang and Jones 2005: 80), and food festivals are able to emphasize the localness of the food on display. These events may also have long-term production effects when they result in increased demand for local goods (Hede 2008) and as people desire to return to buy additional local products in the future and attend similar events again. Likewise, such events can 'brand' locales and their food items that will enable products to be purchased further afield beyond the celebratory venue (Hall and Sharples 2008c). Food and wine festivals may serve as off-season occasions to draw out-of-town consumers during periods of low tourist demand (Ioannides and Timothy 2010).

The second purpose, and part of economic development, food festivals are organized in many rural areas is to counter agricultural decline (Timothy and Ron 2013). They have the potential to offset some of the fiscal losses incurred with agricultural decline while at the same time helping to support local producers (Çela et al. 2007; Mason and Paggiaro 2009) and diversify rural economies (Hall and Sharples 2003).

Third, culinary celebrations highlight what is unique and special about a place (Einarsen and Mykletun 2012; Long 2004). This is particularly important today when international boundaries have diminished and every place is more globally connected, and each destination has become more familiar, mundane and standardized, reflecting the inherent predictability denoted by Ritzer and Liska's (1997) notion of McDisneyized tourismscapes. Every destination now clamors to be exceptional, and food festivals have the potential to distinguish one place from another in an increasingly competitive tourism marketplace (de la Barre and Brouder 2013; Haven-Tang and Jones 2005). Many small communities boldly claim to be the most superlative place in the world regarding a specific food item. The 'garlic capital', 'strawberry central', or the 'home of the watermelon' in any given country are various places' own calculated claims to fame and provides a unique selling proposition (USP) (Hall and Sharples 2008b).

Destination branding in this way is key in establishing a place's position in the global hierarchy of must-visit locations. Food festivals can help provide an identifiable brand and create an identifiable USP (Blichfeldt and Halkier 2014; Kalkstein-Silkes et al. 2008; Lee and Arcodia 2011). Sharples (2008) explains that apple festivals in the United States, of which there are many, frequently use the famous mythical figure Johnny Appleseed to brand, interpret and market the importance of apples in that country's horticultural heritage, creating their own USP. A critical mass of food festivals in a region can create 'festival-scapes' (Einarsen and Mykletun 2012) that will appeal to casual visitors and 'gourmet tourists' (Hall and Sharples 2003). An important part of destination branding is building a new image or enhancing an existing one. Food and drink festivals can enrich the image of a place and create widespread awareness of what it has to offer (Mason and Paggiaro 2009; Park et al. 2008). Festivals showcase quality and uniqueness in local foods (Lee and Arcodia 2011).

The fourth rationale for hosting culinary festivals is that they may be instruments for protecting cultural heritage. By providing economic ends and boosting a collective sense of nostalgia, gastronomical events can help residents and tourists appreciate and value edible local patrimony. This is discussed in detail later in the chapter.

The market for food festivals

Most food festival attendees are local residents and day-trippers from nearby areas (Çela et al. 2007; Hall and Sharples 2008b; McAndrews 2004). Rural events commonly attract urban dwellers who want to get away from the city to enjoy a countryside experience. Other participants include tourists (often foodies or Hall and Sharples's (2003) 'gourmet tourists') from faraway places who travel between festivals to partake of local specialties, staying in a region for extended periods of time and returning to food events multiple times (Chang 2014; Kim et al. 2009). Food lovers will often make a point of traveling for food encounters, "and events figure prominently in their desired experiences" (Getz and Robinson 2014: 328), although most food enthusiasts appreciate having a multisensory experience beyond just that of food. Many visitors stop by a festival unplanned on their way to another destination. All of these markets are important for the economic stimulation, agricultural support, branding and image enhancement and cultural preservation goals of culinary events.

Recent research on people's motives for attending food festivals has shed some interesting, albeit predictable, light on this element of demand (e.g. Çela et al. 2007; Chang and Yuan 2011; Xie 2004). In common with many other types of jubilee occasions, attendance at culinary events is motivated by a wide range of factors, including having fun, being outdoors, the reputation of the event and the variety of things to see and do, to socialize and to experience a change from one's ordinary routine (Chang and Yuan 2011). Gastronomy-specific reasons for attending a culinary fête typically include a desire to taste local food, including regional specialties that have developed a known reputation and become a 'must-try' attraction. Purchasing local foodstuffs, supporting local producers and sellers and having a chance to buy farm-fresh and organic foods are also vital motives. Importantly, there is an educational element that causes people to attend events to observe or learn about production processes, increase knowledge about food and regional food traditions, appreciate the cultural heritage context, and learn about recipes and cooking (Çela et al. 2007; Chang and Yuan 2011; Hall and Sharples 2008c; Mason and Paggiaro 2009; Xie 2004). Some culinary festivals incorporate cooking schools for children and cookery lessons for adults to satisfy visitors' interest in culinary learning (Einarsen and Mykletun 2012). There is also a significant nostalgic component, particularly for attendees who might have grown up on a farm or in a rural area but who now live in the city. Taking their children to the countryside, to farms and food events can help urbanites teach their children about rural living and their own personal heritage (Timothy and Ron 2009).

Food festivals as channels of heritage

There are probably as many different categories of food festivals as there are food festivals themselves. As already noted, Getz and Robinson (2014) described several types of gastronomic events in general, but of greatest concern in this chapter are their food competitions, indigenous food experiences and food festivals. Hall and Sharples (2003) identified five other types of culinary events based upon the product being celebrated and the scale of the event's appeal. They pinpointed generic events with no local product focus, generic events with a local product focus, multiple-themed categories, single categories of products and single specific products.

While acknowledging that every sort of food festival/event can be a purveyor of heritage principles, Figure 11.1 identifies seven different categories of food festival based specifically upon the notion of food as heritage. We recognize that these classifications are not mutually exclusive. The types of heritage food festivals of concern in the following section include indigenous, immigrant, harvest, iconic food, cooking competitions, special-purpose events and festivals where food is secondary to other heritage characteristics. These groupings represent a mix of both Udell and Wilson's (1978) commercialized indigenous festivals and Lewis's (1997) rationally constructed or intentionally planned food festivals.

Indigenous food fêtes are most common in immigrant societies, where there is significant cultural distance between the natives and the émigrés, and usually where the aboriginal population is now the minority. These culinary festivals highlight traditional foods, and many accentuate the differences between the food of the visited and the tastes of the visitors. The Poke Festival in Hawaii, for instance, celebrates traditional island foods and underscores the islands' dependence on the sea. Many of the dishes better suit the tastes of local Hawaiians than they do

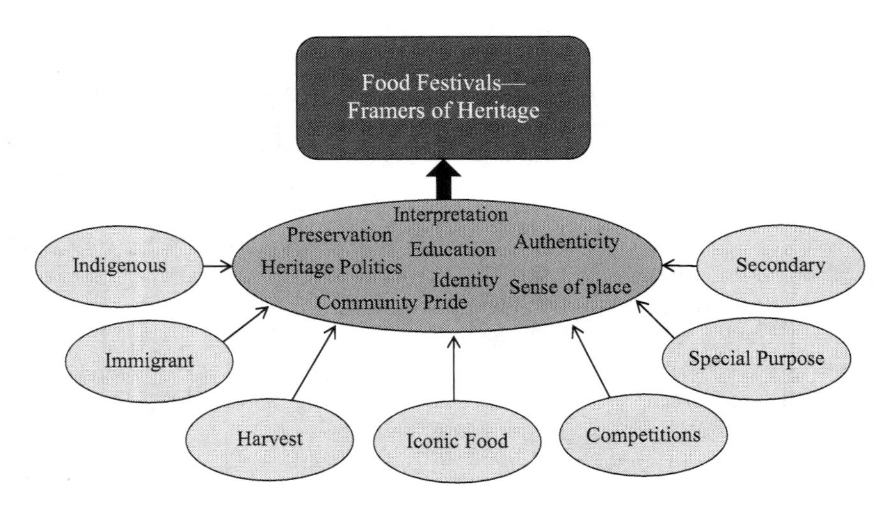

Figure 11.1 Food festival categories based on the notion of food as heritage

outsiders, so the primary aim of the festival has been to attract Hawaiians rather than non-resident tourists (McAndrews 2004). Gyimóthy and Mykletun (2009) similarly discuss local *smalahove* – traditional roasted sheep's head – which is celebrated in the Norwegian *Smalahovesleppet* Festival. It is 'scary' to outsiders but the fodder of pride for the natives of Voss, Norway.

There are many aboriginal food festivals on Native American lands and in Canadian First Nations. The Celebration of Basketry and Native Foods Symposium and Festival in Tucson, Arizona, encourages visitors to "taste foods that have sustained Native peoples for generations. Witness and taste traditional and innovative preparations of Native foods by top chefs and traditional Native cooks" (Arizona-Sonora Desert Museum 2015: n.p.). An Indigenous Food Festival was held on October 21–22, 2011, to observe the inauguration of Indigenous Food Day in Lawrence, Kansas, celebrated with food demonstrations, cooking contests and a community potluck feast. The objective of the festival was "to restore balance in our relationship with the earth and our communities by increasing awareness of food, environment and health. By honoring the traditional teachings of our indigenous relatives we restore respect for the blessings of food, soil, water, and air that we must have to ensure a healthy life for the next … generations" (Indian Country 2011: n.p.). Annual Māori kai festivals in New Zealand are prevalent and celebrate traditional and modern Māori food from the sea and from the land (McKerchar et al. in press). Food festivities are essential among the indigenes of Mexico, more so for the natives than for tourists. The annual indigenous Traditional Food Festival in Michoacán state attracts cooks and eaters from throughout the region who meet to share their ancestral recipes.

The second type of gastronomic festival commemorates the cuisines of diasporic or immigrant populations (Shortridge 2004). These ethnic food festivals are commonplace in settler societies and can focus on specific immigrant ethnic groups, refugee cultures or colonizers. These tend to highlight the foods and recipes brought from the motherland to the new country and appeal significantly to first- and second-generation immigrant residents, regional visitors and tourists from the homeland. In addition to satisfying the curiosity of outsiders, ethnic food festivals are fundamental for immigrant groups in maintaining their own connections to the homeland (Shukla 1997). Some visitors from the 'old world' attend these events to experience old-fashioned gastronomic delights that might be better preserved in the émigrés' new country than in the homeland (Shortridge 2004).

Many cities and small towns celebrate immigrant culinary cultures through festive celebrations (Hashimoto and Telfer 2006; McClinchey 2008; Rivera et al. 2008; Zeitler 2009). These focus largely on individual nationalities or ethnicities in areas and urban neighborhoods that are known to have high concentrations of diasporic populations. In most instances, ethnic cuisines and émigré foodways are the centerpieces of these events, with music, dance, language lessons, poetry, art and costumes being of secondary importance (Ioannides and Timothy 2010). Vendors, sampling stations and cooking competitions characterize many ethnic festivals in immigrant societies, and demonstrations of traditional foods and hunting and gathering techniques are regular parts of the festivities. For African-American descendants of slave immigrants, Juneteenth celebrations take place each year in the United States to celebrate the end of slavery and feature barbeques, which are often connected with slave cuisine and African-American fare (Donovan and de Bres 2006).

Many attendees at immigrant ethnic food festivals are interested in tasting another culture. This alimentary immersion can help them feel "Swiss or Swedish for a day" in the American Midwest (Shortridge 2004: 268). Immigrant celebrations are attractive because outsiders see them as authentic or nostalgic representations of juxtaposed cultures or romanticized concepts of the 'Other' (Chhabra et al. 2003; Laing and Frost 2013). In addition to the aliment itself, the music and clothing, eating utensils, menus and staging help create an 'authentic' ambience, whether real or perceived, for visitors. When attendees perceive an authentic experience, there is a higher likelihood they will return (Robinson and Clifford 2012) because this perceived 'genuine' gastronomic encounter brings them closer to the culture on display (Çela et al. 2007; Clarke 2014; Mason and Paggiaro 2009).

Harvest celebrations, the third type of culinary festival, are observed in almost all societies (Hashimoto and Telfer 2006; Tellstrom et al. 2005). Religious and spiritual beliefs and practices were historically an important part of these events, as in most traditional societies, harvest festivities were an opportunity to demonstrate gratitude to Mother Earth or the divine for the blessing of a bounteous yield (Sahu 2015). In addition to crop yields, harvest celebrations commemorate livestock and poultry products, gathering of wild foods and hunting and fishing (Janiskee 1980). Harvest jubilees are sometimes heavily influenced by immigrant and indigenous cultures as well, and they are determined by climatic conditions, physical geography and social practices (Hashimoto and Telfer 2008). As a result of the reality of geography, harvest festivals in most cases have seasonal characteristics. They usually take place as certain food items come into season. This reflects the natural cycle of sowing and harvesting on land and in the sea (Lyons 2008; Rotherham 2008), although as Lyons rightfully points out, given the expansion of neoliberal trade and globalized economies, foods can be sourced from all over the world. Today, therefore, even harvest festivals are no longer necessarily constrained by the availability of food in the festival locale.

The fourth type of food festival focuses on local specialty produce or iconic foodstuffs. The celebrated commodity is normally raised, gathered or processed in the community that hosts the celebration or is otherwise connected in some way. These communities tend to select the products that clearly identify with their locale and have a high novelty value (Janiskee 1980: 98). Specialty-item festivities are extremely common in the US Midwest and are growing in popularity in Canada, Australia, New Zealand, Japan and Western Europe. The Gilroy Garlic Festival (California) is an oft-cited example, as are product-specific events such as the Dairy Parade, Peach Days, Strawberry Days, Turkey Testicle Festival, Sauerkraut Days, Annual Honey Fest, Chocolatefest, Watermelon Days, the Great Wisconsin Cheese Festival, the Central Maine Egg Festival and the North Ridgeville Corn Festival. Of this type, and in the setting of the Stockton Asparagus

Festival (California), Lewis (1997: 76) argues that these events are some of the most 'invented'. They are "economically important for the community, but are not, really, culturally significant in any indigenous sense. The festival does not resurrect age-old traditions . . . nor of any sub-cultural groups. . . . It celebrates asparagus because the vegetable is grown in the area".

Relatedly, festivals based on iconic food items occur when a place is world renowned for a specific cuisine or food product. Chocolatefest in Hershey, Pennsylvania, home of one of America's oldest and most revered chocolate producers, the yearly Pierogi Festival in Krakow, Poland (Figure 11.2), the Paprika Days Festival in Hungary (Smith and Jusztin 2014) and the Pure Grenada Nutmeg Spice Festival – Grenada being the most recognizable source of the world's nutmeg supply – (Thomas-Francois and Francois 2014) are prominent examples of iconic food festivals.

Food-related competitions are the fifth type of culinary festival that displays elements of cultural heritage. They are closely related to the iconic food examples in the fourth category but are different in that their main purpose is to promote contests for supremacy and trophies in the culinary world. Foods are prepared by various contestants and judged by a panel of adjudicators. Chili cook-offs, many of which are organized by the International Chili Society, are the most popular of these in the United States. Many competitive galas center on seafood and barbeques, such as various ribfests throughout North America (Steinbacher 2007).

Figure 11.2 Advertisement for the annual Pierogi Festival in Krakow, Poland (Photo: Dallen J. Timothy)

The International Soup Festival in Krakow, Poland, features chefs from all over Europe vying to be the 'King of Soups'. Fishing and hunting contests are celebrated in many Native American nations. Although much of its roots derive from North America, the competitive fête is becoming more fashionable in Europe and the United Kingdom, prompting the production of competitive cooking television shows in Great Britain, the United States and parts of Asia.

Sixth, special purpose food festivals have developed in recent years in response to organizations' or communities' desires to spread a certain message or to set an agenda (Frost and Laing 2013; Laing and Frost 2010). Organic and sustainable food events have grown in number and intensity in recent years with the point of encouraging the growth and consumption of local, GMO-free and heirloom produce. Vegetarian and vegan fiestas promote animal rights and the healthful qualities of eating plant-based diets. Slow food festivals are gaining traction all over the world, as the Slow Food Movement is embraced by more practitioners, members and related organizations (Frost and Laing 2013; Hall and Sharples 2008c; Laing and Frost 2010) in an effort to quell the proliferation of unhealthy fast food and non-local products. Other special-purpose food festivals are also used by international tourism destinations, such as Barbados's Food & Wine and Rum Festival, which is hosted in the island nation every November. The Food & Wine and Rum Festival was strategically developed "to maintain its [Barbados's] ownership of the food niche in the [Caribbean] region" (Vicky Chandler, personal communication, June 3, 2015) and was created through an alliance between the Barbados Tourism Authority (now the Barbados Tourism and Marketing Inc.) and the epicurean magazine *Food & Wine* in 2009. The festival is viewed as being the finial iteration of Barbados's exploration of its food and cuisine product, which commenced in the 1980s.

Finally, non-food food festivals are events whose primary raison d'être is not directly food oriented, but where comestibles play a strong equal or secondary role in the celebration. There are dozens of Aboriginal Australian cultural festivals each year that focus primarily on art and music, but indigenous bush tucker also features prominently as an essential part of the culture on display. Hannam and Halewood (2006) examine the characteristics of various Viking festivals that provide 'authentic' Viking atmospheres where performances, music, theater, lectures, exhibitions, handicrafts and shipbuilding feature, alongside Viking aliment. They declare that at one event, "all food must be served on typical Viking plates. No modern packages of any kind and no beer cans. The foods should be cooked with typical Viking tools and if possible use typical Viking food" (Hannam and Halewood 2006: 28). Food plays a prominent role at most dance festivals, jazz festivals, other musical events and cultural celebrations (Way and Robertson 2013; Zeitler 2009), not only to nourish visitors and performers but to connect the people, place and music to the cultural heritage of the place.

All of these festival types have the potential to magnify the characteristics and principles of cultural heritage (see Figure 11.1): authenticity, protection/preservation, interpretation, education, political manipulation, identity, community pride, sense of place and others. The contemporary concept of authenticity has been well debated in the heritage studies literature. Several different kinds of authenticity have been identified (c.f. Chhabra et al. 2003), but for our purposes, objective and subjective authenticity are the most critical, with some observers suggesting that the authenticity of places, events and objects can be documented and verified objectively. Others argue that authenticity is in the eye of the beholder and therefore subjective (Timothy 2011). The majority of food festivals contain elements of both authenticities, but even the most purposively developed, or invented, festival traditions can, through time, like many other forms of 'invented pasts', become the celebratory heritage of an area and through an authentication process become a genuine part of the marketable patrimony (Timothy and Boyd 2003). In the words of Lewis (1997: 76–77), even contrived events such as iconic food fêtes, competitions and special-purpose events can "become, over time, accepted as authentic both by outsiders, who come to enjoy the good times and by the community members who participate in them", particularly in communities that traditionally have had little sense of their own historic identity.

While many culinary celebrations try to be as authentic as possible, most food festivals, like many other planned events, care little about the objective reality of what they are providing. Instead, they exaggerate the 'otherness' of jovial times and places; they provide outlets for carnivalesque and silly behavior that attendees would rarely exhibit in the confines of their home places. Food fêtes accentuate the bizarre elements of local traditions and attendees' behavior, and they provide a channel for the extraordinary or abnormal to become ordinary or normal (Lewis 1997). They also have a tendency to "exoticize the familiar" and "present the mundane as celebratory" (Long 2004: 37–38). Festivalgoers can "gobble gobble" some "hot nuts" at a turkey testicle festival and "have a ball" at other testicle festivals in the United States and Europe. Eating garlic ice cream at the Gilroy Garlic Festival, partaking of "road kill chili" or "wearing silly asparagus caps or getting drunk and eating chocolate-dipped asparagus spears becomes, in the festival context, 'normal' behavior" (Lewis 1997: 75) and perhaps 'authentic behavior' for some.

As explained previously, food festivities are also a tool for preserving the cultural heritage of a place or a people (Hashimoto and Telfer 2008). This is particularly important for immigrant cohorts as they struggle to maintain a dual identity in their adopted country and in rural areas where certain gastronomic traditions may be declining. Culinary events can help locals embrace their own alimentary heritage and appreciate the urgency of preserving what could be lost through acculturation. In food events, reenactments of traditional fishing and farming methods help keep heritage alive (Valadares Teixeira and Ribeiro 2013). Likewise, city-based food festivals can be a justification for urban regeneration and heritage preservation (Hollows et al. 2014; Kim 2015; McClinchey 2008). They may provide a financial justification for investing in gentrification projects, cleaning and greening programs and protecting historic urban landscapes that will provide scenic backdrops to these occasions. Food events can also help preserve and protect food cultures (Çela et al. 2007; Hede 2008), some of which, including immigrant cuisine, may be on the verge of disappearing or being permanently altered by the dominant gustatory culture that surrounds them (Avieli 2005). As well, festivals help reinforce an 'imagined community', or collective identity, among immigrant groups (Laing and Frost 2013; Shukla 1997). Involvement in local festivals, particularly as volunteers, can help youth understand and appreciate their roots and intergenerational traditions (Kim 2015).

Interpretation helps festival managers and community members tell their story and explain why their culinary heritage is important for them and for others. In the festival setting, this is often done by costumed actors, signage, lectures, brochures and websites, poetry, music and reenactments, although the food itself is considered the best educator of all as it tells stories of taming nature, settling in a new land or living under colonial repression. These stories are figuratively and literally told through the flavors, smells and appearances of the food, some of the most salient manifestations of intangible culture (Chang and Yuan 2012; Timothy 2014). The preeminent goal of interpretation is education. Interpretive programs at gastronomic celebrations can provide considerable edification for visitors and volunteers. In some instances, research is a crucial component of authentic events. Many festivals, such as the Viking festivals noted earlier, require extensive research to discover how and what people ate centuries ago. In this regard, there is a clear educative element to consuming heritage cuisines.

All heritage has deep political undertones. Decisions have to be made regarding which heritage of many will be preserved, sold and interpreted, and this is inherently a political process (Timothy 2011). In multi-ethnic societies, citizen groups may contend or compete over times, spaces and priorities in promoting culinary events. In a climate of 'competitive cultural pluralism' and competing social hierarchies, dissonance may occur as one group contends its comestible heritage is more important than that of another. Ruling elites can even determine, through food events and gastronomic ritualization, iconic national cuisines through politicized processes of exclusion and inclusion (Chen 2011). Even relatively homogenous communities must decide what product(s) they should commemorate. What food item best showcases local gastronomy? What is our most important agricultural product? Do we really want to allow outsiders to see this part of our heritage? These are questions every community must navigate as it turns existing events into visitor spectacles or when it makes decisions to plan an event from scratch. These situations can aggravate or alleviate intrinsic tensions between different stakeholders (Blichfeldt and Halkier 2014).

Food events can also be exploited for political ends, such as the Singapore Tourism Board's efforts to encourage all Singaporeans to be proud of their edible cultures and to be proactive ambassadors for the country's diverse cuisines through the annual Singapore Food Festival (Brien 2014) (Figure 11.3). Underlying tensions in multi-ethnic Singapore may be alleviated in part at least through this festival, which aims to build cohesion and a sense of nationalism. Similarly, Lewis (1997: 73) reasoned that maltreatment of Native Americans through America's early history might be "masked somewhat by celebrations of difference in the relatively neutral area of food preferences". In like manner, this configuration of 'societal amnesia' (Timothy and Boyd 2003) allows food festivals to mask many realities of life in the homeland, which numerous people sought to escape by emigrating (e.g. war, famine, oppression or violence). This festivalization process glosses over the deleterious realities of life in the primordial homeland, as culinary celebrations underscore immigrants' 'idyllic', if unrealistic, congenial memories of home (Shukla 1997). The Holiday of Holidays is a festival that brings together the three main religions of the Holy Land – Judaism, Islam and Christianity – in Haifa. It focuses on universal cultural elements such as food and art in an effort to disengage from the conflicts in the region and create amity among hostile parties through a food event (Sharaby 2010).

Events that memorialize successful harvests and iconic food items can both be key in promoting the nostalgic element of agricultural heritage. As noted previously, day trips to the countryside can help urbanites feel like 'farmers for a day' and experience romanticized nostalgia for more innocent times and places (Timothy and Ron 2009). Rural food festivals connect urban areas and city dwellers with their rural hinterlands.

Gastronomic events and food festivals play powerful roles in community development far beyond their economic impacts. Perhaps the most obvious of these is that they help enhance community cohesion and pride (Avieli 2005; Çela et al. 2007; Hall and Sharples 2008b; Hashimoto and Telfer 2008; Hjalager and Corigliano 2000; Lewis 1997). By exposing outsiders to local food traditions, festivals help raise awareness of traditional food products, local food culture(s),

Figure 11.3 Promoting Singapore's food festival in the Little India area (Photo: Dallen J. Timothy)

tastes and innovation (Amilien et al. 2005). In sharing their edible patrimony, and seeing visitors' interest in what they do well, residents appreciate and take pride in their own heritage (Timothy 2015). This promotes solidarity, collaboration and a stronger sense of place, which reinforces place-specific uniqueness (Haven-Tang and Jones 2005; Hede 2008). This fosters local support for heritage foods and facilitates communities in building solidarity and pride in their comestible heritage (Timothy 2015; Valadares Teixeira and Ribeiro 2013). Profiling local food producers via culinary events draws attention to their importance in the community and connects them to the area's broader socio-economic development (usually through tourism) beyond their day-to-day agricultural operations.

Conclusion

The elements of both supply and demand in this context reflect heritage narratives. However, the challenge of this chapter, and indeed the challenge all of the other constituent chapters of this book has been, and will be, to convince readers of the importance of food and cuisine as a manifestation of human heritage. In doing so, several critical issues and concepts that relate to food as heritage must be addressed. At the top of this list are the several categories of food festivals identified in this chapter, including indigenous, immigrant, harvest, iconic foods, culinary competitions, special-purpose food events and secondary events such as carnivals and music festivals where, though food is not the core focus, it supports the primary element of the event. As mentioned earlier, all of these categories share overlaps and commonalities but none more important to this book than the fact that they are all channels of heritage through food and foodways.

Also presented is the argument that all of the categories of food and cuisine festivals outlined respond to the agendas of their respective organizers, be they indigenous groups attempting to preserve or revive foodways and their attendant traditions which are in danger of disappearing or have vanished completely, regions attempting to promote the food or food products which can be most identified with that particular place or a government seeking to create an event to fill a trough in a calendar year as it relates to tourist arrivals. All of these channel heritage and, more specifically, culinary heritage. Interconnected to this idea is that not only are agendas met, but so are demands by those who patronize food festivals.

As with all heritage discourses, notions of authenticity are paramount to defining the heritage being discussed. This is clearly also true of cuisine and food festivals and the food heritages they promote. The pursuit of authenticity is also the pursuit of the objective and of the subjective. We have seen how both Native American food celebrations, as well as some festivals where food plays a secondary role, such as certain Viking heritage events, are particularly interested in presenting food traditions as authentically as possible. Perhaps the most important example in the gambit of food festivals that is most heavily critiqued in terms of authenticity are special-purpose food events, such as the Food & Wine and Rum Festival in Barbados. Some might argue that festivals of this sort are not authentic; instead, they are essentially faking it. However, the counter school of thought is that given time these staged festivals will become authentic events to their loyal patrons who eagerly anticipate them.

Perhaps one of the most critical views presented in the evaluation of cuisine as heritage is the idea that food celebrations are the finest examples of heritage interpretation. In this chapter the idea of food being used to interpret human experiences and values is argued as being important to the community hosting the festival and the message received by those who visit. Indeed in many cases interpretation can become a politicized matter, ranging from culturally important questions (particularly for indigenous and immigrant groups) such as what heritages are shared and not shared, to the macro political level such as the Singapore Tourist Board which, through food, promotes that nation's ethnic diversity.

Finally to researchers and other observers, the power of food and cuisine festivals in promoting solidarity and group identity, and ultimately a greater sense of place, is paramount to many, if not everyone associated with gastronomic festivals. Of final import is the often, yet not readily seen, multiple partnerships that food festivals can create. These range from the chefs cooking at serving stations right through to the local farmers who are actually growing and harvesting the produce consumed by eager patrons, thereby highlighting the many socio-economic linkages that food as heritage as presented in food festivals achieves.

References

Amilien, V., Torjusen, H. and Vittersø, G. (2005) From local food to terroir product? Some views about Tjukkmjølk, the traditional thick sour milk from Røros, Norway. *Anthropology of Food*, 4: n.p. (online). Available at: https://aof.revues.org/211

Arizona-Sonora Desert Museum (2015) Celebration of basketry and native foods symposium and festival. Available online at http://www.desertmuseum.org/visit/basketry.php Accessed June 10, 2015.

Avieli, N. (2005) Roasted pigs and bao dumplings: festive food and imagined transnational identity in Chinese-Vietnamese festivals. *Asia Pacific Viewpoint*, 46(3): 281–293.

Blichfeldt, B.S. and Halkier, H. (2014) Mussels, tourism and community development: a case study of place branding through food festivals in rural North Jutland, Denmark. *European Planning Studies*, 22(8): 1587–1603.

Brien, D.L. (2014) A Taste of Singapore: Singapore food writing and culinary tourism. *M/C Journal*, 17(1): n.p. (online). Available at: http://journal.media-culture.org.au/index.php/mcjournal/article/viewArticle/767

Çela, A., Knowles-Lankford, J. and Lankford, S. (2007) Local food festivals in northeast Iowa communities: a visitor and economic impact study. *Managing Leisure*, 12(2/3): 171–186.

Chang, S. (2014) The spillover effects of wine and harvest festivals on other festivals. *Tourism Analysis*, 19(6): 689–699.

Chang, W. and Yuan, J. (2011) A taste of tourism: visitors' motivations to attend a food festival. *Event Management*, 15(1): 13–23.

Chen, Y. (2011) Ethnic politics in the framing of national cuisine: state banquets and the proliferation of ethnic cuisine in Taiwan. *Food, Culture and Society*, 14(3): 315–333.

Chhabra, D., Healy, R. and Sills, E. (2003) Staged authenticity and heritage tourism. *Annals of Tourism Research*, 31: 702–719.

Clarke, A. (2014) Culture and authenticity in food and wine events. In A. Cavicchi and C. Santini (eds) *Food and Wine Events in Europe: A Stakeholder Approach*, pp. 45–57. London: Routledge.

de la Barre, S. and Brouder, P. (2013) Consuming stories: placing food in the Arctic tourism experience. *Journal of Heritage Tourism*, 8(2/3): 213–223.

Donovan, A. and de Bres, K. (2006) Foods of freedom: Juneteenth as a culinary tourist attraction. *Tourism Review International*, 9(4): 379–389.

Einarsen, K. and Mykletun, R.J. (2012) Exploring the success of the Gladmatfestival (The Stavanger Food Festival). In T.D. Andersson, D. Getz and R.J. Mykletun (eds) *Festival and Event Management in Nordic Countries*, pp. 203–226. London: Routledge.

Frost, W. and Laing, J. (2013) Communicating persuasive messages through slow food festivals. *Journal of Vacation Marketing*, 19(1): 67–74.

Getz, D. (2005) *Event Management & Event Tourism*. New York: Cognizant.

Getz, D. and Robinson, R.N.S. (2014) Foodies and food events. *Scandinavian Journal of Hospitality and Tourism*, 14(3): 315–330.

Gyimóthy, S. and Mykletun, J. (2009) Scary food: commodifying culinary heritage as meal adventures in tourism. *Journal of Vacation Marketing*, 15(3): 259–273.

Hall, C.M. and Sharples, L. (2003) The consumption of experiences or the experience of consumption? An introduction to the tourism of taste. In C.M. Hall, L. Sharples, R. Mitchell, B. Cambourne and N. Macionis (eds) *Food Tourism around the World: Development, Management and Markets*, pp. 1–24. Oxford: Butterworth Heinemann.

Hall, C.M. and Sharples, L. (2008a) Food events and the local food system: marketing, management and planning issues. In C.M. Hall and L. Sharples (eds) *Food and Wine Festivals and Events around the World: Development, Management and Markets*, pp. 23–46. Oxford: Butterworth Heinemann.

Hall, C.M. and Sharples, L. (2008b) Food events, festivals and farmers' markets: an introduction. In C.M. Hall and L. Sharples (eds) *Food and Wine Festivals and Events around the World: Development, Management and Markets*, pp. 3–22. Oxford: Butterworth Heinemann.

Hall, C.M. and Sharples, L. (2008c) Future issues and trends: food events, festivals and farmers' markets. In C.M. Hall and L. Sharples (eds) *Food and Wine Festivals and Events around the World: Development, Management and Markets*, pp. 330–348. Oxford: Butterworth Heinemann.

Hannam, K. and Halewood, C. (2006) European Viking themed festivals: an expression of identity. *Journal of Heritage Tourism*, 1(1): 17–31.

Hashimoto, A. and Telfer, D.J. (2006) Selling Canadian culinary tourism: branding the global and the regional product. *Tourism Geographies*, 8(1): 31–55.

Hashimoto, A. and Telfer, D.J. (2008) From saké to sea urchin: food and drink festivals and regional identity in Japan. In C.M. Hall and L. Sharples (eds) *Food and Wine Festivals and Events around the World: Development, Management and Markets*, pp. 249–278. Oxford: Butterworth Heinemann.

Haven-Tang, C. and Jones, E. (2005) Using local food and drink to differentiate tourism destinations through a sense of place: a story from Wales – dining at Monmouthshire's Great Table. *Journal of Culinary Science & Technology*, 4(4): 69–86.

Hede, A. (2008) Food and wine festivals: stakeholders, long-term outcomes and strategies for success. In C.M. Hall and L. Sharples (eds) *Food and Wine Festivals and Events around the World: Development, Management and Markets*, pp. 85–100. Oxford: Butterworth Heinemann.

Hjalager, A.M. and Corigliano, M.A. (2000) Food for tourists – determinants of an image. *International Journal of Tourism Research*, 2(4): 281–293.

Hollows, J., Jones, S., Taylor, B. and Dowthwaite, K. (2014) Making sense of urban food festivals: cultural regeneration, disorder and hospitable cities. *Journal of Policy Research in Tourism, Leisure and Events*, 6(1): 1–14.

Indian Country (2011) Haskell Indigenous Food Festival. Available online at http://indiancountrytodaymedianetwork.com/2011/10/19/indigenous-food-day-kansas-59067 Accessed June 3, 2015.

Ioannides, D. and Timothy, D.J. (2010) *Tourism in the USA: A Spatial and Social Synthesis*. London: Routledge.

Janiskee, B. (1980) South Carolina's harvest festivals: rural delights for day tripping urbanites. *Journal of Cultural Geography*, 1(1): 96–104.

Kalkstein-Silkes, C., Cai, L.A. and Lehto, X.Y. (2008) Conceptualizing festival-based culinary tourism in rural destinations. In C.M. Hall and L. Sharples (eds) *Food and Wine Festivals and Events around the World: Development, Management and Markets*, pp. 65–77. Oxford: Butterworth Heinemann.

Kim, S. (2015) Understanding the historical and geographical contexts of food festival tourism development: the case of the Tatebayashi Noodle Grant Prix in Japan. *Tourism Planning & Development*, 12(4): 433–446.

Kim, Y., Kim, M., Goh, B. and Antun, J. (2009) A comparison between first-timers and repeaters at a food event. *Journal of Culinary Science & Technology*, 7(4): 239–249.

Laing, J. and Frost, W. (2010) How green was my festival: exploring challenges and opportunities associated with staging green events. *International Journal of Hospitality Management*, 29(2): 261–267.

Laing, J. and Frost, W. (2013) Food, wine … heritage identity? Two case studies of Italian diaspora festivals in regional Victoria. *Tourism Analysis*, 18(3): 323–334.

Lee, I. and Arcodia, C. (2011) The role of regional food festivals for destination branding. *International Journal of Tourism Research*, 13(4): 355–367.

Lewis, G.H. (1997) Celebrating asparagus: community and the rationally constructed food festival. *Journal of American Culture*, 20(4): 73–78.

Long, L.M. (2004) Culinary tourism: a folkloristic perspective on eating and otherness. In L.M. Long (ed) *Culinary Tourism*, pp. 20–50. Lexington: University Press of Kentucky.

Lyons, H. (2008) Food festival research methods and approaches. In C.M. Hall and L. Sharples (eds) *Food and Wine Festivals and Events around the World: Development, Management and Markets*, pp. 311–330. Oxford: Butterworth Heinemann.

Mason, M.C. and Paggiaro, A. (2009) Celebrating local products: the role of food events. *Journal of Foodservice Business and Research*, 12(4): 364–383.

McAndrews, K. (2004) Incorporating the local tourist at the Big Island Poke Festival. In L.M. Long (ed) *Culinary Tourism*, pp. 114–127. Lexington: University Press of Kentucky.

McClinchey, K.A. (2008) Urban ethnic festivals, neighborhoods, and the multiple realities of marketing place. *Journal of Travel and Tourism Marketing*, 25(3/4): 251–264.

McKerchar, C., Bowers, S., Heta, C., Signal, L. and Matoe, L. (in press) Enhancing Māori food security using traditional kai. *Global Health Promotion*.

Muhammad, R., Zahari, M.S.M., Othman, Z., Jamaluddin, M.R. and Rashdi, M.O. (2009) Modernization and ethnic festival food. In *Proceedings of the International Conference of Business and Economics*, pp. 1–14. Kuching, Malaysia.

Park, K., Reisinger, Y. and Kang, H. (2008) Visitors' motivation for attending the South Beach Wine and Food Festival, Miami Beach, Florida. *Journal of Travel and Tourism Marketing*, 25: 161–181.

Ritzer, G. and Liska, A. (1997) 'McDisneyization' and 'post-tourism': complementary perspectives in contemporary tourism. In C. Rojek and J. Urry (eds) *Touring Cultures: Transformations of Travel and Theory*, pp. 96–109. London: Routledge.

Rivera, M.A., Hara, T. and Kock, G. (2008) Economic impact of cultural events: the case of the Zora! Festival. *Journal of Heritage Tourism*, 3(2): 121–137.

Robinson, R.N.S. and Clifford, C. (2012) Authenticity and festival foodservice experiences. *Annals of Tourism Research*, 39(2): 571–600.

Rotherham, I.D. (2008) From haggis to high table: a selective history of festival and feast as mirrors of British landscape and culture. In C.M. Hall and L. Sharples (eds) *Food and Wine Festivals and Events around the World: Development, Management and Markets*, pp. 47–61. Oxford: Butterworth Heinemann.

Sahu, C.K. (2015) Makar Festival of Mayurbhanj at a glance. *International Journal of Research in Social Sciences*, 5(1): 163–172.

Sharaby, R. (2010) Bridge over the Wadi: a festival of coexistence in Israel. *Middle Eastern Studies*, 46(1): 117–130.

Sharples, L. (2008) Apples, cider and celebration. In C.M. Hall and L. Sharples (eds) *Food and Wine Festivals and Events around the World: Development, Management and Markets*, pp. 133–145. Oxford: Butterworth Heinemann.

Sharples, L. and Lyons, H. (2008) Ludlow Marches Food and Drink Festival. In C.M. Hall and L. Sharples (eds) *Food and Wine Festivals and Events around the World: Development, Management and Markets*, pp. 101–112. Oxford: Butterworth Heinemann.

Shortridge, B.G. (2004) Ethnic heritage food in Lindsborg, Kansas, and New Glarus, Wisconsin. In L.M. Long (ed) *Culinary Tourism*, pp. 268–296. Lexington: University Press of Kentucky.

Shukla, S. (1997) Building diaspora and the nation: the 1991 'Cultural Festival of India'. *Cultural Studies*, 11(2): 296–315.

Smith, M.K. and Jusztin, M. (2014) Paprika: the spice of life in Hungary. In L. Jolliffe (ed) *Spices and Tourism: Destinations, Attractions and Cuisines*, pp. 53–71. Bristol: Channel View Publications.

Steinbacher, J. (2007) *Food Fest! Your Complete Guide to Florida's Food Festivals*. Seminole, FL: Bee Cliff Press.

Tellstrom, R., Gustafsson, I.B. and Mossberg, L. (2005) Local food cultures in the Swedish rural economy. *Sociologia Ruralis*, 45(4): 346–359.

Thomas-Francois, K. and Francois, A. (2014) Spices and agro-tourism on Grenada, Isle of Spice in the Caribbean. In L. Jolliffe (ed) *Spices and Tourism: Destinations, Attractions and Cuisines*, pp. 17–32. Bristol: Channel View Publications.

Timothy, D.J. (2007) Let them eat Moussaka: cuisine and foodways as cultural heritage. Invited keynote address at the Philoxenia International Symposium on Gastronomy and Wine Tourism, Thessaloniki, Greece, November 1–4.

Timothy, D.J. (2011) *Cultural Heritage and Tourism: An Introduction*. Bristol: Channel View Publications.

Timothy, D.J. (2014) Views of the vernacular: tourism and heritage of the ordinary. In J. Kaminski, A. Benson and D. Arnold (eds) *Contemporary Issues in Cultural Heritage Tourism*, pp. 32–44. London: Routledge.

Timothy, D.J. (2015) Cultural heritage, tourism and socio-economic development. In R. Sharpley and D.J. Telfer (eds) *Tourism and Development: Concepts and Issues*, 2nd Edn, pp. 237–249. Bristol: Channel View Publications.

Timothy, D.J. and Boyd, S.W. (2003) *Heritage Tourism*. Harlow: Prentice Hall.

Timothy, D.J. and Ron, A. (2009) Farmers for a day: agricultural heritage and nostalgia in rural Israel. Paper presented at the annual conference of the Association of American Geographers, Las Vegas, Nevada, March 26.

Timothy, D.J. and Ron, A.S. (2013) Heritage cuisines, regional identity and sustainable tourism. In C.M. Hall and S. Gössling (eds) *Sustainable Culinary Systems: Local Foods, Innovation, Tourism and Hospitality*, pp. 275–290. London: Routledge.

Udell, L. and Wilson, J. (1978) *Presenting Folk Culture*. Washington, DC: National Council for the Traditional Arts.

Valadares Teixeira, V.A. and Ribeiro, N.F. (2013) The lamprey and the partridge: a multi-sited ethnography of food tourism as an agent of preservation and disfigurement in central Portugal. *Journal of Heritage Tourism*, 8(2/3): 193–212.

Wargenau, A. and Che, D. (2006) Wine tourism development and marketing strategies in southwest Michigan. *International Journal of Wine Marketing*, 18(1): 45–60.

Way, K.A. and Robertson, L.J. (2013) Shopping and tourism patterns of attendees of the Bikes, Blues & BBQ Festival. *Journal of Hospitality Marketing & Management*, 22(1): 116–133.

Xie, P.F. (2004) Visitors' perceptions of authenticity at a rural heritage festival: a case study. *Event Management*, 8(3): 151–160.

Zeitler, E. (2009) Creating America's 'Czech Capital': ethnic identity and heritage tourism in Wilber, Nebraska. *Journal of Heritage Tourism*, 4(1): 73–85.

12 Reflections on slow food

From 'movement' to an emergent research field

Stephen W. Boyd

Introduction

Food is a basic physiological requirement to sustain life; it was one of Maslow's lowest-order needs. The manner in which food has been consumed throughout history has been shaped by wider societal traditions, customs and fashions, and it would not be overgeneralising to say that it was reflective of a shared experience of enjoying meals with family members, friends and relatives. Since industrialisation, the quicker pace of postmodern societies has witnessed a shift toward faster food production and consumption, the increased importance of fast foods in western societies and increasingly so in developing societies and, for some people, a key part of their overall eating practices. Quicker cooking processes and the acceptance of homogenised foodstuffs that lack flavour, taste and quality are perhaps symptomatic of the increased pace at which people live their lives today wherein the basic tasks of food preparation and cooking time are not as easily accommodated (Petrini 2001, 2007).

Reversing this pace and advocating a slower lifestyle was at the heart of the slow movement, in particular the focus on slow food. The purpose of this chapter is to examine slow food, examining how the idea of slow food transformed into a movement with a distinct philosophy of food and food production. Attention is given to the structure of the Slow Food Movement and the distinct strategies adopted to connect plate, planet, people and culture. The movement is often held up by scholars as an exemplar of slow consumption and the wider concept of slow thinking, but it would be remiss at the start of this chapter not to acknowledge that the slow movement over time developed into a subculture that includes Cittaslow (Slow cities), slow tourism, slow fashion, slow parenting and slow technology, to reflect a few of the more prominent areas. The discussion of the scholarly research on slow food reflects the diversity that comes with thinking slow. This examination of slow food commences with the genesis of slow food and the development of a distinct movement connected to it.

A history of a movement

Like all revolutionary ideas, slow food started from the reaction of one individual to a singular event that would evolve into a distinct global movement. That person was Carlo Petrini. The event was the 1986 opening of a McDonald's fast-food chain restaurant in Piazza di Spagna, near the Spanish Steps in Rome. This crusade became known as the Slow Food Movement, out of which would evolve a much broader movement known as the 'Slow Movement', eventually embracing many facets of peoples' lives beyond food (Jones et al. 2003; Leitch 2003; Miele 2006; Petrini 2001).

A strong political activist and member of the communist Partito di Unita Proletaria, Petrini came to prominence in food circles first in the late 1970s for his culinary articles in a number of communist papers (e.g. *il manifesto* and *l'unita*), and as one of the leading founding members of *Arcigola*, the Italian nonprofit food and wine association established in 1983. Following resistance to the opening of the McDonald's branch, Petrini, along with a group of other Italian activists, started the idea of slow food with the initial aim of defending regional traditions, good food and gastronomic pleasures, alongside promoting a slower pace of living (Slow Food 2015). By 1989, this idea had evolved into an international movement that was launched in Paris with the signing of the 'Slow Food Manifesto'. The manifesto had strong communist undertones, critical of modern advances starting from the industrialisation era to the present trends in globalisation that have ushered in 'fast food'. The movement adopted the snail as both its patron and symbol, recognising it as 'an idea and a way of life that needs much sure but steady support'. The snail was chosen as the symbol for slow food as it moves slowly, calmly eating its way through life; it is also a culinary specialty around the northern Italian town of Bra where the Slow Food Movement was born.

The movement's manifesto railed against a fast-paced lifestyle, stating that this factures customs. The faction's starting point was in the kitchen with food that would 'let us rediscover the rich varieties and aromas of local cuisines', and be the alternative, the avant-garde's riposte to the 'fast life' which had "changed our lifestyle and now threatens our environment and our land and cityscapes" (Slow Food 2015: n.p.).

From its early beginnings when only 15 countries were signatories to the founding manifesto, the Slow Food Movement has grown over the past quarter century into a global grassroots organisation of more than one million supporters and 100,000 members across 150 countries who aim to link the pleasures of good food with a commitment to their community and its environment (Slow Food 2015). The Slow Food Movement campaigns to prevent the disappearance of local food cultures and traditions, aims to counteract the rise of fast lifestyles and combats people's lack of interest in the food they consume (Jones et al. 2003; Miele 2006; Miele and Murdoch 2002; Pilcher 2006; Timothy and Teye 2009). It promotes locally grown food and challenges increased food miles and carbon footprints created through ever-increasing networks linking production with consumption. Food is viewed as being tied to other aspects of life, including culture, agriculture, the environment, politics and political culture. On its website, the Slow Food Foundation states "through our food choices we can collectively influence how food is cultivated, produced and distributed, and as a result bring about great change" (Slow Food Foundation 2015: n.p.). The change being advocated is a political one directed against the globalisation of agricultural products, with the goal of sustainable foods, the promotion of local small food-related businesses (Figure 12.1), and making the connection between food enjoyment and the need to be responsible, act sustainably and behave in harmony with nature (Pietrykowski 2004).

The slow food ethos from its outset was based on a philosophy of food and food production defined by three interrelated principles or tenets of *good, clean* and *fair*:

- Good: fresh and flavoursome seasonal diet that satisfies the senses and is part of our local culture, as well as being natural, both in terms of choice of raw materials and production methods used;
- Clean: respect for the environment, including sustainable farming practices, animal husbandry and an agro-industrial production chain (processing, marketing and consumption) that protects ecosystems and maintains biodiversity, and;
- Fair: accessible prices for consumers and fair conditions and pay for small-scale producers.

All three tenets are interconnected prerequisites for the Slow Food Movement, which envisages them achieving three objectives: a pledge for a better future, an act of civilisation and a tool to improve the current food system (Slow Food 2015).

Figure 12.1 River Cottage Canteen and Deli in Devon, England, is closely linked to the Slow Food Movement, focusing on seasonal, local, organic and wild (Photo: C. Michael Hall)

The movement has evolved at international, national and local levels. Slow Food International is headquartered in Bra, Italy, the town where the movement had its genesis. The association is coordinated by an international council and steered by an executive committee of which Carlo Petrini is the president. The association's role is to plan and promote the development of the global network and its projects worldwide. At a national level, more than 150 countries have established their own organisational structure to coordinate slow food activities within their respective countries, support local activities and organise events. While they have decisional autonomy, they are required to follow the political guidelines as set forth by Slow Food International. At the local level, members form groups known as convivium/convivia (local chapter(s)) which are responsible for coordinating activities and organising events that can range from putting on simple dinners and tastings and visits to local producers and farms to more complex events such as convening conferences or running educational programmes for the local community. At the time of writing there are more than 1,500 conviva worldwide; more than 350 exist in Italy alone. In sum, slow food operates through a decentralised structure to promote good, clean and fair local food.

To plot the evolution of slow food as a movement over the past three decades, it is useful to subdivide its history into a number of distinct phases. The first phase of the movement (1986–1999) was its formation, setting out its manifesto (all of which has been previously discussed), and moving from a national (Italy) to an international focus with the establishment of biennial events. In its early years, the movement was European in focus; the first international congress was held in Venice in 1990, which was followed by the establishment of Slow Food Germany and Switzerland, in 1992 and 1993, respectively. The slow food organisation held its first international fair (Salone del Gusto), in Turin in 1996 where the organisation launched its Ark of Taste project – a celebration of local (ecoregion) culinary traditions and foods (Miele and Murdoch 2002). This international fair became a biennial event for the movement, where the focus was on artisanal, sustainable food and small-scale producers who were viewed as safeguarding local traditions and maintaining high-quality products (Meneley 2004). The following year (1997), Slow Food's first international fair dedicated to dairy products, titled 'Cheese' was held in the town of Bra in Piedmont, Italy, the home of Petrini and the main headquarters of Slow Food International. This too became a biennial event; the ninth hosting of this event returned to Bra in 2013.

The second phase of the Slow Food Movement is discernible across the first decade of the new millennium (2000–2010) when the organisation, in an effort to realise its ambitions, created a number of entities that operated alongside its international, national and local structural framework. First, in 2000 the Slow Food Presidia project was launched, designed to be a network of grassroots organisations with the purpose of promoting slow foods to the public. Slow Food Presidia aims to sustain "quality production at risk of extinction, protect unique regions and ecosystems, recover traditional processing methods, safeguard native breeds and local plant varieties" (Slow Food 2015: n.p.). At the time of writing there are more than 450 Presidia worldwide, involving more than 13,000 producers. Second, the Slow Food Foundation for Biodiversity was formed in 2003 as the operational body for the protection of food biodiversity and local traditions (Pilcher 2006). This involved the previously addressed Ark of Taste project, first launched in 1996, which is an international catalogue of endangered heritage foods that is maintained by the global Slow Food Movement (Leitch 2003). According to the foundation's website, the Ark is designed to preserve at-risk foods that are sustainably produced, are unique in taste and form part of the heritage of a distinct ecoregion. The wider aim of the project is to encourage their cultivation for consumption, in view of promoting growing and eating foods that are both sustainable and protective of biodiversity within the human food chain. By mid-2015, more than 1,000 products (including prepared foods, vegetables, fruits and livestock breeds) from more than 50 countries were registered in this international catalogue, with the largest number being in Italy (375 foods), the United States (205 foods), Spain (61 foods), the United Kingdom, France and Japan (21 foods), Switzerland (16 foods) and Austria, Germany and Brazil (15 foods). The remaining countries on the register have 10 or fewer foods identified as endangered heritage foods (Slow Food Foundation 2015). To protect food biodiversity across the world, the Slow Food Foundation set in place the following during the first decade of the new millennium:

- *Earth Markets* (2008) – a global network of farmers' markets that respect the Slow Food philosophy. The intention here was to establish a network where the consumer recognises quality food that can be bought directly from the producers. The network's focus was also to foster an environment where fair prices can be set for both the consumer and the producer to the benefit of local economies.
- *Slow Food Chefs' Alliance* (2009) – a network of chefs defending food biodiversity across the world. The aim here was to commit chefs and cooks to using products from Presidia projects and the Ark of Taste, as well as local fruits, vegetables and cheeses and offering them to the public in their restaurants, bistros and street kitchens. As of mid-2015, there are more than 400 Alliance chefs (Slow Food, 2015).
- *The Thousand Gardens in Africa* project (2010) – the intention of this effort was to create 10,000 good, clean and fair food gardens in African schools and communities. The project had multiple aims. First, it was designed to raise awareness among African youth regarding the importance of food biodiversity. Second, it provided access to local, healthy and fresh food. Finally, it aimed to teach the next generation of leaders about the value of their lands and cultures, encouraging them to become protagonists for change across the continent.

A third significant development during the first decade of the millennium was the establishment of the Terra Madre (Mother Earth) Foundation. It was founded in 2004 to support the growth of what was emerging as a global network of food communities, chefs, academics and young people working for a sustainable food system. The first world meeting of food communities was held concurrently with the Salone del Gusto (international food fair) in Turin, Italy, and attracted more than 5,000 delegates from 130 countries. It was set up to foster discussion and introduce innovative concepts in the field of food, gastronomy, globalisation and economics. Convened every two years, the Turin Terra Madre meeting drew more than 9,000 participants, focusing on the relationships among food communities, cooks, universities and scientists. The movement quickly branched beyond Italy to regional Terra Madres taking place in Brazil and Belarus (2007), Ethiopia, the Netherlands and Ireland (2008), Tanzania, Argentina, Bosnia and Herzegovina, Norway and Austria (2009) and Azerbaijan, Canada, South Korea, Georgia, Kazakhastan and Bulgaria (2010), all demonstrating a global network established over a very short period of time. The national and regional Terra Madres are designed to work closely with the Slow Food conviva with the aim of increasing the capacity of local communities to provide good, clean and fair food (Terra Madre Foundation 2015).

Fourth, a number of national Slow Food organisations were set up between 2000 and 2010. These included Slow Food USA (2000), Slow Food Japan (2004), Slow Food UK (2006) and Slow Food Netherlands (2008). Fifth, in 2004 the University of Gastronomic Sciences (UNISG) was opened at Pollenzo in Piedmont and Colorno, in Emilia-Romagna, Italy. The university aims to educate future food professionals and promote awareness of wholesome food and nutrition. Carlo Petrini and Piercarlo Grimaldi, the latter a member of the International Council of the International Slow Food Association, are the leading figures in the establishment and operation of the university.

Finally, two additional notable events occurred before the end of 2010.The first was the ratification of the 2007 Declaration of Puebla, signed during the fifth International Slow Food Congress, held in Puebla, Mexico, that ensured the mission statement and aims of the Slow Food Movement outlined under the original manifesto of 1989 would continue to be met. The second event was the twentieth anniversary of Slow Food in 2009, which witnessed the first Terra Madre Day; around 200,000 people came together in 1,000 events in 150 countries to promote good, clean and fair food (Slow Food 2015).

The third and current phase of the Slow Food Movement exists from 2010 to present. During this period, the Slow Food Movement has been recognised for its importance at a transnational and international level, and its principles have garnered a great deal of respect and acceptance by international organisations, leaders and policy makers. Four landmarks characterise this period:

- The Slow Europe campaign was launched in 2011 and calls for European legislators to foster policies that promote sustainability, biodiversity protection and support for small-scale farmers.
- Carlo Petrini was invited to speak at the Global Food Security and Nutrition Dialogue at the 2012 United Nations Conference on Sustainable Development Rio+20.

- Slow Food joins a range of nongovernmental organisations (NGOs) to campaign for a better Common Agricultural Policy (CAP) for Europe.
- In 2013, Carlo Petrini received the highest United Nations Environment Award: a Champion of the Earth.

In the space of three decades, what started as a protest against the opening of a fast-food outlet has developed into an well-established and pervasive movement and political agenda against the globalisation of agricultural products in pursuit of promoting a new philosophy of food and food production which has good, clean, fair and sustainable principles at its heart (Pietrykowski 2004). Over time the Slow Food Movement has shifted from emphasising neo-gastronomy to promoting eco-gastronomy, the former being a multidisciplinary approach to food that recognises the strong connections between plate, planet, people and culture where a slower pace of life is encouraged. The latter embraces broader human-environmental issues such as quality of life and the health of our planet.

From theory to praxis: slow food research trends

This section now discusses the critique of slow food that has emerged in the scholarly literature in recent years. Since the Slow Food Movement began, several strands of slow food research have emerged, including research specific to the movement itself and the connections between slow food and tourism, sustainability, quality and the local production of food. To assess the extent of research undertaken on each of these strands, CABI's Leisure and Tourism abstract base was used to examine publications during the period when Petrini coined the term 'slow food' in 1986 until 2015.

Table 12.1 illustrates that the majority of research has taken place since 2000. This is not surprising, as it takes time for studies to emerge on new concepts and ideas, but it also requires scholars to become interested in particular niche areas, in this case slow food. But as the frequency of research output increases, as Table 12.1 reveals, slow food has been a rich area of academic inquiry, not just

Table 12.1 Slow food research and related themes[1] 1980–2015

Year	*Slow Food*	*Slow Food Movement*	*Slow food + tourism*	*Slow food + sustainability*	*Slow food + quality*	*Slow food + local food*	*Slow food + heritage (cuisine)*
1980–89	0	0	0	0	0	0	0 (0)
1990–99	3	0	3	0	0	0	0 (0)
2000–09	44	5	22	4	2	12	2 (0)
2010–15	64	14	39	10	3	19	14 (3)

[1] numbers do not cumulate, as several themes are identified in the same abstract

Source: author's own tabulation

focused on the movement itself but also on its connections to tourism and other related areas of inquiry (Hall 2006). What is somewhat surprising is that with the key tenets of slow food being good, clean and fair, there is less focus on research on the linkages with quality, sustainability, localness and heritage, and particularly heritage cuisine. That being said, the pace of research on these interconnections with slow food has picked up over the past decade and a half, with a slight exception on research that examines the quality dimension, as revealed in the table. When all of the sub-areas are considered, slow food is developing a distinct research culture of its own.

One of the earliest publications associated with a slower life and food was Silverstone's (1993) paper titled 'Whither fast food?' The author does not make any specific connection to the idea of slow food or the Slow Food Movement, despite the fact the paper came out several years after the movement was formally started. Instead he points out that catering experiences were starting to shift towards a market that was seeking sophistication, novelty and variety, which would necessarily involve policy shifts towards improving the quality of product and service, thereby slowing the speed of service. The remainder of this section provides a general critique of slow food as it relates to each of the sub-themes shown in Table 12.1.

A first strand of research examines the Slow Food Movement itself, including the behaviour of its members and consumers. This has been a relative dearth of focus, and when the movement is examined it is often in connection with a range of diverse issues. For example, works published in the journal *Espaces, Tourisme and Loisirs* in 2006 linked the movement to safeguarding culinary traditions and promoting high-quality agricultural production; it was also one of the earliest collections of works that made the connections to quality, local food and heritage cuisine.

Mair et al. (2008) studied the Slow Food Movement as part of a wider assessment of the political connections between leisure and food, where the pleasure of food is linked to a political practice grounded in reflection. Dunlap (2012) suggests that the Slow Food Movement is best understood as a crusade that addresses crises in societies' use of leisure, in particular how food is consumed during the mealtime and the need to create meal experiences that are convivial, mindful and ethical. Hall (2012: 62) was critical of slow food, as it lacks the radical dimension of any movement, stating rather it is "focussed on more of a lifestyle reinvention approach, that is more inward looking and focussed on the transformation of personal values and practices", reflective of its objective of education and knowledge transfer through development of its network and its hosting of food festivals and events. Hall does not see the Slow Food Movement radically changing food systems, as it largely focuses on food practices that are localised with limited impact on wider consumption practices. In contrast, Nilsson et al. (2011) regard slow food as a social movement that is trying to counteract increasing globalisation in eating habits and food production.

Somewhat surprising has been the absence of much research on slow food programmes for specific countries. One exception is the research by Erdös (2004), who provides a brief outline of programmes in Germany, Italy, the Netherlands and Portugal, against which he suggests the Hungarian food industry could learn from the Slow Food Movement with regard to the development of traditional Hungarian foods and cuisine for the purposes of developing recreational and tourism activities. There is some evidence to imply that the Slow Food Movement is attracting a growing interest, particularly with leisure scholars. For instance, Dunlap's (2012) paper in a special issue on leisure education examines the movement from the perspective of linking leisure education to a wider societal context.

A few scholars have examined the practices of slow food consumers/participants, examining their eating activities when they are away and at home, adopting the Fits-Like-A-Glove (FLAG) model to suggest that their behaviour is shaped by *habitus*, with decisions taken based on prior social and historical factors (Lee, Scott and Packer 2014a; Lee, Scott and Packer 2015). The authors compared the preferences of slow food consumers and non-slow-food consumers and found that slow food participants differed significantly in both their travel-related lifestyle preferences and destination activity choices, favouring local cultural immersion over more comfortable travel experiences (Lee, Packer and Scott 2015).

A second strand of research examines the connections between slow food and tourism. Of all the subcultures that have emerged from the slow movement, this area has received perhaps the most academic attention, derived from thinking about slowness, the travel experience and environmental consciousness (Lumsdon and McGrath 2011). The earliest work focused on case studies to reinforce the Slow Food Movement in the development of food guides (Ulloa district, Galicia), establishing culinary regions and using restaurant guides to promote slow food along with other food trends such as 'Nouvelle cuisine' (Pereiro and Conde 2005; Lemasson 2006). More recent research has been more disparate, examining the challenges slow food providers face against fast-food restaurant competitors in upmarket resort destinations (see Mkono 2012 on Victoria Falls in Zimbabwe), the contribution of the Slow Food Movement to developing more sustainable forms of tourism and hospitality (Hall 2012; Jung, Ineson and Miller 2014) and with slow food events as part of a destination's strategy development, as in the case of Bario, Sarawak (Adeyinka-Ojo and Khoo-Lattimore 2013).

Kosnik (2014) assesses the opportunity that World Wide Opportunities on Organic Farms (WWOOF) presents as an alternative form of travelling and hospitality, where people work for food and accommodation. As well, there is an emergent interest in how food can act as both an experience, which is central to all tourism, as well as a key ingredient of storytelling. De la Barre and Brouder's (2013) research is important in this regard as they make the connection that consuming food is also about consuming stories.

A third line of research to emerge has focused on the interconnections between slow food and sustainability. Mayer and Knox's (2010) examination of Italy's slow food and slow city (Cittaslow) movement pointed to the value of small communities benefiting from the partnerships and networks that facilitated growth beyond the local to an international level. In contrast, Hall (2012) was critical of the movement because travel is at the heart of sharing best practices, of attending annual food fairs and events (e.g., Salone del Gusto, Turin), or in the words of Petrini (2007: 241, cited by Hall 2012), "[I]t is necessary to move, to meet people, to experience other territories and other tables . . . the right to travel becomes fundamental, a premise on which to base cultural growth and self-nourishment of the network of gastronomes". Hall (2012) argues that the movement appears unaware of the contradictions that exist between mobility and sustainability, and that there is a danger that slow food consumers appear as elitist travellers or the latest trend among foodies and gourands. Petrini (2007), after all, refers to slow food enthusiasts as the 'inclusive elite'. However, Hall (2012) does accept that the movement has been successful in raising the issue of fair trade in the production and consumption of food (Figure 12.2).

With regard to achieving profitable, just and sustainable hospitality services, Moskwa, Higgins-Desbiolles and Gifford (2015) point to the evolution of sustainable cafes as forums in which the restaurateur can engage in conversation to transform food cultures. Part of this conversation centres on slow food, which the authors see as offering a systemic alternative to narrow-focused initiatives, such as promoting organic produce and fair trade. The importance of developing communication channels is also evident in Kosnik's (2014) research on the WWOOF movement, but Kosnik goes further by arguing that there is a need to establish reciprocity between hosts and helpers (those engaging in work for food and accommodation), to break down the boundaries between production and consumption by establishing, negotiating and nurturing a work-exchange relationship based on barter and gift exchange.

A fourth emergent research area examines quality issues and local food. With regard to the former, the concept of quality has been linked with food marketing

Figure 12.2 The Fair Trade Café and Community Kitchen in Phoenix, Arizona, United States, supports the tenets of fair trade and slow food (Photo: Dallen J. Timothy)

and fast food for a long time (Panyko 1990; Petrini 2001; Silverstone 1993), but there is limited research on quality with respect to slow food (see Table 12.1). One exception is a recent study by Nelson (2015) that examines place reputation and its management, where innovative chefs have been instrumental, often inspired by slow food thinking, to create a vibrant culinary creative destination that focused on quality food and gastronomy. Earlier work by Telfer and Wall (1996) studied a very similar, albeit nascent, situation in Lombok, Indonesia. Although they did not refer to it yet as 'slow food', the chef-inspired program of direct farm-to-resort food production highlighted the same principles of fresh, local and vibrant and was an early example of successes and failures of such a program in the developing world context.

With regard to local food, the importance of local food emerged in slow food consumers' travel preferences (Lee, Packer and Scott 2015; Lee, Scott and Packer 2014b), forms an integral part of current thinking about sustainable tourism development (Adeyinka-Ojo and Khoo-Lattimore 2013; Jung, Ineson and Miller 2014), is part of the conversation between restaurateurs and clients (Moskwa, Higgins-Desbiolles and Gifford 2015), lies at the core of many gastronomic events (Pereiro and Conde 2005), and is integral to how local food can both form a movement and appeal to visitors interested in experiencing new tastes (e.g. circumpolar foods) (de la Barre and Brouder 2013).

The final topic of study to emerge in recent years focuses on the connections between slow food and heritage, in particular heritage cuisines and foodways. Hall (2012) noted that a major contribution of the Slow Food Movement was maintaining heritage varieties through the Ark of Taste project, the Terra Madre (Mother Earth) network and various education programmes. Heritage cuisines emerged as a central element in shaping visitors' experiences by linking food to the storytelling of traditions (de la Barre and Brouder 2013), or found expression as part of cultural festivals and events (Adeyinka-Ojo and Khoo-Lattimore 2013; Nilsson et al. 2011). Frost and Laing (2013) examined how the message of slow food can best be communicated by hosting food-themed festivals, noting the existence of varying levels of cultural heritage as expressed in distinct regional cuisines. They point to the value of using well-known local media food personalities as champions, alongside strong marketing of slow food as authentic, artisanal and high status.

Conclusion

Slow food remains an emergent area for scholarly inquiry, particularly among those who are interested in food studies and culinary tourism. It is not surprising that only in the past decade and a half have we witnessed an uptake of research. Sufficient time has now elapsed in the evolution of the Slow Food Movement for scholars to engage with the topic, debate what it stands for, examine how it compares to other food movements and evaluate it on the basis of a range of consumerist, heritage, political and cultural criteria. At present, research has focused on assessing the movement, its philosophy and strategies, the connection to slow travel and in particular food tourism and the extent to which the ideas behind slow food complement or contradict thinking on sustainability, quality, the value of local food and the role it plays in maintaining and celebrating a region's comestible heritage.

The Slow Food Movement values and promotes local heritage. Part of its mandate is to protect traditional foods, highlight regional tastes, underscore the importance of historical horticultural and preparation methods, support artisanal culinary experiences, safeguard cultural diversity and biodiversity and enhance the identity of places (Meneley 2004; Miele and Murdoch 2002; Petrini 2001; Pilcher 2006). Many of its principles, including localness, wholesomeness, locational identity, the importance of aesthetics and conservation and sustainable growth parallel the tenets of sustainable forms of heritage tourism (Timothy and Boyd 2003). Also from a heritage perspective, 1986 marks an important point in time for the heritage of the Slow Food Movement. The campaign itself has gained its own heritage ethos in terms of its origins and its research and practice. It has gained considerable strength during the past quarter century and will no doubt continue to garner support far into the future.

In today's harried society where the focus is on all things fast and global, it may now be time to put on the brakes and enjoy life more slowly, including the food we eat, celebrate and share with others as part of the experience of the places we consume.

References

Adeyinka-Ojo, S.F. and Khoo-Lattimore, C. (2013) Slow food events as a high yield strategy for rural tourism destinations: the case of Bario, Sarawak. *Worldwide Hospitality and Tourism Themes*, 5(4): 353–364.

de la Barre, S. and Brouder, P. (2013) Consuming stories: placing food in the Arctic tourism experience. *Journal of Heritage Tourism*, 8(2/3): 213–223.

Dunlap, R. (2012) Recreating culture: slow food as a leisure education movement. *World Leisure Journal*, 54(1): 38–47.

Erdős, Z. (2004) Foods, meals and globalisation: the 'slow food' movement. *Elelmezesi Ipar*, 58(2): 38–41.

Frost, W. and Laing, J. (2013) Communicating persuasive messages through slow food festivals. *Journal of Vacation Marketing*, 19(1): 67–74.

Hall, C.M. (2006) Culinary tourism and regional development: from slow food to slow tourism? *Tourism Review International*, 9(4): 303–305.

Hall, C.M. (2012) The contradictions and paradoxes of Slow Food: environmental change, sustainability and the conservation of taste. In S. Fullagar, K. Markwell and E. Wilson (eds) *Slow Tourism: Experiences and Mobilities*, pp. 53–68. Bristol: Channel View Publications.

Jones, P., Shears, P., Hillier, D., Comfort, D. and Lowell, J. (2003) Return to traditional values? A case study of slow food. *British Food Journal*, 105(4/5): 297–304.

Jung, T.H., Ineson, E.M. and Miller, A. (2014) The slow food movement and sustainable tourism development: a case study of Mold, Wales. *International Journal of Culture, Tourism and Hospitality Research*, 8(4): 432–445.

Kosnik, E. (2014) Work for food and accommodation: negotiating socio-economic relationships in non-commercial work-exchange encounters. *Hospitality and Society*, 4(3): 275–291.

Lee, K., Packer, J. and Scott, N. (2015) Travel lifestyle preferences and destination activity choices of slow food members and non-members. *Tourism Management*, 46: 1–10.

Lee, K., Scott, N and Packer, J. (2014a) Habitus and food lifestyle: in-destination activity participation of slow food members. *Annals of Tourism Research*, 48: 207–220.

Lee, K., Scott, N and Packer, J. (2014b) Where does food fit in tourism? *Tourism Recreation Research*, 39(2): 269–274.

Lee, K., Scott, N. and Packer, J. (2015) The Fits-Like-A-Glove model and destination activities of slow food members. *Current Issues in Tourism*, 18(3): 286–290.

Leitch, A. (2003) Slow food and the politics of pork fat: Italian food and European identity. *Ethnos*, 68(4): 437–462.

Lemasson, J.P. (2006) Thinking about gourmet tourism. *Téoros, Revue de Recherche en Tourisme*, 25(1): 3–49.

Lumsdon, L.M. and McGrath, P. (2011) Developing a conceptual framework for slow travel: a grounded theory approach. *Journal of Sustainable Tourism*, 19(3): 265–279.

Mair, H., Sumner, J. and Rotteau, L. (2008) The politics of eating: food practices as critically reflexive leisure. *Leisure/Loisir*, 32(2): 379–405.

Mayer, H. and Knox, P. (2010) Small-town sustainability: prospects in the second modernity. *European Planning Studies*, 18(10): 1545–1565.

Meneley, A. (2004) Extra virgin olive oil and slow food. *Anthropologica*, 46(2): 165–176.

Miele, M. (2006) Consumption culture: the case of food. In P. Cloke, T. Marsden and P. Mooney (eds) *The Handbook of Rural Studies*, pp. 344–354. London: Sage.

Miele, M. and Murdoch, J. (2002) The practical aesthetics of traditional cuisines: slow food in Tuscany. *Sociologia Ruralis*, 42(4): 312–328.

Mkono, M. (2012) Slow food versus fast food: a Zimbabwean case study of hotelier perspectives. *Tourism and Hospitality Research*, 12(3): 147–154.

Moskwa, E., Higgins-Desbiolles, F. and Gifford, S. (2015) Sustainability through food and conversation: the role of an entrepreneurial restaurateur in fostering engagement with sustainable development issues. *Journal of Sustainable Tourism*, 23(1): 126–145.

Nelson, V. (2015) Place reputation: representing Houston, Texas as a creative destination through culinary culture. *Tourism Geographies*, 17(2): 192–207.

Nilsson, J.H., Svärd, A.C., Widarsson, A. and Wirell, T. (2011) 'Cittáslow' eco-gastronomic heritage as a tool for destination development. *Current Issues in Tourism*, 14(4): 373–386.

Panyko, F. (1990) Challenging directions in food marketing. *Cornell Hotel and Restaurant Administration Quarterly*, 31(1): 52–55.

Pereiro, X. and Conde, S.P. (2005) Tourism and gastronomic offerings in the district of Ulloa (Galicia): analysis of a local development experience. *PASOS: Revista de Turismo y Patrimonio Cultural*, 3(1): 109–123.

Petrini, C. (2001) *Slow Food: The Case for Taste*. New York: Columbia University Press.

Petrini, C. (2007) *Slow Food Nation: Why Our Food Should be Good, Clean and Fair.* New York: Rizzoli International.

Pietrykowski, B. (2004) You are what you eat: the social economy of the slow food movement. *Review of Social Economy*, 62(3): 307–321.

Pilcher, J.M. (2006) Taco Bell, maseca, and slow food: a postmodern apocalypse for Mexico's peasant cuisine? In R. Wilk (ed) *Fast Food/Slow Food: The Cultural Economy of the Global Food System*, pp. 69–82. Lanham, MD: AltaMira Press.

Silverstone, R. (1993) Whither fast food? *International Journal of Contemporary Hospitality Management*, 5(1): i–iii.

Slow Food (2015) Slow Food. Available online at http://www.slowfood.com/ Accessed May 1, 2015.

Slow Food Foundation (2015) Slow Food Foundation for Biodiversity. Available online at http://www.slowfoodfoundation.org Accessed May 3, 2015.

Telfer, D.J. and Wall, G. (1996) Linkages between tourism and food production. *Annals of Tourism Research*, *23*(3): 635–653.

Terra Madre Foundation (2015) Terra Madre. Available online at http://terramadre.org Accessed May 3, 2015.

Timothy, D.J. and Boyd, S.W. (2003) *Heritage Tourism*. Harlow: Prentice Hall.

Timothy, D.J. and Teye, V.B. (2009) *Tourism and the Lodging Sector*. Oxford: Butterworth Heineman.

13 Conclusion

Heritage cuisines and the patrimony of food

Dallen J. Timothy

The contents of this book have collectively argued that cuisine, foodways, epicurean traditions and gastronomic patterns are critical elements of cultural heritage deserving of additional research attention. The relationships between heritage and food are extremely complex and multidimensional, but what they boil down to essentially is that cuisine is a rich and varied keeper of the past, a veritable archive of information about evolving human relations and forces of nature.

As repositories of cultural knowledge, native food and foodways can shed considerable light on indigenous people and their efforts to maintain at least basic elements of their aboriginal heritage in an increasingly modernized and technology-dependent world. While technology can help maintain some of their traditional ways through information sharing and preservation, modernization in general terms presents obstacles when fast food replaces long-held traditions, and foreign ingredients replace native flavors. Colonialism was perhaps, more than any other force, the fount of change for many gastronomic foodways in the colonies and in the metropoles. Today we see a resurgence of culinary pride among indigenes throughout the world to counter the effects of colonialism, acculturation and modernization, who seek to relearn lost traditions or educate younger generations to prevent the losses that are occurring with other elements of culture, such as language. In the Arctic and parts of the tropical world, native peoples continue ancient hunting and gathering practices as a means of survival and a way of preserving intergenerational knowledge. As well, indigenous restaurants are beginning to crop up in various locations such as the Aboriginal Restaurant near Sun Moon Lake, Taiwan, and the Nili Restaurant in Rovaniemi, Finland, both of which serve traditional meals based on aboriginal gastronomy.

We still know relatively little about the influences of technology on conserving traditional foodways, and comparative studies between the influences of different colonial realms (e.g. Portuguese, British, French, Dutch, Italian, etc.) would provide interesting insight into how colony-metropole relationships varied between different regions and colonial cases. As well, with growing numbers of aboriginal restaurants and stronger assertions of indigenous identities and intellectual property rights over their own patrimony, questions need to be raised about how native peoples are able to withstand external pressures, or not, and how they have adapted to preserving their foodways in the midst of McDonaldized culinary climates everywhere.

Like colonialism, migration has had salient implications for food throughout the world, not least of which is the proliferation of ethnic cuisines to places far away from the diasporic homeland. Indian, Italian, Chinese, Mexican, Thai and Middle Eastern food shops and restaurants are some of the most omnipresent ethnic food vendors in the Western world. In areas with smaller emigrant populations, such as Finns in the Great Lakes area of the United States and Canada, Afghanis in San Francisco, Ethiopians around Washington, DC, and Turks in Berlin, other ethnic food providers have developed in more geographically centered locales. Continued scholarly inquiry into the geography of migration and heritage cuisine would also be a fruitful subject for additional long-term analysis.

The proliferation of diasporic cuisines is indicative of differentness or the novelty effect of foreign cuisines compared to the dominant food of the surrounding population, the sheer size and ubiquity of certain diasporas and the propensity of some migrant populations to promote their ethnic food and at reasonable prices. Large cities throughout the world are more prone to host a wider diversity of ethnic restaurants owing to a larger assortment of ethnic concentrations and a broader consumer base. While it is clear that diasporic and migrant peoples help redesign the cultural foodscapes of their adopted countries, it is less clear whether or not their mobility patterns and return visits home have any implications for changing tastes and gastronomic traditions in the original motherland, or is the influence only one-way? We still know very little about the culinary experiences of different, especially lesser-known, diasporas throughout the world and their gastronomy-related acculturation processes. As well, given that different types of diasporas have different experiences in their scattering from the homeland and in their adopted lands (e.g. victim, labor, imperial, trade and cultural diasporas (Cohen 1997)), it is likely that their experiences with cuisine and foodways are also distinctive. For example, the malevolent history of slavery in the United States (a victim diaspora extraordinaire) severely impacted the foodways of African Americans in a variety of ways that are still discernible in the gastronomy of the Deep South (Bower 2007; Witt 2004).

Indigeneity, colonialism and migration raise many questions regarding the disputed notion of authenticity (Chhabra 2012; Timothy and Boyd 2003; Timothy 2011; Wang 1999) in the gastronomic context. Some disputants believe that authenticity is intrinsic within objects, places or events and that it can be measured and delineated objectively. On the contrary, others believe that no element of heritage can be truly authentic in a world of constant change and outside influence, and therefore authenticity is a subjective notion that varies by object and by person. Compared to other elements of heritage, as it relates to cuisine, authenticity is fundamentally a moot point because even the most authentic foods (whatever that means) have at some time been influenced by the practices and products of neighboring tribes or nations. As a result, authenticity in the context of food is extremely elusive, if it can possibly exist at all. What was, gastronomically speaking, authentic a millennium ago, last year or yesterday may not be authentic today, but it may nonetheless be 'traditional', local and acceptable to the majority of its producers and consumers. Thus, it is more accurate to speak of traditional rather than authentic cuisines.

The European Commission's PDO, PGI and TSG labels make a valiant attempt to preserve the traditional values of various agricultural and food items (Jordana 2000). Similarly, the slow food Ark of Taste catalogue is a list of endangered heritage food items that aims to distinguish, encourage the cultivation of and draw international attention to at-risk food products that epitomize *terroir* and other characteristics of defined ecoregions, to safeguard heirloom foods and Earth's biodiversity and to sustain heritage foodways (Lotti 2010; Scaffidi 2014). There is much more work to be done to help preserve endangered agricultural and food products given the pressures of modernization and globalization.

Regardless of its inadequacy for describing gastronomy, the word 'authentic' is frequently used by producers and marketers to peddle their gustatory wares because authenticity sells (Timothy and Boyd 2003). Nascent research is beginning to show that eating in perceived 'authentic' ethnic restaurants can instill a desire within diners to visit the country whose food they are eating (Min and Lee 2014). Thus, dining on the immigrant food of others in one's own country can potentially become a 'conversion' tool to sway people's holidaymaking decisions. As well, immigrants may choose to dine in restaurants that sell the most representative food from the homeland as a way of maintaining a connection to the homeland (Chhabra et al. 2013). Studies on representations of nation and authenticity through culinary heritage are sorely needed beyond the use of 'authenticity' as a marketing buzzword.

As neoliberal processes continue to usurp the local with the global, modern societies are becoming increasingly displaced from their direct food sources. Prevailing economies of scale mean that most supermarket items are manufactured or harvested far from where they are consumed. This is a reality of the contemporary world, yet it often results in people feeling disconnected from their gastronomic roots. Since the 1980s, growing numbers of people have become more distrustful of their food sources, realizing what is missing is the heritage or time-honored heirloom element, which entails freshness, traditions and terroir. Genetically modified foods (genetically modified organisms (GMOs)) are perhaps the best example of this heritage disconnect. GMOs are pervasive in foods consumed in the developed world today, yet we still do not know the long-term implications of consuming GMOs. This and other concerns have led to a wave of recent socio-gustatory back-to-basics crusades, such as the Slow Food Movement, the Ark of Taste, organic eating, buying local and other related efforts (Wilk 2006).

Concerns about GMOs and the questionable quality of imported foods, together with recent volatile global economies, are increasing numbers of people in urban areas allotting more yard space to vegetable gardens, planting edible landscaping and raising backyard chickens (Schindler 2012). Correspondingly, farmers' markets and fresh fish markets are becoming a more prevalent part of the foodscapes of cities and rural areas, and increasing numbers of people are taking advantage of pick-your-own farms to harvest their own fruits and vegetables in an effort to ensure their food sources, to bypass the middle person (which better ensures freshness) and as a way of preserving an agrarian heritage (Griffin and Frongillo 2003). Agritourism is a similar manifestation of people's interest in getting closer to their food sources, appreciating the cultural heritagescapes of farming and helping to produce their comestibles. An incipient concept related to this in the US Midwest is the growth of 'pizza farms' (Malley 2015). Playing into Americans' love of pizza, several farms have been inviting families to enjoy a pizza picnic – pizza made from fresh ingredients such as homemade cheese, farm-produced organic meats and homegrown vegetables. Parents enjoy these summer picnics for their nutritional value, and children enjoy them because they can eat pizza outdoors in a rural setting. Many such trends are emerging, but researchers have yet to identify them and how they comingle cultural heritage and agricultural production into farm-fresh culinaria.

Societal angst about modern life in general, which uncertainties about food and its production accentuate, leads to a sense of longing for simpler times past, especially among Baby Boomers and Generation Xers. In traditional societies, foodways and family recipes are common knowledge that is imparted orally from one generation to the next. In Western societies, ancestral culinary heritage is a source of comfort in a tumultuous and uncertain world. Family recipes, holiday occasions and other aliment-oriented practices are salient parts of people's own personal heritage. Thoughts of a grandmother's cooking, rekindled tastes of a faraway homeland or smells of holiday cookery can trigger vital memories that help people identify with their past and cope with their present (Coblentz and Williams 2013; Lowenthal 2015), much the same way visiting ancestral homelands on genealogical pilgrimages can do (Timothy 2008).

Every place is unique, and so are the ways in which food products are raised and processed. Through time, regions or countries become recognized and even branded for their specialty food items. This can be a source of great pride and solidarity when people realize what they have is one-of-a-kind, extraordinary and of interest to outsiders. Nationally branded foods, such as goulash in Hungary, fondue in Switzerland, spaghetti and pizza in Italy, *cou-cou* and flying fish in Barbados, *nasi lemak* in Malaysia, *empanadas* in Argentina and *pad thai* in Thailand, are iconic cuisines that brand places by their culinary heritage. These 'brands' are important underlying elements of national and regional identity, often with political overtones. Some of these iconic foods are 'officially' designated national cuisines, occasionally sparking political divisions and contention.

Tourism and gastronomic heritage are inseparable (Yeoman et al. 2015). Special interest travel, including food tourism, has been around for centuries, but it has only been identified as a way of classifying tourism since the 1980s. Culinary tourism has received a great deal of attention in recent years, but now we see that even this type of tourism appears to be too broad, as specialized food enthusiasts begin to travel to see and sample specific items – wine, coffee, tea, cheese, sausages, olives, mushrooms and caviar to name but a few. As part of their broader travel itineraries, food enthusiasts may choose holiday destinations for beach going that also offer tea (e.g. Sri Lanka) or sport destinations that also offer wine and cheese (e.g. France). However, there is a growing market segment that chooses its vacation spots based entirely on food preferences. These clearly represent Hall and Sharples's (2003) 'gourmet tourists' or 'foodie tourists' (Getz and

Robinson 2014; Getz et al. 2014) who are hard-core culinary enthusiasts, many of whom travel to experience specific food items, such as the national cuisines noted earlier or even more specific products such as chocolate, cheese, tea, coffee, sugar or spices (Jolliffe 2007, 2010, 2012, 2014; Van As 2012), not necessarily just for the food item but also to learn about its production process and to see its cultivation firsthand.

These consumables and the heritage tales they tell are key cultural resources in many destinations (Aslam and Jolliffe 2015). For example, Jolliffe's (2012) book about sugar and tourism goes far beyond loose descriptions of the sweet stuff, its production and tourists eating candy. Instead, the work looks at sugar as an impetus for the genesis and growth of various heritages, including Caribbean slavery and rum production and all that these relations entail. Lee Jolliffe and a handful of others (e.g. Anbalagan and Lovelock 2014; Cheng et al. 2012; Frost et al. 2010; Kraftchick et al. 2014; Lyon 2013) have only recently begun to look at specialized food item–tourists, their motives and their experiences as they interact with heritage foods and drinks.

Festivals and food trails also play into the notion of food tourism as they celebrate alimentary themes, iconic food places and memory. There are thousands of taste trails and gustatory celebrations through the world, with only a small portion of these ever receiving global recognition. Instead, they cater largely to a local market, aiming to enrich a sense of place, collective nostalgia and nationalistic feelings of pride, while simultaneously creating a marketable brand in hopes of eventually drawing outsiders and their purses.

The agricultural and culinary past tells countless personal and shared stories of humankind's intercourse with nature, our efforts to eke out a living, regardless of how meager or lavish it might be, and the socio-political tensions that have long underscored intergroup relationships. Many scholars have examined heritage cuisines from historical, geographical, political, anthropological, economic, touristic, sociological, nutritional and business perspectives, and we now know much (e.g. Bell and Valentine 1997; Fishler 1988). However, there are multitudes of latent narratives remaining to be unveiled as empirical research continues to peel back the layers and meanings of heritage cuisine.

References

Anbalagan, K. and Lovelock, B. (2014) The potential for coffee tourism development in Rwanda–neither black nor white. *Tourism and Hospitality Research*, 14(1/2): 81–96.

Aslam, M.S.M. and Jolliffe, L. (2015) Repurposing colonial tea heritage through historic lodging. *Journal of Heritage Tourism*, 10(2): 111–128.

Bell, D. and Valentine, G. (1997) *Consuming Geographies: We Are What We Eat*. London: Routledge.

Bower, A. (ed) (2007) *African American Foodways: Explorations of History and Culture*. Urbana: University of Illinois Press.

Cheng, S., Hu, J., Fox, D. and Zhang, Y. (2012) Tea tourism development in Xinyang, China's stakeholders' view. *Tourism Management Perspectives*, 2: 28–34.

Chhabra, D. (2012) Authenticity of the objectively authentic. *Annals of Tourism Research*, 39(1): 499–502.

Chhabra, D., Lee, W., Zhao, S. and Scott, K. (2013) Marketing of ethnic food experiences: authentication analysis of Indian cuisine abroad. *Journal of Heritage Tourism*, 8(2/3): 145–157.

Coblentz, E. and Williams, K. (2013) *The Amish Cook: Recollections and Recipes from an Old Order Amish Family*. New York: Random House.

Cohen, R. (1997) *Global Diasporas*. London: Routledge.

Fishler, C. (1988) Food, self and identity. *Social Science Information*, 27: 275–292.

Frost, W., Laing, J., Wheeler, F. and Reeves, K. (2010) Coffee culture, heritage and destination image: Melbourne and the Italian model. In L. Jolliffe (ed) *Coffee Culture, Destinations and Tourism*, pp. 99–110. Bristol: Channel View Publications.

Getz, D. and Robinson, R.N. (2014) "Foodies" and their travel preferences. *Tourism Analysis*, 19(6): 659–672.

Getz, D., Robinson, R.N., Andersson, T.D. and Vujicic, S. (2014) *Foodies and Food Tourism*. Oxford: Goodfellow.

Griffin, M.R. and Frongillo, E.A. (2003) Experiences and perspectives of farmers from upstate New York farmers' markets. *Agriculture and Human Values*, 20: 189–203.

Hall, C.M. and Sharples, L. (2003) The consumption of experiences or the experience of consumption? An introduction to the tourism of taste. In C.M. Hall, L. Sharples, R. Mitchell, B. Cambourne and N. Macionis (eds) *Food Tourism around the World: Development, Management and Markets*, pp. 1–24. Oxford: Butterworth Heinemann.

Jordana, J. (2000) Traditional foods: challenges facing the European food industry. *Food Research International*, 33(3): 147–152.

Jolliffe, L. (ed) (2007) *Tea and Tourism: Tourists, Traditions and Transformations*. Bristol: Channel View Publications.

Jolliffe, L. (ed) (2010) *Coffee Culture, Destinations and Tourism*. Bristol: Channel View Publications.

Jolliffe, L. (ed) (2012) *Sugar Heritage and Tourism in Transition*. Bristol: Channel View.

Jolliffe, L. (ed) (2014) *Spices and Tourism: Destinations, Attractions and Cuisines*. Bristol: Channel View Publications.

Kraftchick, J.F., Byrd, E.T., Canziani, B. and Gladwell, N.J. (2014) Understanding beer tourist motivation. *Tourism Management Perspectives*, 12: 41–47.

Lotti, A. (2010) The commoditization of products and taste: Slow Food and the conservation of agrobiodiversity. *Agriculture and Human Values*, 27(1): 71–83.

Lowenthal, D. (2015) *The Past is a Foreign Country, Revisited*. Cambridge: Cambridge University Press.

Lyon, S. (2013) Coffee tourism and community development in Guatemala. *Human Organization*, 72(3): 188–198.

Malley, D. (2015) Fresh trend: pizza farms have become a Midwestern ritual. Available online at http://www.cnn.com/2015/07/02/travel/best-of-usa-pizza-farms/index.html Accessed July 2, 2015.

Min, K. and Lee, T.J. (2014) Customer satisfaction with Korean restaurants in Australia and their role as ambassadors for tourism marketing. *Journal of Travel & Tourism Marketing*, 31(4): 493–506.

Scaffidi, C. (2014) Slow food: the politics and the pleasure. *Development*, 57(2): 257–261.

Schindler, S. (2012) Of backyard chickens and front yard gardens: the conflict between local governments and locavores. *Tulane Law Review*, 87(2): 231–296.

Schlosser, E. (2012) *Fast Food Nation: The Dark Side of the All-American Meal*. Boston: Mariner Books.

Timothy, D.J. (2008) Genealogical mobility: tourism and the search for a personal past. In D.J. Timothy and J. Kay Guelke (eds) *Geography and Genealogy: Locating Personal Pasts*, pp. 115–135. Aldershot: Ashgate.

Timothy, D.J. (2011) *Cultural Heritage and Tourism: An Introduction*. Bristol: Channel View Publications.

Timothy, D.J. and Boyd, S.W. (2003) *Heritage Tourism*. Harlow: Prentice Hall.

Van As, H. (2012) The cows, the cheese, the mountain: on the farm. *Farmlink*, 2(4): 26–27.

Wang, N. (1999) Rethinking authenticity in tourism experience. *Annals of Tourism Research*, 26: 349–370.

Wilk, R. (ed) (2006) *Fast Food/Slow Food: The Cultural Economy of the Global Food System*. Lanham, MD: AltaMira Press.

Witt, D. (2004) *Black Hunger: Soul Food and America*. Minneapolis: University of Minnesota Press.

Yeoman, I., McMahon-Beattie, U., Fields, K., Albrecht, J. and Meethan, K. (eds) (2015) *The Future of Food Tourism: Foodies, Experiences, Exclusivity, Visions and Political Capital*. Bristol: Channel View Publications.

Index

Note: Page numbers for figures and tables are in italics.